Her Brilliant Career

Her Brilliant Career

TEN EXTRAORDINARY
WOMEN OF THE FIFTIES

◆

RACHEL COOKE

virago

VIRAGO

First published in Great Britain in 2013 by Virago Press
Reprinted 2013 (three times)

A CIP catalogue record for this book
is available from the British Library.

Hardback ISBN 978-1-84408-740-2

Typeset in Spectrum by M Rules
Printed and bound in Great Britain by
Clays Ltd, St Ives plc

Papers used by Virago are from well-managed forests
and other responsible sources.

MIX
Paper from
responsible sources
FSC® C104740

Virago Press
An imprint of
Little, Brown Book Group
100 Victoria Embankment
London EC4Y 0DY

An Hachette UK Company
www.hachette.co.uk

www.virago.co.uk

For TQ,

And in memory of my grandmothers,

Madge Cooke and Elsie Goodson

The fact that I was a girl never damaged my ambitions to be a pope or an emperor.

Willa Cather

Funny business, a woman's career.

Margo Channing, as played by Bette Davis
in All About Eve (*1950*)

Contents

Introduction

Where does a book begin?

This one began with a piece of furniture. Not so long ago, I bought a sideboard on eBay. I was very pleased with it: I'd got myself a lovely piece of fashionable-again early Ercol at a bargain price, and it looked so wonderfully pale and interesting, standing there in a corner of the kitchen. I relished telling people how little I'd paid for it; I loved watching them run their hands enviously over its warm beech and elm curves.

Friends who admired this sideboard were always surprised by its age – the man who sold it to me believed that it dated from 1954 – and after a while I began to share their amazement. The more I lived with it, the more timelessly modern it seemed; it was difficult to picture it in the comfortable but old-fashioned living rooms of my grandparents, who would have been about the same age as I am now when it was made – they favoured fitted carpets, cut-glass rose bowls and what used to be known somewhat unappetisingly as 'brown furniture' – and because of this I began to wonder about the Fifties. In my mind, they split in two. There were the Sepia Fifties, all Linoleum and best china; and there were the Technicolor Fifties, all atomic prints and Swedish-inspired modernism. Ercol, whose designs were exhibited at the Festival of Britain in 1951, was not the cheapest of the new-style post-war furniture, but nor was it impossibly expensive; though beautifully made, it was certainly mass-produced. I wanted to know: what kind of people had first bought it, and what were they telling the world about themselves

My Ercol sideboard

when they did? It wasn't too long after this – aspiration of one kind surely signifying ambition of another – that I had the idea of trying to write a book about the career women of the Fifties.

The more I thought about it, the more I questioned our idea of Fifties woman – so inflexible, so monolithic, a cultural symbol of all that we are most grateful to have sloughed off. As she is portrayed everywhere from Ian McEwan's *On Chesil Beach* to Matthew Weiner's *Mad Men,* she is a compliant, smiling creature who knows little or nothing of sex, and stands no chance at all of getting to the top of advertising or any other career. She must marry or die. (McEwan's novel, like the second series of *Mad Men,* is set in 1962, aka the last year of the Fifties; the Sixties, by general consent, only began in 1963, when Philip Larkin enjoyed his *Annus Mirabilis* and Betty Friedan published *The Feminine Mystique.*) In newspaper columns and magazine articles, the phrase 'like the Fifties' has become a kind of shorthand, especially when it comes to the lives of women, doing the work of at least a dozen other words, some of them contradictory. The phrase means, or can mean: old-fashioned, unambitious, docile, emollient, inhibited, clenched, prudish, thwarted, frustrated, repressed and, most recently, obsessed with baking (those who rage against the cult of the cupcake often marshal the backwards Fifties in their cause). But what if there was another side to the story? What if this collective readiness to move on has tilted history too far in one direction? Some people idealise the past, but far more common is the tendency to patronise it. We can't help ourselves. We make it one thing, or another, and then we set about considering ourselves superior to it.*

At first, I must admit, it seemed as though I might have set out on a wild goose chase. Many, if not most, of the heftiest histories of the Fifties were written by men, and while they have, for instance, an awful lot to say about Anthony Eden and the Suez Crisis, they are rather less forthcoming about the lives of women, especially the kind who might have longed for Ercol furniture. The male historians' favourite resource, when it comes the female Fifties, is Mass Observation, the research organisation founded in 1937 to record everyday life via legions of diary-writing volunteers. And while the journals people wrote under MO's auspices are vivid and fascinating, and often extremely moving, their female authors were mostly housewives and secretaries: women rather like my grandmothers, in fact. Still, I read on, and eventually was rewarded with a few names. Several weeks into the new Queen's reign in 1952, I learned, the *Picture Post* ran a feature entitled 'The New Elizabethans'. On the magazine's list were forty-two men (among them Nye Bevan, Benjamin Britten, Graham Greene and Henry

---

* In November 2011 around two thousand women marched through the City of London to protest against government cuts to benefit payments and publics services – cuts which, according to the march's organiser, the Fawcett Society, disproportionately affect women and risk setting back the battle for equality by several decades. To illustrate this point, many of those who took part had come dressed as Fifties housewives in twin sets and red lipstick, mushroom-shaped hats and leopard-print coats, pink rollers and silk scarves. Already hard at work on this book, I looked on with mixed feelings.

Moore) and five women. Two of these women were actresses: Glynis Johns, star of the 1948 mermaid hit *Miranda*, and Celia Johnson, whose performance in *Brief Encounter* had proved so resonant for a generation of women dealing with the return of the men from the war. A third was the ballet dancer Margot Fonteyn. Actresses and dancers probably weren't, I felt, illustrative of anything very much – they are surely anomalies, whatever the age – but the last two names caught my eye: Barbara Ward, an economist, and Rose Heilbron, then Britain's only female QC. They sounded interesting. Then, six hundred pages into David Kynaston's amazing panorama *Family Britain*, there came a couple more. 'Contrary to subsequent mythology,' writes Kynaston, 'the 1950s were not entirely bereft of ambitious, independent-minded women.' His examples were Sheila van Damm, the rally-car driver and theatre manager, and Margery Fish, the gardener and writer.

I took these names – new to me – as a gauntlet, thrown down. I would investigate (and celebrate) their achievements, and I would find others like them. I understood that I wouldn't be rewriting the decade: the facts would see to that. It *was* a time when most women were married (75 per cent of adult women in 1951); when relatively few women worked (though not, perhaps, as few as you might think: in 1956, women comprised about 30 per cent of the workforce); and when, whether thanks to expectation or necessity, a huge amount of energy was devoted to housework (full-time housewives spent between sixty-one and seventy hours a week on washing, ironing and the rest). Women could not take out mortgages in their own name, even if they had a job, and if they wanted to be fitted with a diaphragm, one of the few forms of contraception then available, they had first to produce a marriage certificate. Abortion was illegal. But we need to be clear: the end of the war did not send every female hurrying back into the kitchen, just as the feminism of the Sixties did not spring from the minds of women who had spent the last decade in an apron and rubber gloves. As Katharine Whitehorn, who graduated from Cambridge in 1950, puts it in her memoir *Selective Memory*, 'There's been a tendency to look on the Fifties as simply a damp patch between the battleground of the Forties and the fairground of the Sixties; yet it was anything but . . . We had the heady sense that everything was getting better.' It goes without saying that Austerity Britain could be grim: all that smog and rubble, the feeling that rationing would last for ever. Yet perhaps we underestimate the sense of excitement many people, especially the young, felt about what lay ahead. Margaret Steggles, the heroine of Stella Gibbons 1946 novel *Westwood*, can't help but think of the ruins of post-war London as 'sombre and thrilling, as if History were working visibly, before one's eyes'. Elaine Dundy, the actress and novelist, arrived in London from America in 1949; the city was, she later wrote, 'a place where young people, besieged for six years of war, could finally see that they had a future. You could fairly feel the rush of air as they raced forward to greet it.' I suppose you could say that I wanted to stir up that breeze all over again.

At the start, my aim was to bag ten of these women because that seemed like a good, round number, but also because I feared I would struggle to find more. In the end, though, I was quite wrong on that score. When I finally sat down to write this book my poor heroines found themselves in a beauty contest; somewhat to my amazement they were too many, not too few. So many pioneers! Forced to make hard choices about who was in and who was out, I went mostly with those whose private lives were as modern as their professional lives. (Though this only narrowed things a little: the more successful career women of the Fifties were not often the spinsters I had been expecting.) Of the ten who survived, then, seven were married and the other three were lesbians. Six had children. Two worked in professional partnership with their husbands. Three were divorced and another separated from the father of her children, a man she never married. Several had extra-marital affairs. Three of the women lived together, bringing up two unrelated children as brothers. This interest in love and sex and all the permutations of the family, a sacred institution in post-war Britain, wasn't prurience on my part. I wanted to know how these women solved the problems that most of us still struggle with today: the balance of work and the rest of life. So much was stacked against them. Were they lonely? Did they sacrifice love for ambition, or did fulfilment at home lead naturally to fulfilment at work? Who looked after their children? And how did they run their homes when they were so busy?

For me, this is, I suppose, a sly kind of feminism – by which I mean that my message, in as much as I have one, is intended to hit the reader side on. Polemical books that tell us how we might close the pay gap, become FTSE directors and put an end to sexual harassment at the office are all very fine and important, but the truth is that they are rarely much fun to read. I prefer the idea of role models, inspirational figures who make you want to cheer. The extraordinary, mould-breaking women you will find in the pages that follow weren't perfect. They were, like all human beings, flawed. They doubted themselves, they got in muddles, they made mistakes; feeling defensive, they sometimes seemed difficult and distant even to those who loved them. They certainly did not – dread phrase – 'have it all', or not all of the time, at any rate. Their children sometimes had a hard time of it. But they loved what they did and they got on with doing it as best they could in far less equal times than our own. If that isn't encour-aging – a kind of rallying call to the twenty-first-century battle-weary – I don't know what is.

'Everyone has an age when they are most themselves,' says the nar-rator of Elizabeth Bowen's first novel, *The Hotel*. For Bowen, that era was the Blitz. For the women in this book, it was the Fifties. The youngest of them was twenty-two when the decade began; the oldest, fifty-eight. Most were in their thirties. They were stoical and rather tough, but also hopeful, full of expectation. Their characters had, after all, been informed by two wars: the horror and privations of the first they had experienced vicariously through their parents (though the oldest, Margery Fish, was twenty-two in 1914, when she had bravely crossed the Atlantic at a time when the U-boats were doing their very worst); the second they had endured themselves and, perhaps, had even enjoyed at times.

The Second World War had kicked open the door to another life. Some of them had joined one of the women's auxiliary services (the ATS, the WAAF or the WRNS) and found themselves suddenly driving an ambulance or sitting behind a big desk in a government ministry. Others had been able to take advantage of the men's absence. After 1939 more university places had become available to women; a young woman barrister like Rose Heilbron, meanwhile, found herself newly in demand with solicitors whose preferred male lawyers had all disappeared to fight. On a practical level, dress codes had relaxed. During the war, girls had worn trousers and flat shoes; those who couldn't get hold of decent stockings – from 1942, nylon was used exclusively in the production of parachutes – had simply gone bare-legged. On an emotional level, restraint had been exercised more infrequently than before, and the chastening crimp of disapproval felt much less often. In Britain's bombed cities people had slipped their moorings, falling in love easily and, sometimes, inappropriately. Future-less, couples had lived in the moment. Temporarily husband-less, wives had sought solace in the arms of others.* In

* For a good sense of this, try the novel *To Bed with Grand Music* (1946) by Marghanita Laski, in which a young mother, Deborah Robertson, embarks on a series of affairs while her husband is serving in Cairo. She neglects her son and spends her money on nightclubs and fripperies, and in doing so falls into debt. Although Laski, who published the book under a pseudonym, exaggerates for effect, her story makes for a bracing antidote to the stoical and loyal wife who holds everything together in the most trying of circumstances. No wonder the (male) critics hated it.

London the joke had been that everybody was having at least one affair – and that some were enjoying two or three. All of these things together added up to something quite significant: the sense that there was a world out there, and that a woman was entitled to move through it as easily and as confidently as any man.

During the war the numbers of women working had peaked at nearly eight million, but within a year of VE Day that figure had fallen by a quarter. The men wanted their jobs back, and the usurpers were expected to beat a nifty but decorous retreat. Of course, there were some women who longed for nothing more than to be a housewife again: the safety, the security and no officer or factory boss barking orders in your face. But for others, post-war retrenchment came as a shock. Those women who were accommodating returning husbands did not always manage to meet their expectations (and vice versa), the joy of reunion fading when couples woke up and realised they were strangers. In *One Fine Day*, a novel by Mollie Panter-Downes published in 1947, Laura and Stephen Marshall grapple with this altered landscape over the course of twenty-four hours. They must deal with a new world order, running their house without help, their girls Ethel and Violet having escaped to a 'big bright world where there were no bells to run your legs off'. Laura knows they'll have to adjust, but her husband is in denial: 'He talked the situation over with other men on the train, and they reported that things were getting easier. Bellamy's wife had got a cook immediately the other day by an advertisement in the *Bridbury Herald*.' Stephen, the reader gathers, is in for a disappointment at some point quite soon. Even if he secures the longed-for domestic, this isn't going to right the listing ship that is his marriage, post-war wives being almost as uppity as post-war servants. The novel reflected the reality. Nineteen forty-seven was a great marrying year, with 401,210 weddings, but at the same time the divorce rate began to rise, the number of Maintenance Orders made by magistrates courts

almost doubling to twenty thousand (it had stood at 11,177 in 1938).
Cut to 1954 and there were six times the number of divorces (27,417)
as there had been before the war.

But the lives of single women were also in flux. 'What to do
with my day, jobless and faced by the awesome prospect of endless leave?' wrote Joan Wyndham, wartime diarist extraordinaire.
'I was beginning to realise that now I was no longer in the WAAF
I would have to recreate my world from scratch every morning.'
Joan was a twenty-two-year-old girl about town, whose sex life
during the war had been both busy and exciting ('the happiest
time of my life'). The more determined among these young
women refused to feel guilty for wanting to 'steal' men's work,*
and were fast learning to be on their guard when it came to the
matter of their future. In 1951, twenty-one-year-old Grace
Robertson, soon to embark on a remarkable career as a photo-
journalist, saw a woman in one of the full skirts made popular by
Christian Dior and his New Look struggling to get on a London
bus: 'A crowd had gathered. Her skirt was so wide, she couldn't
negotiate the door. At first, I laughed with everyone else. But
then I suddenly thought: are they putting us into these clothes
so we can't get on buses, and take their jobs?'†

The question was: how should a woman who wanted to have
a career conduct herself? Should she fly below the radar, or above
it? Some didn't bother to hide their ambition: 'I knew exactly
what I was going to do, and that was art,' says Wendy Bray, who

---

* Though this was difficult. 'You couldn't avoid the men who had been hurt in the war,'
Grace Robertson told me. 'They were everywhere, blind or scarred, on crutches or in wheel-
chairs.' This made women less voluble when it came to the subject of equality than they
might otherwise have been. 'I could no more have thought of feminism in the face of what
I could see in the streets than I could have flown to the moon. It would have been indecent
as far as I was concerned.'
† Robertson wasn't the only one to worry about the New Look. Mabel Ridealgh, the Labour
MP, railed against it, saying, 'Our modern world has become used to the freedom of short,
sensible clothing ... the New Look is too reminiscent of a caged bird's attitude.' Bessie
Braddock, also a Labour MP, called it 'the ridiculous whim of idle people'.

Penelope and John Mortimer at home

began a career as a textile designer at Courtaulds soon after leaving art school in 1951. 'And I was going to kill in order to do it. I had to fight my father every inch of the way.' Others tried to disguise it: 'I wanted to be a perfect housewife *and* a successful actor,' says Sylvia Syms, who in 1953 had recently graduated from RADA. 'I would be away on tour, and I would rush back the following week to cook all the food for my husband. I mean ... what was *wrong* with me?' Still others worked in snatched moments, as if they weren't really working at all, with the inevitable result that they often felt thwarted and resentful. In December 1957 the novelist Penelope Mortimer wrote in her diary that she was finding it increasingly difficult to run her family – by this time, she was a mother of six – and find the space to write: 'I wake radiant to the thought of a peaceful work day ... I long for it and can't bear it to end – which it does with the key in the lock: *"Hullo? What's the*

plan?" We must have people in or go out, my room invaded, all
routed and nothing left in its place.'* (All the same, her work was
going well. She was delivering a steady stream of stories to the
New Yorker, for which she was well paid. A useful side-effect of the
way society was changing was that women longed to read about
experiences like their own, and said so. Even the 'dreariest days'
could, she found, be profitably mined for irony and farce.) Finally,
there were those who only leapt into the fray when Plan A had
failed. In *Millions Like Us*, her excellent book about women's lives
during and just after the war, Virginia Nicholson cites the example of Margery Baines. Abandoned by her husband – since their
marriage in 1940, she and he had spent barely a year together – and
with a young child to bring up, in 1946 Margery opened a one-
woman typing agency in a tiny Mayfair room. This business
would one day become the Brook Street Bureau, the first employment agency to be listed on the London Stock Exchange.

Those who embarked on careers had to be thick-skinned:
immune to slights and knock-backs, resolute in the face of
tremendous social expectation and prepared for loneliness. When
she began working at *Picture Post* at the age of just nineteen, the first
consequence for Grace Robertson was that she lost two of her girlfriends. 'Their parents stopped them seeing me. You could be a
nurse, a secretary or a teacher while you waited to get your man.
But a photographer? That sounded off-putting. I might be a bad
influence. I was cut dead.' In the office she grew accustomed to
visitors assuming she was a secretary. Her colleagues treated her
well, mostly, but on work trips they would inevitably attempt to
get her into bed. 'They would try and get you blotto, and then
turn up at the door of your hotel room. Luckily, I could out-drink

* Mortimer hated to feel thwarted; she feared it. 'Frustration is a greater poison than jealousy, which at least recognises the existence of someone else,' she once wrote – and she was
in a position to know, given the reputation of her husband John Mortimer.

any man in Fleet Street.' Her mother worried about such preda-
tors. She insisted that Robertson go to work in a hat and gloves
like a 'nice' girl. (The gloves lasted about as long as it took her
daughter to peel them off.) In 1954 Claire Tomalin, future biographer of Dickens and Pepys, went for a job interview at the
publisher Heinemann. A few minutes into her conversation with
a man called Roland Gant, a younger man, 'thick-set and wearing heavy glasses', came in without a word and put a piece of paper
on Gant's desk. 'He was James Michie, the poet,' she writes in her
book *Several Strangers*. 'Later, he told me he had been awarding me
marks for my looks. Seven out of ten, he gave me, just enough for
the job of secretary/editorial assistant, at £5.10s a week. This was
how things were done in 1954.'

It was, of course, impossible to fight back. It wasn't only that
sexual harassment had yet to be invented; women were expected
to know their place, irrespective of their talents and experience,
of the fact that they had won their jobs on merit. In 1959 the influential costume designer Jocelyn Rickards* was hard at work on
the film of John Osborne's *The Entertainer* when Michael Balcon,
the famous producer, questioned the casting of Joan Plowright as
Jean Rice. Rickards made the mistake of sticking up for her. Soon
afterwards, Balcon asked the film's director, Tony Richardson, to
sack Rickards. He would not, Balcon said, 'be spoken to like that'
by a woman.† But this was a mild example (and in any case,
Richardson refused to relinquish her). Others had it far, far worse.
One thinks of Rosalind Franklin, the crystallographer whose X-
ray photographs were crucial in establishing the structure of
DNA in 1953. At one end of the scale, her male colleagues persisted
in referring to her as 'Rosy', though this was not a name used

* Rickards, an Australian-born artist and costume designer, went on to dress some of the
most iconic films of the Sixties, among them *Blow-Up* and *From Russia With Love*.
† Balcon was an implacable enemy of women at work. For more on this, see Chapter 5, The
Brontës of Shepherd's Bush.

even by those closest to her. At the other, they repeatedly refused to acknowledge her outstanding contribution to the discovery of the double helix.*

Those who were mothers had also to worry about childcare – and it was at this point in history that many women first learnt to juggle, even if that wasn't the word they used. Anne Scott-James, the journalist who spent the Fifties first as the editor of *Harper's Bazaar* and then as the women's editor of the *Sunday Express*, described her own routine as 'a sort of miracle of slotting in' (her son Max was born in 1945; her daughter Claire in 1951). In her 1952 memoir-disguised-as-a-novel *In the Mink*, she carefully describes the battle that raged inside her as she tore herself away from the nursery each morning, an account that would not look out of place in a glossy magazine today. 'Up to now I'd always started out eagerly to work,' she writes. 'Ever since my apprentice days, the office front door had been an agreeable sight to me, and I had looked forward with pleasure to the jolts, excitements and interchanges of the day's work. Now, I banged the door of the flat behind me with something of a pang.' Every day she promised herself – and 'James' (aka Max) – that she would get home in time for tea. And every day she failed: 'Half-past five would find me with three or four people still to see, and the letters still to sign, and I would think: "Bang goes my meringue" – and all it stood for.'

But, in the end, such struggles were worth it. The bliss of work! The balm of it, and the satisfaction. 'I was so pleased to have found what it was that I really wanted to do, and to be paid for it,' says

---

* The canon of sexist slights against Franklin is miserably extensive. (Most recently, it was revealed that shortly before she left King's College London in 1953, her colleague Maurice Wilkins wrote to James Watson and Francis Crick in Cambridge to say that 'the smoke of witchcraft will soon be getting out of our eyes'.) When Watson, Crick and Wilkins were awarded the Nobel Prize for their work on DNA in 1962 only Wilkins made mention of Franklin's role in his acceptance speeches. Many books have been written about Franklin, who died of cancer in 1958, but the best is probably the 2002 biography by Brenda Maddox.

Anne Scott-James

Grace Robertson. Wendy Bray found it 'thrilling': 'I was well aware that I was doing a good job which I enjoyed, and which used my skills.' (She still remembers the first major purchase she made with her new salary: a purple velour coat, which – so much for the brown Fifties – she teamed with yellow shoes and a lime green hat.) 'I loved my job,' says Sylvia Syms. 'Any aspect of it. I needed to work for money, but I wouldn't ever have given it up.' In *Selective Memory* Katharine Whitehorn notes admiringly that in 1956 her former flatmate Sheila Gibson became a partner in the architectural firm Carden & Godfrey. 'She had a life she relished,' she writes. 'She said once about her work: "This is what I am *for*."' For her own part, Whitehorn, who was then working as a journalist on a small magazine called *Home Notes*, was about to hit what she regarded as the big time. 'HAVE GOT JOB ON PICTURE POST WHICH I WANTED MORE THAN HEAVEN' said the telegram she sent to her parents. I don't mind telling you that I have a copy of this message by my desk as I write. Even after all this time, I still can't see it without smiling.

I feel I should say something about the culture of the Fifties. It seems so masculine, its principal literary heroes being Jim Dixon (*Lucky Jim*, 1954) and Jimmy Porter (*Look Back in Anger*, 1956). Doris Lessing published her first novel (*The Grass is Singing*) in 1950, and Iris Murdoch hers (*Under the Net*) in 1954, but it's Kingsley Amis, John Osborne and the Angry Young Men we most strongly associate with the era – a tone that may be traced all the way back to 1950, when William Cooper published *Scenes from Provincial Life*, whose hero, Joe Lunn, is so strikingly determined not to marry his girlfriend Myrtle.* In some ways this heightens our sense of what women's lives must have been like – on the receiving end of a great deal of repression and rage – but it also, I think, warps it. So many of these books and plays, and the films adapted from them, have for an engine the sexual frustration of men; it's sometimes hard to see beyond this. And then there is the inescapable fact that their authors were applauded for their radicalism! If this is what passed for revolution, you think, the situation must have been even more stifling than you thought.†

---

* Women are just there to stop these men from getting what they want, aren't they? I can't stand Jimmy Porter. It's not only that he flays poor Alison; he's nothing more than a peevish Little Englander, secretly relishing the status quo, for all that he rails against it. *Lucky Jim* makes me laugh – I love a good madrigal joke as much as the next woman – but I can't bear the way the women are portrayed. I'm especially offended by the monstrous Margaret Peel, who was based on Philip Larkin's girlfriend Monica Jones. Larkin should have taken Amis out and shot him. Incidentally, the sequel to *Scenes from Provincial Life*, though written in the mid-Fifties, remained unpublished until 1982 for legal reasons; the real-life model for Myrtle had threatened to sue.
† 'For my generation, John Osborne was a heroic figure,' the actor Ian McKellen told Osborne's biographer, John Heilpern. But not everyone bought into this so-called heroism. Jocelyn Rickards walked out of *Look Back in Anger* when it opened at the Royal Court. 'It was all those fucking bears and squirrels,' she told Heilpern. (She never told Osborne, later her lover, about this.)

Monica Jones

I say: take the 'realism' of these novels, plays and films with a pinch of salt. For all their humble roots, for all that they were often threatened by the opposite sex, their authors knew a great many interesting, clever, sexually liberated women. In 1962 Kingsley Amis would leave his wife for the novelist Elizabeth Jane Howard: successful, coolly intelligent, already twice-married. In 1950 Amis's friend Philip Larkin began his long and complex relationship with Monica Jones, who had a first-class degree from Oxford, a lectureship in the Department of English at Leicester University and a stubborn mind of her own. By 1959 John Osborne had left his second wife, Mary Ure, for the bookish, free-spirited Jocelyn Rickards, whose friends included Lucian Freud, Ben Nicolson and Cyril Connolly, and among whose former lovers were the philosopher A. J. Ayer and Graham Greene. It was, moreover, Osborne who wanted his new girlfriend to fall pregnant, not Rickards herself. 'I'm not sorry it happened,' she writes of the miscarriage she suffered during their relationship in her memoir, *The Painted Banquet*. 'I cannot think of myself as one of nature's mothers, and I suspect nature dealt kindly with me on that occasion.' Before the pill, certainly, sex was often fraught with danger. 'We were terrified,' says Sylvia Syms. 'You had to be *very* careful,' says Wendy Bray. But this didn't mean that the life of every woman was dedicated entirely to withholding sex from men. 'If you were a naughty girl, you could sleep around,' says Bray. 'Art school was lovely and naughty [for some people].' When Grace Robertson wanted to sleep with her boyfriend she simply 'stayed at a friend's house'; the girl knew to lie for her if her father rang.*

For the middle classes, or those with enough money, abortion was a possibility. You just had to know the right people. In 1955 Diana Dors had her third abortion, having discovered she was pregnant shortly before *Yield to the Night*, a film in which she had been cast as the lead, went into production (she could not bear to lose the part just because she was pregnant; this was to be her breakthrough as a serious actress, or so she hoped). Nor was the subject taboo.† In Penelope Mortimer's 1958 novel *Daddy's Gone A-Hunting*, Ruth, its main character, helps her daughter Angela, who has returned from university pregnant, to arrange an abortion – and their collusion brings them closer: 'She trusts me and I am justified.' (Ruth decides that, if he asks, she will tell her husband she has spent the money on an abortion for herself, since he would regard another baby for them as a disaster.) Angela isn't agonised by her decision, nor is she frightened, since a doctor is to perform the operation. 'Just think,' she says to her mother. 'Tomorrow I'll wake up and it will all be over. I can't wait. I'm *happy*. You see?'

* Of course, some men still prized virtue. 'I had one who, strolling together across Wimbledon Common, tried to wrestle me to the ground and have his way with me,' says Grace Robertson. 'I fought him off, and the next time I saw him, well, he wants me to meet his mother. I'd kept my virtue, you see.'
† Abortion was not legalised until 1967. But women, and some men, were already agitating for change. As far back as 1934, the Women's Co-operative Guild had passed a resolution in favour of the legalisation of abortion at its AGM (in 1939, incidentally, it was estimated that some 20 per cent of pregnancies ended in abortion). The Abortion Law Reform Association was established in 1936. By the Fifties, led by the redoubtable Alice Brook Jenkins, it was actively campaigning in Westminster.

Mortimer* isn't much read now (though she is still in print) – and this is another problem. The Fifties canon, as it exists today, is too narrowly defined. The narrative that has Rattigan giving way to Osborne, and Waugh to Sillitoe, and the Ealing Comedies to the New Wave has blotted so much out. I could have written a whole book (or at least a PhD thesis) about this alone, but here are a few examples. *Daddy's Gone A-Hunting*, plangent and excoriating, is surely one of the decade's very finest novels, and it's twice as 'modern' as most of the books by her male contemporaries (or at any rate, it has dated far less). At its heart is Ruth, who finds herself trapped at home all day in a stockbroker village, while her paunchy, self-centred husband messes about with girls in London, a confinement Mortimer contrasts with her daughter's escape to university. It's not an awful life, hers; it's prosperous and safe: 'The wives conform to a certain standard of dress, they run their houses along the same lines, bring their children up in the same way; all prefer coffee to tea, all drive cars, all play bridge, own at least one valuable piece of jewellery and are moderately good-looking.' But still, Ruth is going mad. She is suffering from what, just five years later, Betty Friedan would call 'the problem that has no name'. She is isolated and frustrated, cut off from all the things that once defined her character. Mortimer's next novel, *The Pumpkin Eater*, about a woman with too many children and a husband just as unfaithful as Ruth's, moves the story on, in the sense that its narrator (who also, incidentally, has an abortion towards the end of the novel) has already had her breakdown and is telling her story from the psychiatrist's couch. 'Almost every woman I can think of will want to read this book,' said Edna O'Brien when it came out in 1962.

You see the same kind of desperation, albeit in a much less

---

*Mortimer, by the way, had six children by four different men. In 1961, at the suggestion of her husband, John Mortimer, she aborted her eighth pregnancy.

Yvonne Mitchell as the depressed housewife Amy in Woman in a Dressing Gown

wealthy household, in J. Lee Thompson's *Woman in a Dressing Gown* (1957), a wonderful, melancholy film that has never had half so much attention as *Room at the Top* and *Saturday Night and Sunday Morning*, perhaps for the simple reason that its main role is played by a woman. Yvonne Mitchell is Amy, a housewife; Anthony Quayle her husband Jim. Outwardly, Amy is cheerful, a chatter-box and a music lover. But it is clear that she has depression. She is unable to keep her tiny new London council flat clean and tidy, and spends most of the day in her dressing gown, her face unmade, her hair a mess. Jim tolerates this, but he is having an affair with his beautiful, organised secretary Georgie, and when she asks him to make his choice he is tempted . . . Sylvia Syms, who played Georgie, doesn't doubt that Thompson and his screenwriter, Ted Willis, had proto-feminist ideas, though they might not have described it that way themselves. 'It was time to make films in which working-class women had problems in their lives that weren't necessarily solved by a joke and going out to the pub,' she says. 'Amy is desperate, and Georgie is only in love with Jim, the most boring man in the world, because her horizons are so limited. He's her boss; he's the only man she knows.'

Such books and films reflected, to a degree, something that was in the air. Simone de Beauvoir's *The Second Sex*, don't forget, first came out in English in 1953; and in 1956 the sociologists Alva Myrdal and Viola Klein published *Women's Two Roles*, which warned women of the dangers of the new cult of motherhood and home-making: 'The sentimental cult of domestic virtues is the cheapest method at society's disposal of keeping women quiet without seriously considering their grievances, or improving their position . . . it has been successfully used to this day and has helped to perpetuate some dilemmas of home-making women by telling them on the one hand that they are devoted to the most sacred duty, while on the other hand keeping them on a level of unpaid drudgery.'* By the end of the Fifties the subject of working mothers was one of the most talked-about moral issues of the day. It was in 1957 that the term 'latch key child' was first coined – by a

---

* Myrdal and Klein had been provoked, in particular, by the public response to the ideas of the psychiatrist John Bowlby, whose book *Child Care and the Growth of Love* described the damage done to babies and infants by early and prolonged separation from their mothers ('the absolute need of infants and toddlers for the continuous care of their mothers will be borne in on all who read this book, and some will exclaim, "Can I then never leave my child?"'). The public had applied his theories to situations they simply did not cover, and which Bowlby himself had specifically excluded.

magistrate who reported his distress at the numbers of delin-
quents he found before him, 'mostly because post-school and
holiday hours meant all the temptations of street life, with the
home motherless, cold and often locked up . . . '

On the flip side, there were plenty of books and films about the
lives of single, liberated girls. Elaine Dundy's 1958 novel *The Dud
Avocado*, which became a best seller, has for its heroine the
adorable Sally Jay Gorce, who is alone in Paris, indulging her
'predilection for being continually on the wing'. Most of the book
is devoted to her romantic encounters. Sally Jay sleeps with her
boyfriends, thinks nothing of it and (crucially) *no harm comes to her*.
J. Lee Thompson's *Yield to the Night* (1956) is an anti-death penalty
film, made against the backdrop of the hanging of Ruth Ellis. It
tells the story of the last weeks on earth of Mary Hilton (Diana
Dors), who is to be hanged for the murder of the woman with
whom her lover, Jim, was unfaithful. This film, a commercial flop
in its day, has long since been reduced to a footnote in the dustier
shelves of film studies, perhaps because it is about an Angry
Young Woman rather than an Angry Young Man. In its flashback
scenes, which depict Mary's life before she committed the
murder, she is shown to be a liberated (and hard-working) young
woman. She has left her boring husband and is renting herself a
flat using her own money (she has a good job in a perfume store);
the film makes it clear that she sleeps with Jim. She wants a better
life, and when she shoots Lucy it is out of jealousy and curdled
love, but also of class rage (Lucy is wealthy; Jim was her bit of
rough). Powerful and terrifying, *Yield to the Night*, whose screenplay
was written by a woman, Joan Henry, is remarkable in a dozen
different ways. Above and beyond its contribution to the debate
about hanging, it is a film whose central message seems to be that
it is stupid and dangerous to think of women only as pretty things
to have about the place. This applies as much to Dors, its wasp-
waisted star and the greatest sex symbol of her day, as to anyone.

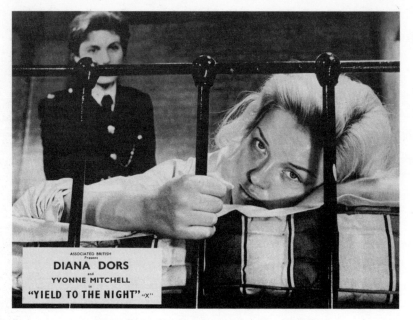

ASSOCIATED BRITISH
Present
DIANA DORS
and
YVONNE MITCHELL
in
"YIELD TO THE NIGHT" "X"

Mary (Diana Dors) in the condemned woman's cell

Save for the flashback scenes, she looks terrible throughout. Sullen and unsmiling, she wears no make-up and her roots are growing out. Her eyes are shadowed with grey. Her face is greasy. She puts in a blazing performance, and you ache for all that she might have been as an actress, had the men around her only given her more of a chance.*

Nineteen fifty-six. If this, as the historians suggest, is the year that marks the point the decade changed, austerity giving way to prosperity and deference to a new kind of confidence, then let us see what the women were up to. Across Britain they were

---

* In the US, the film was given the more blunt – and deeply unfair – title of *Blonde Sinner*. For more about *Yield to the Night* see Chapter 5, The Brontës of Shepherd's Bush. Dors's career was more or less over by 1960, by which time she had been reduced to selling sordid stories about her private life to the *News of the World*.

returning to work in ever larger numbers. The boom had created more jobs, and since there was already full employment women were once again in demand. Some of these women were wives too: by 1957, 33 per cent of married women worked. They wanted, many of them, to improve their family's standard of living, to be able to buy the shiny new consumer goods then becoming available: the country's hire-purchase debt rose to £784 million in 1959 (the figure had stood at £100 million before the war). And though disapproval of those women who worked had certainly not gone away, even the naysayers and doom merchants had to admit it was becoming ever easier to work and also have a family. Life was smoothed by, among other things, the rise of freezers, supermarkets, labour-saving devices in the kitchen and convenience foods. Fish fingers arrived on the market in 1955.

Other women, though, worked for its own sake, wanting their lives to be interesting, satisfying, *replete*. Their careers had taken them over, in the best sense. At Pinewood Studios Jocelyn Rickards was working on her costume designs for Laurence Olivier's film *The Prince and the Showgirl*. At the Royal Court Jocelyn Herbert was beginning her professional life at the age of almost forty with a job painting scenery; in less than twelve months' time she would produce her first major design, for the British premiere of Ionesco's *The Chairs*, and her career as the most celebrated and innovative theatrical designer of her day would be under way. At the Theatre Royal, Stratford, in the East End of London, the director Joan Littlewood and her company, the Theatre Workshop, were staging Brendan Behan's bawdy play, *The Quare Fellow*, a scathing indictment of the death penalty. Two years later Littlewood would stage *A Taste of Honey* by the eighteen-year-old Shelagh Delaney. The play, set in Salford, depicted working-class women from a working-class point of view, and would portray a gay character and a black character sympathetically. It would also be a smash hit.

Lucienne Day with a bolt of one of her Miró-inspired fabrics; her daughter Paula peeks out

In Stoke-on-Trent twenty-eight-year-old Jessie Tait, who'd trained at the Burslem School of Art and had begun her career as a junior to the great Charlotte Rhead, continued to design revolutionary abstract patterns for Midwinter Pottery: Savannah, in minimalist yellow and black; Zambesi, inspired by zebra stripes; Festival, which looked like cells seen through a microscope. In Chelsea, west London, in the studio she shared with her husband Robin, Lucienne Day was producing distinctive and fashionable textile designs inspired by painters such as Kandinsky and Miró. Calyx, the fabric she designed for the Festival of Britain, had made her a celebrity, and by this time she was everywhere: her house and even her recipes appearing in magazines, her face in an ad campaign for Smirnoff vodka. Across London, in the East End, Rosamind Julius continued to work to ensure that Hille, her family furniture company, was seen as the leading purveyor of contemporary style in Britain. She and her husband Leslie had furnished both the Royal Festival Hall and Gatwick Airport, and they had commissioned Robin Day to design furniture for them, including the moulded plywood Hillestak chair in 1950. At the *Guardian* the newsroom had a new architecture correspondent:

Diana Rowntree, who had won her job after sending its editor an excoriating analysis of the Shell building, which was shortly to be built on London's South Bank. 'No one at the *Guardian* wanted to learn about architecture,' she said. 'Only the women journalists warmed to the subject.' Nevertheless, she would remain at the newspaper for the next fourteen years.

In public and academic life, women were increasingly prominent. In 1956 Barbara Wootton, the sociologist and criminologist, was a governor of the BBC and had just finished serving on the Royal Commission into the civil service (this was her third Royal Commission). A Nuffield research fellow at Bedford College, she would soon be made a life peer. Edith Summerskill, the Labour MP for Warrington and a well-known campaigner on women's issues, was in the shadow Cabinet and had spoken at the famous rally against the Suez War in Trafalgar Square. Summerskill was also at work on *Letters to my Daughter*, a book that would, among other things, discuss frankly female sexuality. The distinctive voice of the novelist and campaigner Marghanita Laski was often heard on the BBC's *The Brains Trust*. In Jericho, Palestine, the archaeologist Kathleen Kenyon was hard at work on the Neolithic

Corrugated Fence by Prunella Clough

excavations that would make her internationally famous. Among her team was Honor Frost, a keen diver, who would later make her name as an underwater excavator. At Birkbeck College in London Rosalind Franklin was now working on tobacco mosaic virus and would soon reveal the structure of the ribonucleic acid of the virus, the carrier of its infectivity. In Oxford the chemist Dorothy Hodgkin, a mother of three, was close to solving the full structure of vitamin B12.*

The list goes on. Some marvellous novels by women, of course: Rose Macaulay's *The Towers of Trebizond*, Sybille Bedford's *A Legacy* and Mary Renault's *The Last of the Wine* all came out in 1956 – a year that was rather a poor one for fiction by men. Mary Quant had opened her first shop, Bazaar, in Chelsea. Barbara Hepworth was at the height of her powers, casting her first bronzes, having built her reputation as a carver. At Erica Brausen's† Hanover Gallery in Piccadilly Magda Cordell had a successful show of her abstract work. According to the architect Peter Smithson (the husband of one of the women at the heart of this book), Cordell was 'a force who had the capacity to turn her willpower to anything'. Her paintings were bloody and brutal; when it came to the female body she subscribed not at all to conventional ideas of beauty. Meanwhile, another artist, Prunella Clough, had embarked on her extraordinary and very fine depictions of industrial landscapes. Her subjects: cranes, cooling towers, fences of corrugated iron.

The women I interviewed for this introduction were all hard at work too. Grace Robertson had just been offered a job by *Life* magazine (she turned it down). Many of her assignments, now, were about the lives of women: party girls, childbirth, ribald seaside outings. Wendy Bray, having left Courtaulds, was pursuing a career as

---

* In the Forties, one of Hodgkin's students had been Margaret Roberts, the future Margaret Thatcher, who would enter parliament as a Conservative MP in 1959. Margaret Thatcher died on the day I finished writing this book.
† Brausen was Francis Bacon's first patron and gallerist.

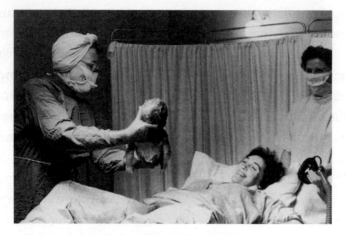

New Born Baby by Grace Robertson

a freelance textile designer, her portfolio bulging more with every day that passed. Both were recently married. Sylvia Syms was shortly to marry her childhood sweetheart, Alan – and to be cast in her first film, *My Teenage Daughter*, in which she would play a rebellious girl alongside Anna Neagle. And the women whose stories I tell in the coming pages – Rose Heilbron, Nancy Spain, Joan Werner Laurie, Sheila van Damm and Jacquetta Hawkes; Muriel and Betty Box, Margery Fish, Alison Smithson and Patience Gray – were up to all sorts of things, as you will shortly discover.

A word on how this book should be read. It is a group biography, but not in the traditional sense. These women were not friends, or members of the same gang or organisation. A few of them knew each other, it's true, but not well. Fame was often the only thing they had in common. Each of the essays in this book, then, stands alone, making perfect sense even if yanked from its neighbours. But if you read all seven of them there will, I hope, be a cumulative effect, the culture of the Fifties – its food, its architecture, its popular culture, its habits and its opinions – revealed through the lives of ten revolutionaries and taste makers who just happen to have been women. I hope these stories make people reconsider the 'lost' decade between the end of the war and feminism. But more than that, I hope they pull the reader along. As I researched them, piecing lives together by means of interviews, diaries, letters, photographs and memoirs, I was mostly goggle-eyed, *in awe*. These are, above all, tales of derring-do. Records will be broken, and hearts.

Timeline

1950

Ken Wood launches his electric mixer – later to be known as the Kenwood Chef – at the Ideal Home Exhibition.

Elizabeth David publishes *Mediterranean Food*.

Doris Lessing publishes her first novel, *The Grass is Singing*; set in Southern Rhodesia, it examines racial politics and causes a sensation.

1951

The first Miss World competition is held. It is won by Miss Sweden.

1952

On the death of her father King George VI, Princess Elizabeth ascends to the throne.

1953

Women teachers are awarded equal pay.

Lita Rosa is the first British woman to have a number-one hit, with 'How Much is That Doggy in the Window?'

The Second Sex by Simone de Beauvoir is published in English for the first time.

1954

Iris Murdoch publishes her first novel, *Under the Net*, the story of a struggling young writer called Jake Donaghue.

At the Alexander Sports Ground in Birmingham, Diane Leather becomes the first woman to break the five-minute mile.

1955

Dame Evelyn Sharp is appointed the first woman Permanent Secretary, at the Ministry of Housing and Local Government.

Barbara Mandell is the first woman to read the news on ITN.

Mary Quant opens her shop Bazaar.

Birds Eye launches Fish Fingers.

Ruth Ellis, a nightclub hostess, is hanged for the murder of her lover David Blakely.

1956

Tesco opens its first supermarket in Maldon, Essex.

Women's Two Roles by Alva Myrdal and Viola Klein, an academic study that allows for the possibility that women should be able to combine family life and work, is published.

1957

The *Guardian* starts its women's page.

Hubert de Givenchy designs a dress called the 'sack', an unstructured column that allowed for the possibility that women might want to move around (and which hid their curves from view).

1958

Hilda Harding becomes Britain's first female bank manager, at Barclays in Hanover Street, Mayfair.

Shelagh Delaney's controversial play *A Taste of Honey* opens at the Theatre Royal, Stratford.

Three women take their seats in the House of Lords, following the passing of the Life Peerages Act: the sociologist and criminologist Barbara Wootton (Baroness Wootton of Abinger); Stella Isaacs, the Marchioness of Reading, founder of the Women's Voluntary Service (created Baroness Swanborough); and the Conservative politician Katharine Elliot (Baroness Elliot of Harwood).

1959

The American pharmaceutical company, Searle, seeks Food and Drug Administration approval for the pill.

1960

Sylvia Pankhurst dies.

Coronation Street begins, and with it the reign of Ena Sharples and Elsie Tanner.

1961

The pill is made available on the NHS.

The first branch of Mothercare opens.

1962

Elizabeth Lane is appointed the first woman county court judge.

The TV satire *That Was the Week That Was* begins; one of its stars is Millicent Martin.

Doris Lessing publishes *The Golden Notebook*, the story of writer Anna Wulf.

1963

Betty Friedan publishes *The Feminine Mystique*, which identified 'the problem that has no name' and marked the beginning of second-wave feminism.

In the Kitchen with . . .

Patience Gray

'Large fishes are best left unscaled . . .'

Rationing. How miserable it was. 'Shoot straight, lady,' urged one of the Ministry of Food's many wartime posters. 'FOOD is your munition of war.' It was up to women to keep the nation fighting fit. But how few weapons the housewife infantry had at their disposal! No meat, no eggs, no butter, no sugar, no cream and barely any fruit. The cookbooks of the day, so chipper it makes you want to weep, are full of ideas for mock foods: marzipan cobbled from haricot beans and almond essence; eggs that are really tinned apricots fried in bacon fat. One cold afternoon in the

..Shoot straight, Lady

British Library I opened one of these books and realised with a start that I was looking at advice for cooking crow. 'Boil it up with suet,' said the writer, 'to keep the meat as white as possible.' There was a recipe for sparrow pie too – though the Ministry of Food did not 'encourage' the eating of these tiny birds.

Reams have been written about snoek, an imported tinned fish no one cared to eat. Ditto Woolton pie, a concoction of boiled vegetables named for the Minister of Food. But you get a truer sense of the privations of rationing by thinking about what people missed than by how they made do (or not). Oh, the *longing* that was there. On 5 March 1944 Vere Hodgson, who worked as a social worker during the war, recorded in her diary that a shop near her flat in Notting Hill had got hold of some oranges. 'We have seen orange peel in the street,' she wrote. And then: 'Most refreshing *even to look at it.*' In 1946 Elizabeth David, the future author of *Mediterranean Food*, returned to London from India, where she moved in with her pregnant sister Diana and promptly took over the shopping. 'One day, I took back to her, among the broken biscuits and the tins of snoek . . . one pound of fresh tomatoes. As I took them out of my basket to show her, I saw that tears were tumbling down my sister's beautiful and normally serene face.' Elizabeth asked Diana what on earth was wrong. 'Sorry,' she was told. 'It's just that I've been trying to buy fresh tomatoes for five years. And now it's you who've found them first.'

Things did not improve after the war; they got worse. In 1946 bacon, poultry and egg rations were all reduced, and the National Loaf shrank; far more shockingly, bread, flour and oatmeal were rationed for the first time (the government had agreed to donate part of the nation's wheat crop to Germany, the price of America supplying the bulk of what was needed to the starving nation). In 1947 a bad winter led to restrictions on potatoes. Milk was also in short supply, and canned meat and fish no longer coming in from America. Bread was removed from the ration in 1948, along with jam, but there then followed a long and dreary wait. Tea was not de-rationed until 1952; sweets, cream, eggs and sugar until 1953; butter, cheese, margarine, cooking fats and meat until 1954. At this point the cookbook-writers went into celebratory mode. Suddenly it was glamorous to be at the stove: new homes were being built at a rate of three hundred thousand a year, with new kitchens full of new appliances – and now, just in the nick of time, food was abundant once more, which meant that these colourful new work surfaces (Formica!) could be put to good use. People could *entertain*. They could be *adventurous*. A trickle of books turned into a deluge, one that has been unstoppable pretty much ever since.

Of course, it was a while before most people would be eating, say, pasta as a matter of course. I was born in 1969, and into a family that cared about food, but it was 1977 at least before I tasted an avocado, 1978 before I tried lasagne and some years after that before my stepmother first attempted to cook a risotto. We were deep into the Eighties before most of us ate a salad leaf other than butter lettuce, and nudging the Nineties when pesto became a craze (and only then the ersatz kind, in little glass jars). This is why we must take cookbooks, whether written in 1945 or 2005, with a pinch of salt: they tell us more about our aspirations than about our daily lives (and this, perhaps, is why I remain unconvinced that anyone ever cooked a crow for their dinner – though I hope the thought of its black feathers shocked you as you read about it). Fifty years from now people will look at the cookbooks in kitchens like yours and mine and assume that our lives were one long celebration of spelt and sea bass, samphire and salsify. But the truth is that I can't tell you when I last used any of these things. Indeed, I have never knowingly cooked salsify.

It is in this context that we must consider Elizabeth David and her vastly less well-known but equally talented peer Patience Gray.

David's ambition, her sheer chutzpah, cannot, I think, be under-estimated; outrageously, she published her first cook book, *Mediterranean Food*, in 1950, four long years before rationing ended. But her *influence* surely can. This book and those that followed it were only ever read by a small, select crowd, and even after rationing ended its fans would not have been able to get hold of many of the things she described: the figs and the aubergines, the polenta and the pistachio nuts. But, of course, that hardly mat-tered. She was not writing for the masses – she was too grand for that – and nor, in all honesty, was she writing a handbook. As Rosemary Hill has pointed out, David was to cooking what Bernard Leach was to ceramics: *A Potter's Book*, published in 1940 but unexpectedly popular after the war, offered a similar kind of par-adise in its description of the lives of Oriental craftsmen to the one David evoked in the olive groves of Europe. Just as the majority of Leach's readers had no intention of building themselves a kiln, so David's were mostly not about to make a bouillabaisse for dinner. David was certainly prescient. The food she wrote about is everywhere today. But in her own time she fed fantasies, not families.

Perhaps because she is still so famous, people often assume that David was the Fifties' best-selling food writer. In fact that acco-lade must go to Patience Gray and her 1957 book, *Plats du Jour*, some hundred thousand copies of which were sold before the decade was out. It is said that David and Gray met just once, in 1961, for dinner in the flat of their mutual acquaintance, an antiquarian book dealer called Irving Davis. But if this is so neither one of them recorded the occasion. What would such a meeting have been like? Terrifying, one imagines. For one thing, they were the kind of women who mostly preferred male company to that of their own sex; impossible to imagine them, heads bent, sharing baking tips. For another, they were too similar for each to have taken the other for a kindred spirit; as every junior science

PATIENCE GRAY · 7

student knows, like poles repel. If such an encounter did happen, one hopes that Davis was more than usually circumspect with the claret.

Both came from the upper middle classes, growing up in large Jacobean manor houses in Sussex where legendarily bad nursery food was cooked by cooks and served by maids, and both were famously beautiful and intelligent. Compared to most British women their age they were well travelled and in possession of complicated, bohemian private lives. Elizabeth David, as all the world surely knows by now, spent the war abroad, travelling to Greece in a small boat in 1939 with Charles Gibson Cowan, an actor and writer, and thence to Egypt; Patience Gray was in London and Sussex for the duration of the war, sharing her life with a badly behaved man called Thomas Gray, but she went to Romania in 1938, and later to France, Italy and Yugoslavia. Most significant of all, both women enjoyed a brief period in thrall to older mentors who would have a profound influence on their careers as food writers. David met the writer Norman Douglas in Antibes when she was twenty-six and he was seventy-two; he is the dedicatee of *Mediterranean Food*. Patience Gray met Irving Davis when she was forty and he was sixty-nine; the seventh chapter of her masterpiece *Honey from a Weed* is a tribute to him, and in 1967, after his death, she edited his Catalan cookery book, *A Collection of Impossible Recipes*.

What about their work? Both women were extremely clear-sighted about what it was that they wanted their books to do. Controlling, you might say. You see this in their prose (bracing), in their recipes (sophisticated, unapologetic) and even in the illustrators they chose starting out (John Minton in the case of David, and David Gentleman in the case of Gray: neo-Romantics, the pair of them). David was first into print, but Gray beat her to it when it came to French *cuisine bourgeoise*; David's *French Provincial Cooking*, the most accessible of her books, was published some four years after the chic but unprecedentedly user-friendly *Plats du Jour*.*

And yet, as I have said, we know so much about one – Elizabeth David's story has been told many times, in print and on screen – and so little about the other. Gray, perhaps because she was the more unconventional of the two, and perhaps because she followed her heart in a way that David never did, remains in the shadows. This is not a competition, and I am not about to make it one. They were both glorious, fascinating, pioneering. But I will say this. It was Gray who hung on to her ideals right to the end (though this does not mean that her opinions calcified; she never ceased to be interested in the world and in other people). She was a cook *to her bones*: not for her the diet of instant coffee and Ritz crackers Elizabeth David would come to favour in old age. When it came to the details of her life she was, like David, wilfully vague.† The ins and outs could be glossed over, she felt. But when it came to dinner, she meant what she said. She *lived* her words. 'As can be seen, all this chopping and pounding has much to do with health,' she once wrote. She could no more give it up than she could breathing.

Patience Gray was born on 31 October 1917 at Shackleford, near Godalming in Surrey, the second of the three daughters of Hermann Stanham, a major in the Royal Field Artillery, and his wife Olive. The family home was Mitchen Hall, a grand but rather isolated house of peach-coloured brick, whose oak-panelled rooms overlooked 'a world of woods, garden, cherry trees' and beyond

---

* It is striking that Patience Gray is not mentioned at all in *Writing at the Kitchen Table*, Artemis Cooper's authorised biography of Elizabeth David.
† As Artemis Cooper notes, David always behaved 'like a married woman' even when she was not. Her busy private life as a younger woman was tidied away in the assurances of her publisher that 'Mrs David has kept house in France, Italy, Greece and Egypt' – as if she were just another diplomatic wife. (She was a divorcee.)

them the Hog's Back, that part of the North Downs which rises far higher than the countryside around. For Patience, Mitchen Hall was a place of 'wonder and terror' whose every nook and cranny she would remember until the end of her life. 'Mysteries without and mysteries within,' she wrote of it in her maddeningly cryptic collection of essays, *Work Adventures Childhood Dreams*. 'Sunbeams streamed into these rooms, in which the dancing dust particles were so clearly seen against the darkened panelling that they were imagined, then known to be, slides for fairy beings. The passages, concealing cupboards in their walls, the winding stairs with carved balusters, impressed mere infants with uncertain feelings, as if at any moment some terrifying "thing" might appear ...'

Major Stanham was not quite what he seemed. Stanham was his mother's maiden name. His real name was Warschawski, and he was the son of a Jewish professor of Hebrew who had fled persecution in Poland in the middle of the nineteenth century, become active in the London Society for Promoting Christianity among the Jews and had finally been ordained as a Unitarian minister in about 1900. Major Stanham's career in the army, moreover, was running in parallel to a photographic studio he kept up in Brighton – a business his children seem not to have known about until much later, and which operated under his real name.* But outwardly he was an upper middle class Englishman, and this was what his daughters took him for. Thanks to an inheritance his wife had received from her grandfather the family had servants, and the children were brought up in high Edwardian style by their nanny in a nursery at the top of the house; later, there would be governesses, often French. Left alone – Nanny would regularly disappear down the back stairs for tea with Cook –

* A notice in the *London Gazette* of 21 April 1903 announces Hermann's promotion from Captain to Lieutenant. In this, he is referred to as Hermann Stanham Warschawski. Before he joined the army Hermann had trained as a photographer's assistant.

Olive and her daughters. Patience is on the right, Tania on the left, Virginia carried piggyback

Patience would stand on a toy box and gaze on the garden below with its orchard, its enclosing yew walk, its tennis court and its wide lawn on which, in summer, tea would be taken: black lacquer tray, silver pot, cucumber sandwiches, strawberries and cream. 'Nanny's so wonderful!' her mother liked to say. 'She never leaves the children.' Unbeknownst to Olive, Nanny was also in possession of certain 'terror-inducing powers'. Sudden death was a favourite theme: it could, she informed the children, strike at any time, even in the paradise of the garden. Patience knew to avoid the pink-orange berries of the yew and the shiny black berries of the deadly nightshade. But still, magpies had to be saluted, knives and forks immediately straightened, salt handled with extreme care.

With the exception of her father, the household was entirely female. This did not improve Major Stanham's famously bad temper: 'Looking round the table he sighed, then came out with the familiar words: "*Women again . . . always women.*"' As an adult, Patience would lay her refusal to marry firmly at his feet. 'The kneeling upset me,' she wrote. 'I used to suffer appalling embarrassment when my mother got down on her knees to implore my father, who was sitting in a low armchair stretched with well-worn leather and completely absorbed in the *Times* fourth leader, to come to dinner.' Mealtimes were a battlefield. When the children were small he would command the maid to set down the dish of the day in front of one or other of them, knowing full well this would provoke tears (no one liked the look of Cook's spotted dogs and roly poly puddings). When they were older he would ask impossible questions, 'the answer to which was supposed to be a fundament of general knowledge'. There would then follow a lecture, a disquisition that proceeded without interruption because their mother carved the meat herself.

The Major was also mean to his daughters' governesses. One, Miss Collins, used to be teased about the arrival (or non-arrival) of letters from her fiancé in India. Another, Zella, was asked to take his prize boar for a walk – an outing that ended in disaster when the pig lay down in a ditch and refused to budge: the fuming Major, called from the sanctuary of his study to retrieve the hog, condemned this incident as 'a bad case of mismanagement of which only a woman is capable'. It was left to Patience's mother to act as his pacifier, a role on which she seemed to thrive. As her daughter put it drily, '"Pacifying" can also be seen, in retrospect, as "a bad case of masochism".' No one knew why their father was so choleric – though it must have had something to do with the war, it might also have been connected to his strange double life – but his moods were difficult to live with. 'I have listened to other people's accounts of their happy childhoods with sadness mingled with disbelief,' wrote Patience. 'I recognised mine as a snuffing out of every spontaneous impulse to the point where one might have been said to be walking on tiptoe to avoid the detonations.' The only respite came when her parents disappeared to hunt, to swing their golf clubs and, most blessed of all, to ski. (For them, this relatively new sport had an especially romantic aura, for they had first met on the slopes at Gstaad.) At these times a maiden aunt – the kind who lived in fear of draughts – would supervise the household and all would be peaceful, for a while, at least.

When Patience was six, however, the family's fortunes changed dramatically. On his return from the war and a stint in Mesopotamia, the Major had set up a pig farm near Basingstoke. When this failed – according to his middle daughter, he was born with 'zero business sense' and found himself quite unable to market his pigs – he moved the family back to Sussex, the county where he had grown up, buying a 'perfectly inconvenient farmhouse' halfway between a seaside golf club and the Pevensey Marshes. Here he returned to studio photography full time,* at which point Patience's parents' social life became altogether more rackety: 'Divorce, a word hitherto unknown, began to crop up at home in adult conversation, a signal for our dismissal to the schoolroom. Lingering on the stairs, one overheard phrases such as: "The cad! I've a good mind to go and horsewhip him." A supposed victim on one occasion – a rather fast and fascinating woman with [an] Eton crop, low husky voice and nine-inch ivory cigarette holder, who drilled my father through the clockwork paces of the foxtrot and the perilous complexities of the tango – inspired him to dash off and threaten the doubtless cruel but perhaps timid offender ... with a revolver. This high-flown action resulted in a visit from a policeman.'

Patience's maternal grandfather and her mother's sister Dodo began to worry about Olive, 'detecting in my father's indifference to breadwinning a growing threat to my mother's peace of mind and pocket. Our bread and butter could be traced to mysterious "shares" left to her by Grandmother. In the financial landslides of

---

* Patience did not, I think, realise that he was returning to his original trade. Similarly, she did not find out about her Jewish roots until late in life – a discovery that delighted her.

the time, she became the object of their solicitude . . . *poor Olive.*'
It was on her sister's account, then, that Dodo suggested Patience,
a prodigiously intelligent child, should live with her in term time
and attend school in London with her youngest cousin.

For Patience, this was a terrifying prospect. Aunt Dodo, a talented musician, was a 'glittering' figure. She had a large collection
of 'late-afternoon adorers' with whom she liked to discuss Proust
and Wagner, and she was married to the distinguished obstetri-
cian Eardley Holland (later *Sir* Eardley Holland), a saturnine
figure who was 'often reported to be "perfectly charming" to his
female patients'.* At home, Patience was the only daughter
capable of speaking to Major Stanham without stammering or
blushing. But in London – the Hollands lived, in grand style,
close to Harley Street – she found that she could not countenance the idea of uttering so much as a single word to Uncle
Eardley. She had, it seemed, moved out of the frying pan and into
the fire: 'At breakfast, he gloomily, silently, savagely surveyed the
five females [the Hollands also had three girls] from the far end
of the table, frowning, then with a grunted Umph! retired behind
the *Times,* emanating thunderous vibrations.' The family was
always relieved when, at 8.30, his chauffeur arrived to take him to
the London Hospital.

Being 'a half-fledged cuckoo in alternating family nests' gave
Patience a certain detachment. Moving between the two houses
threw all sorts of things into relief, for the contrast between them
was now severe: 'While the tea tray was still being gracefully
borne across the polished parquet in Queen Anne Street [the

---

* This may be code – or sarcasm. Holland had a long affair with the novelist Elizabeth Jenkins,
whom he met during the war, and who described him as the love of her life. 'He wasn't faithful to his wife,' said Jenkins many years later. 'I wondered why she didn't value him more;
so many women, including me, would happily have changed places with her. I offered him
my heart on a plate. He made me unhappy, but it was worth it.' Jenkins wrote one of the
great novels of the Fifties – and one of the great novels of any age about marriage – *The Tortoise
and the Hare.*

Hollands' home], financial extremity faced my mother with new tasks.' Thanks to the Depression, the Stanhams now lacked both cook and housemaid, and Olive was forced to perform their duties herself. By rights Patience should have admired her mother's stoicism, the determined way she learned to make kedgeree, angels on horseback and all the other familiar dishes on the her newfangled gas stove. But somehow she could not. The 'pursed lips of self-immolation' saw to that. When her mother set about the hall gong with the Brasso, she and her siblings would 'linger on the sidelines as spectators'. There was something frantic in these displays of domestic drudgery that Patience disliked. 'I don't exaggerate this obsession with things to be kept up,' she writes in *Work Adventures Childhood Dreams*. 'When Major Blacker, who so recently had flown solo over Everest, a hero, was invited to dinner, my elder sister and I were reluctantly transformed into spotless maids in starched aprons and caps in order to bring on the asparagus, the roast pheasants, and the Stilton cheese.'

At the bridge tables frequented by her father, having a clever daughter was 'a misfortune equivalent to the loss of a dog or an Act of God'. But at least this meant that Patience was spared the fate of her older sister Tania,* shortly to be dispatched to Switzerland to learn household management, and at her new school, Patience thrived. Queen's College in Harley Street,† founded by the Victorian theologian and social reformer Frederick Denison Maurice, was a liberal establishment respectful of the rights of women, having begun its life as a place where governesses might be educated. The atmosphere was serious and

---

* Tania became a photographer. Her work appeared in *National Geographic* and elsewhere. She married the journalist John Midgley, who had a long career at *The Economist*.

† Among her contemporaries at Queen's College were the daughters of the Labour politician Stafford Cripps, and Unity Mitford, who was a boarder: 'Try to imagine an outsize supercilious beautiful doll harnessed inside a gym tunic, aloof and dumb, outraged at being thus confined.'

the teachers able and passionate (save for poor Miss Enderby, a 'well-intentioned, broad-bottomed lady' whom the girls liked to tease, and whom Patience would one day meet again in a short story by Katherine Mansfield, an old girl whose portrait hung in the school's entrance hall). Drawn to the Jewish girls in her class, a group she thought particularly bright and quick, Patience began to feel competitive, and with pleasing results: by the time she was fourteen she had already qualified for university entrance.

She spent her final year at school as a boarder – it's not clear why; perhaps Uncle Eardley had had enough – sharing a top-floor bedroom with a girl from Berlin called Edith Goeritz and Ann Stephen, Virginia Woolf's niece. ('A victim of psychoanalysis', according to Patience, Stephen mistook her narrow bed for the analyst's couch with the result that her dorm-mates had to listen to her droning free associations late into the night.) Patience found boarding ridiculous at times – 'how absurd to remember the midnight feast which, in a childish fit, the boarders had conspired to hold underneath the long table in the library' – but Queen's taught her to be both free-thinking and spirited, and when she went home to Sussex for the holidays she noticed immediately the effect she had on the young men in her parents' social set. The 'least gleam of thought or the slightest satirical inflection' in the direction of these youths, callow or otherwise, caused them both anxiety and irritation. She found their chat – what animals they had shot, what injuries had befallen them when they 'took a toss' from their horses, what miracle they had performed on the billiard table – intensely boring. Her father, meanwhile, regarded these young men as 'undesirable intruders'. He had not left home until he was forty. Wouldn't his daughters be doing the same?

Patience had other ideas. She longed 'for air and flight'. Too young to take up her place at university, she went first to Bonn to learn German and study economics, though she soon swapped

Patience in Germany, 1936

the latter for history of art. Bonn was her father's choice, being a
safe little town; Paris he deemed immoral, and Rome, Florence
and Perugia were 'out of the question.' She lived in a 'kind of
prison', a seventeenth-century observatory in the Poppelsdorfer
Allee which she shared with the professor of astronomy and his
wife and child. To escape the observatory's claustrophobic atmosphere she spent much of her time walking in the old town, and
it was here that she discovered the baroque. 'I was drawn to these
musical façades and domed interiors where imagination could
take off and soar ... ' It was not the gilt and the putti that she
loved but the spaces, and their glorious flowing curves soon
'entered her dreams'. What did these dreams mean? Freedom.
Escape. Or, as Patience put it in her slightly more grandiose style,
'Edwardians! Let me breathe and live!'

In England once more she began her degree at London
University, where her tutor was Hugh Gaitskell, the future
Labour leader. She read economics which was, by all accounts,
Dodo's idea; since her father was not going to be able to support
her – it wasn't only that funds were low; he was now suffering
from cancer and would soon die – she needed to study a subject

that might help her to earn a living. But she knuckled down all the same. Better economics, she thought, than a return to Sussex and the young men with their gumboots and their billiard cues.

In 1938, after she had graduated, Patience and her sister Tania travelled to eastern Europe on a grant from the Society of Quakers, their brief 'to make friends with the Romanians'. From the scant details we have, their three-month stay seems to have been an extraordinary experience – though it's important to bear in mind Patience's tendency to myth-making. Given to making Delphic pronouncements, her writing was often opaque, perhaps because life seemed more interesting that way. 'She had this ... *idea*,' says her daughter Miranda. 'You had a little black dress [among your luggage] that you could wear on any occasion, and then you travelled on carts and met the people.' And so it went. The sisters spent time in Balcic, a formerly Turkish town close to the Black Sea (it's now in Bulgaria), where they drank mazagran (black coffee poured over honey and shreds of ice) and Patience wandered its ancient sites with an archaeologist called Rosetti, whom she hoped, somewhat misguidedly, to use as a human Baedeker (in fact, they got terrifyingly lost). In Bucharest – a city then so elegant it was known as Little Paris – she and Tania stayed in the only 'respectable' hotel, all carmine damask, deep red plush and yellowing marble. In as long as it took to turn the key in the door of her room, she was grown up.

In July Marie of Romania, the Queen consort, died, with the result that Patience was moved to write her first piece of journalism, for a (presumably English language) Bucharest newspaper. The funeral made for great copy. Marie, a granddaughter of Queen Victoria who is sometimes referred to as the jazz-age princess, had led a life full of intrigue and drama and her coffin, followed by an honour guard of hussars, nuns and wounded veterans, moved through a city that the king had commanded to be draped all about with her favourite colour, mauve. (Marie's heart, incidentally, was sent to Balcic, where she had kept a beloved summer palace.) But no sooner had Patience delivered her report than the newspaper's infatuated editor laid siege to her, filling her hotel room with tuberoses, the cloying scent of which would thereafter always fill her with remembered horror. The story goes that she and Tania escaped his attentions by fleeing to the Black Sea in a monoplane piloted by a Romanian prince.

Safely back in London, Patience acquired a job at the Foreign Office. But she held on to it for only a few months: when war broke out in 1939 she was promptly dismissed – well, this was her story – for 'having too many foreign contacts'. Her next job was as a secretary at the Arts Council, and it was there that she met Thomas Gray, a designer and veteran of the Spanish Civil War.* In his spare time, Gray was running a clandestine counter-insurgency course for the Home Guard at Hurlingham in west London. He was married and had two children, but Patience – caught up in what Elizabeth Bowen would call the 'lucid abnormality' of the Blitz – became his lover anyway. And why stop there? She also became the secretary of this somewhat barmy-sounding training school for civilians who wanted to learn 'how to make Molotov cocktails'. Hard to say which was the more exciting.

For a while she and Gray were happy. In January 1941, by which time he and Patience already had a son, Nicolas, she took his name by public announcement in the *London Gazette*. A daughter, Miranda, was born in 1942. But then things changed. Gray was a womaniser, and when he tried to seduce one of her friends Patience resolved to give him up. She left London and moved to her mother's cottage, which stood in a wood on the South

---

* Thomas Gray was the brother of Milner Gray, the artist and designer who founded the Design Research Institute (where Thomas may have worked after the war). The DRI made important contributions to the Britain Can Make It exhibition of 1946, and to the Festival of Britain. He was a close friend of the artist Graham Sutherland.

Downs. The trouble was that she was pregnant again. Believing she could not bring up three children alone she decided to have the baby – a daughter called Prudence – adopted, a decision that turned out to be even more painful than it might ordinarily have been.* The baby was seriously ill, and for a while was returned to Patience so she could nurse her (only mother's milk, it was thought, would see her through). This was agonising. Meanwhile, Gray had been conscripted. Patience was terribly alone, coping with a sick baby and two small children (though Nicolas was eventually evacuated to Fowey) in 'a kind of *Walden* situation, with no telephone, electricity or water laid on'. The cottage didn't even feel that safe. Planes could often be heard overhead, and behind the house was a dirty great bomb crater. In the end Prudence did not survive. As if this weren't bad enough, her adoptive parents would not allow Patience to attend the funeral.

After this, Gray fell out of the picture. Patience never spoke of him, and Nicolas and Miranda did not see him again, though there was an occasion when they found themselves bundled hurriedly on to a number 24 bus in Camden Town. 'That was your father,' said Patience once they were safely on board. In *Work Adventures Childhood Dreams* she refers to him only twice, and then only very briefly. He was, she writes, courageous during the Blitz. In an afterword she notes that she never found, in the Forties and Fifties, 'the propitious moment' for explaining to Nicolas and Miranda, 'who had forgotten they had known their father', why she had not married him, nor anyone else. Towards the end of her life, when she was unwell and her mind wandering, she would watch Nicolas, who resembles Thomas, stoking the fire at her house in Italy and she would say softly, 'There's my husband.' But

---

* I have been unable to find out any more about this adoption drama. Patience never spoke about the baby, and only revealed the adoption to Miranda in old age.

in 1943, when they separated, she thought of him only as a huge mistake. She turned her back on him and on all the trouble he had brought her. From now on, she would live for herself.

Patience remained in Sussex until the winter of 1947, the worst in living memory, at which point the relentless cold and her difficult relationship with the widowed Olive sent her back to London. (Olive, a follower of Krishnamurti, was not judgemental about her daughter's lifestyle; she was delighted to have grandchildren. The problem was more that Patience expected her to disapprove and so bristled anyway.) In the city she hoped to be able to make enough money to educate Nicolas and Miranda, and to keep a roof over their heads. But she also longed for an interesting life. 'There is nothing to say about work,' she once wrote. 'It occupies you intensely if it's what you choose to do.' She wanted to make just such a choice. There followed a series of temporary jobs until, in 1951, she was appointed research assistant to F. H. K. Henrion, designer of the displays inside the Country Pavilion at the Festival of Britain. This was a wonderful opportunity, and not only because of the hullabaloo that surrounded the Festival. Henrion, kind, encouraging and cultivated, was fantastically well-connected: his friends included the writer and naturalist Julian Huxley, the Labour politician Tony Benn and Walter Neurath, the founder of Thames & Hudson. To belong to his circle was to belong to London's intellectual and creative elite.*

What research did Patience do? A good deal of it must have been logistical; the pavilion was an organisational nightmare. It was divided in two: one section, entitled *The Natural Scene*, featured a

---

* Patience loved meeting artistic types, especially writers. In *Work Adventures Childhood Dreams* she describes how she met T. S. Eliot at a Sussex cocktail party in 1950. They talked for a long time – until the curtains were drawn and the lights went up, and all the other guests had gone on their way. They drank many gin and tonics, and talked of London and Henry James, whose 'interminable sentences' muffled Eliot's sense of the present.

huge plaster tree with a woodland garden and pools of water at its foot; visitors gazed at it through a tank of live butterflies. The other, *The Country*, was filled with animals – horses, cows, sheep, goats, chickens, ducks and bees – and a variety of tractors, which moved, bizarrely, up and down on a series of hydraulic columns. The horses had to be transported to Hyde Park every day for exercise, and the fish fed with plankton, deliveries of which came from the Lake District each morning. The butterflies were kept alive with wildflowers, dug up by a network of boy scouts. Slightly less complicated to mount were the geological display and an exhibit of rural crafts,* the highlight of which was a vast narrative stump-work embroidery, *The Country Wife*, designed by the great Constance Howard to depict Women's Institute activities such as baking and weaving (it had been worked by her students at Goldsmiths' College, among them Mary Quant).†

It may have been thanks to Henrion that Patience got her next job, as a secretary at the Royal College of Art (he sometimes used to teach in the design school). But though she somehow hung on to this position until 1953 – according to someone who knew her at the time, she simply wasn't malleable enough to survive for long as a secretary – she had another iron in the fire. At the Festival of Britain an artist called Primrose Boyd had been among her colleagues, and the two women now set up their own

* As one visitor, Dylan Thomas, put it, 'What a pleasure of baskets! Trugs, creels, pottles and punnets, heppers, dorsers and mounds, wiskets and whiskets.' According to her daughter Miranda, Patience was at one point friendly with Thomas.
† Howard, embroiderer and textile designer, won a scholarship to study at the Royal College of Art in the Thirties. She then went into teaching. At Kingston School of Art, where she spent the war, she and her students embroidered maps for the RAF, which were then photographed – a technique that produced great clarity. The students who worked on *The Country Wife* would go to her house in Chelsea both to embroider and to babysit her new daughter Charlotte. Howard would feed them tripe and onions, which she thought good for them. *The Country Wife* was so large it had to be assembled on site. According to the Embroiderers Guild, Howard inspected it every weekend because sections kept disappearing. One, featuring a fish, had to be replaced four times.

freelance research partnership. Their business cards – touchingly and pluckily entrepreneurial, but rather prim – informed potential clients that they would take on 'all kinds' of research and 'report writing' for the rate of five shillings an hour plus expenses, and that commissions would be completed 'accurately, fully and promptly'. When they said all kinds of research, they meant it. The list of their 'SPECIAL SUBJECTS' was extensive: bibliography, cartography, indoor gardening, horticulture, office organisation, kitchen equipment 'and practice'. The last item on this list was opportunist but hardly surprising, for the two of them had also begun work on a cookbook.

Patience's growing interest in cookery had two sources. In Sussex, poverty and rationing had sent her out foraging, which was how she had learned about mushrooms: which ones to pick, and

Foraging in Sussex

how to eat them (she carried them home in a basket lined with moss). But she had by now travelled quite a lot too. In 1947, leaving the children with their grandmother, she had seen Rome for the first time, a city she felt should be approached humbly, 'on one's knees'. She followed this with the first of what would be several visits to Brittany, where she and Nicolas and Miranda stayed in the Hôtel Lautram in a village called Locmariaquer and enjoyed the good Breton butter, the fat, fresh oysters and the 'rosy mullets' fished at dawn and bathed in an equally rosy sauce ('M. Lautram was that mysterious personage, a great cook . . . Fish dishes were his forte.')* In 1951 she had made her way, alone, to Paris, and thence to Yugoslavia on the Orient Express, a route inspired by some of the writers she loved: Gissing, Smollet and Stendhal.

Patience had arrived in London a pretty terrible cook. 'My first introduction [to cooking] was desperate,' she recalled. 'I lived in a sordid square in an old Victorian house and, inspired by a particular article, tried to cook a sheep's head à la Russe. It was absolutely indescribable, and made a frothy scum which filled the whole kitchen.' But when she moved to the Logs, a sprawling Victorian Gothic mansion on the edge of Hampstead Heath – it still stands; Pevsner describes it as a 'formidable atrocity' – her skills began to improve. She and Miranda† lived and worked in its former billiard room; they slept on a mezzanine – little more

---

* *Les rougets au vin blanc de Monsieur Lautram:* For eight red mullets, put 80g butter and a glass of white wine in an oven dish with the fish and cook in a moderate oven for 25 minutes. Thicken the liquor in a pan with good butter and a little flour. Set the fish in a serving dish, cover with the sauce and sprinkle with parsley. Patience adds: 'This is the recipe he gave me written in French in his own hand. What he fails to say is that the sauce, copious and perfectly amalgamated, is achieved by a *tour de main*. A perfect example of a "simple" recipe conveying no idea of procedure, or an instance of a true Breton's reluctance to share his secrets.'

† Nicolas was away at boarding school. According to Miranda, there was no room for him at the Logs. When term was over he and his sister would grab their cat, Pussy Willow, and head straight to their grandmother's in Sussex. The children, incidentally, called their mother Patience.

than a shelf, really – designed for her by Alexander Gibson, one of the architects of the Regatta Restaurant at the Festival of Britain.* The billiard room, for all its obvious drawbacks and eccentricities, suited Patience very well, for she was an early adopter of open-plan living, believing that it was quite wrong for the cook to be marooned in a separate room. Her kitchen, then, was an alcove at one end of the space, and her dining table just a wooden shelf attached to a wall, which she called the Lion's Bar (a lion's head hung on the wall above it – a sculpture constructed by Nicolas and Miranda from lead collected from the crumpled roofs of bombed houses and melted down).

At the Logs she liked to entertain, and gave Sunday lunches oiled with plenty of wine: talky gatherings of Hampstead neighbours such the writer Marghanita Laski and her husband John Howard. Henrion would come, and his colleague John Brinkley, the typographer who'd done the lettering at the Lion and Unicorn Pavilion. Also a young art student, David Gentleman. Patience and Gentleman had grown very friendly, and by the time he went off to Italy on a travelling scholarship in the summer of 1954 it was understood that while he was there he would gather material for Patience's book, which she had asked him to illustrate.

It took a long time to write, this cookbook: she and Primrose began working on it in 1953 or thereabouts, and would not finish it for another four years. Patience was scrupulous about testing its recipes: it made her furious when Primrose failed to do this, and she would often end up dismissing her co-writer's dishes once she'd tried them herself. (She was not, you gather, terribly easy to

---

* Gibson's co-designer at the Regatta Restaurant was Misha Black, Milner Gray's partner at the Industrial Design Partnership – which suggests, perhaps, that she still kept tabs on Thomas's life, or at least that she knew what he was up to. The restaurant sat on the river next to Hungerford Bridge, adjacent to the Skylon. It was the main showcase for the Festival Pattern Group, a selection of futuristic-looking fabrics whose designs were inspired by crystal structures. The food was said to be awful.

*Patience smoking a Craven A at the Logs; on the bentwood hatstand hangs
a winnowing basket, possibly from Madame Cadec's shop on Greek Street*

work with, and because of this it was ultimately Patience who
ended up writing and editing the main body of the book.) Then
there was the shopping involved. Ingredients had to be hunted
down. It's a cliché of food writing to note that in the Fifties olive
oil could only be purchased at a chemist. What people tend to
forget is that the same was also true of – for instance – Tidman's
Sea Salt, an item most people used for bathing but which Patience
recommended for seasoning fish and meat.

The best shops were in Soho: Parmigiani's and Roche's in Old
Compton Street, Schmidt's in Charlotte Street and – for kitchen
kit rather than for ingredients – Cadec's in Greek Street, which
stood next to a 'hospitable place called Rose's, whose horsemeat
steaks and dandelion salads kept a happy few well nourished

during the war'. Cadec's was an emporium that filled Patience with awe. Established in 1862, only master cooks had, she felt, the true right of admission. Sometimes, her nerve having failed her at the last, she would simply remain outside, studying through Madame Cadec's window all her wonderful and exotic wares: 'the beautiful terrines with hares and pheasants moulded in deep relief on their lids, the chef's knives, silver *hatelets* surmounted by cocks' and boars' heads, the embossed tin moulds for iced puddings in the form of pineapples and bunches of grapes . . . '

Inside, the proprietor 'occupied the foreground, an ample figure, her hair piled high and her eyes attentive to every detail behind their rimless pince-nez', while around her stood great cairns of stuff piled high from floor to ceiling. Navigating these finely balanced pyramids of copper and earthenware was perilous, but mysteriously galvanising. 'The essential thing about this charged interior was that it contained nothing which had not a practical significance,' Patience wrote in *Honey from a Weed*. 'But the quality was so superb that the function of the objects seemed to be transcended. Beautiful in themselves, they were an invocation to produce good food.' At home she worked away, practising her *daube de boeuf* and her *pot au feu*, her *bouillabaisse* and her *poulet à l'estragon*. She wasn't a great one for modern gadgets: no mixer, no dish-washer, no ice-cream machine. Her *batterie de cuisine*, however, was a splendid sight to see, and she had Madame Cadec to thank for it.

Plats du Jour, or Foreign Food was finally published by Penguin in 1957. As planned, David Gentleman was its illustrator, and he gave it the adorable cover which was (and still is) so much a part of its appeal.* It was an instant success, selling fifty thousand copies in

---

* Gentleman told me that he 'cribbed' the arrangement of the book from John Minton, Elizabeth David's illustrator. 'An opener for each section of a big picture, and then smaller drawings scattered throughout.' The frontispiece, of a woman lunching outside in the shade of what looks like a wisteria, was a drawing he'd first made in Milan, on his student tour. When I told him how many copies the book sold he looked amazed. 'I'd no idea,' he said.

its first ten months. It isn't difficult to work out why. Of course people liked the recipes, which were pleasingly straightforward, and which came not only from France, but from Spain and Italy too (the book seemed to be doing the work of several volumes twice its size, and at the bargain price of just three shillings and sixpence). *Moussaka, ratatouille, moules marinères*: these things were easy to make, and delicious to boot. But it was also, in its own quiet way, an extremely fashionable book, and it made those who bought it feel modern. It was written for people like its author, who ate in their kitchens (or, if they didn't, *wanted* to), and who owned smart new cookware from Denmark that could be brought from oven to table ('armed with this utensil, it would be possible to produce most of the recipes in this book'). These readers preferred courgettes to marrows and fresh fish to tinned, and they sometimes – oh, the decadence! – drank wine with dinner *in the middle of the week.**

The tone of *Plats du Jour* was sophisticated, but it was rarely bossy and it was never severe. In this sense Patience and her co-author deftly occupied what might be called the middle ground. Consider, for instance, the still controversial issue of garlic. The authors of austerity cookbooks treated garlic with extreme trepidation, knowing that their readers were terrified of it. 'Please try it, just for once,' cajoled Peter Pirbright in his 1946 book, *Off the Beeton Track*. 'Not masses of garlic, just a tiny bit, half a clove, well crushed.' He was at one end of the scale. At the other was Elizabeth David, whose contempt for this kind of attitude rose from her pages like spitting fat from a hot pan. 'The grotesque prudishness and archness with which garlic is treated in this country has led to the superstition that rubbing the bowl with it

* To me, *Plats du Jour* feels more like a book of the Seventies than the Fifties, especially when you reach the chapter on fungi, which seems to have been written for *Good Life* types who combine 'an experimental approach to cooking with an interest in natural history'.

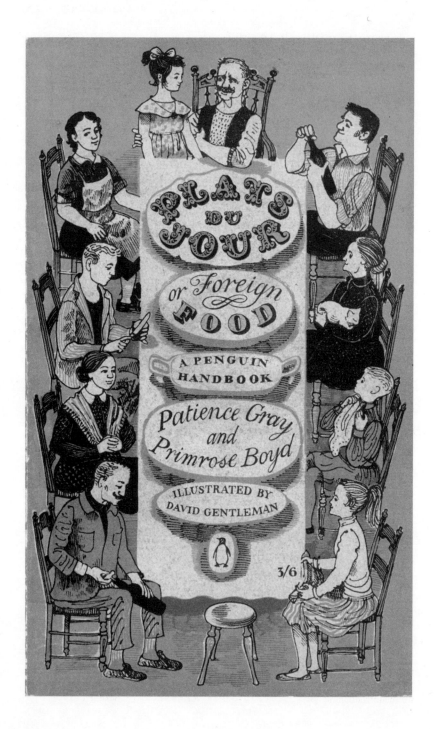

PLATS DU JOUR

or Foreign FOOD

A PENGUIN HANDBOOK

Patience Gray and Primrose Boyd

ILLUSTRATED BY DAVID GENTLEMAN

3/6

before putting the salad in gives sufficient flavour,' she wrote in *Summer Cooking* (1955). And then: 'It rather depends on whether you are going to eat the bowl or the salad.' Patience was in neither of these camps – or at least, not on the page. She would not beg and plead, but nor would she dismiss her readers' anxieties as rank stupidity. Having acknowledged garlic's pungent whiffiness, she set out to reassure: after all, this mighty allium is very easily reduced to 'a molecular state at the point of the knife or in the mortar'.* Try it in pesto, she said, or fried with mushrooms. She did not, of course, provide a recipe for pesto; an important part of the book's flattery is its occasional assumption that the reader knows exactly what its author is talking about.

It was no mean feat to have written what would become the best-selling cookbook of the Fifties, and Patience was thrilled by its success, for all that she would soon turn her back on many (though not all) of its tenets. But one senses that she did not want to be known only as a cookery writer. *Plats du Jour*, a brilliant calling card, now pushed open another door. In 1958 she entered a competition held by the *Observer*, which was in search of an editor for its first woman's page – and won. This was quite astonishing: she had been up against a thousand other entrants and she was not even a proper journalist – though she was not, it seemed, the editor's first choice. When David Astor, the paper's proprietor, told her he would be taking her on, the 'joyful news was mitigated by his adding that the "ideal person" they had endeavoured to persuade [to do the job] was not available'.†

What bliss to have a job with a regular salary that did not involve doing someone else's typing! But still, she mounted the

---

* She took a similar approach with David's beloved olive oil: 'Those who actively dislike the taste of olive oil might try ground-nut oil which is effective and cheaper.'

† Patience believed that the person in question was Anne Scott-James. For more on James, see the Introduction.

stairs at the *Observer*'s offices in Tudor Street with a 'slight tremor', a nervousness that proved to be well founded when she reached the top of them and discovered 'what appeared to be a club for old Etonians'. As she put it, 'A woman was not exactly *persona grata* at Tudor Street. The brilliant and delightful C. A. Lejeune [the film critic] was invisible, at home or watching films. Vita Sackville-West wrote her weekly article at Sissinghurst and posted it. Jane Bown [the photographer], already a wizard, then, was in her dark-room when not on photographic missions. Only Alison Settle,* marooned with her all too female fashion theme in a room apart, was established there.' Settle, the paper's thrusting and opinion-ated fashion editor, promptly invited Patience to lunch at the Women's Press Club: 'Not knowing that I was unclubbable, she invited me to join it. "Women," she said, "in a man's world should stick together." Over a glass of wine she looked at me appraisingly. "It's alright for you," she said, with a trace of acidity, "you have looks. I have had to make my way without them." What Alison had was red hair and character. She outlined her solitary uphill struggle. She was an early fashion pioneer, a quite indomitable profession. She made me realise that I was an amateur.'

The page Patience would edit was to be called 'A Woman's Perspective'. But what exactly did this mean? She wasn't sure. 'Of course I wondered what were women's subjects. In the late Fifties, it was not possible to discuss in print the question of how one might bring up two fatherless children and earn a living while contriving to get home at the precise moment they got back from school. It was this problem that impelled me to send my son to boarding school. I could only follow my own predilections and try to convince Nigel Gosling [her boss] that they might have

---

* Settle (1891–1980) was a former editor of *Vogue*, a vocal champion of women's rights and a contributor to the work of the Council for Art & Industry and the Council of Industrial Design.

some appeal for readers.' The only trouble was that her own predilections were already the province of other experts. The arts, gardening, food and drink: all of these were covered elsewhere, leaving Patience with what she called 'youth', modern architecture, design and 'craftsmanship'. But needs must. As she put it, 'These themes, rather oddly, began to furnish the Women's Page.'

Life at the *Observer* was fraught. Her male colleagues could not be relied upon to act like gentlemen. After long meetings she would sometimes pass Philip Toynbee on her way out; alas, it wasn't always possible to evade the critic's 'bearlike embrace' as she came down the narrow stairs and he came up, roaring drunk after a late lunch in Soho. These same men seemed to think she was there only to help them with their problems. Could she pop over and make their living rooms look more elegant? Could she advise on where they might buy cheap but attractive furniture? David Astor, having read an article she had written about a show of modern jewellery at the Goldsmith's Hall, asked her to choose a birthday present for his wife.

Then there was their response to her ideas. When she reported that she had just seen a brilliant performance by Marcel Marceau in Paris, she was told there was no point in writing it up: mime was so un-English! Only by writing for the *Observer*'s Foreign News Service, which sold stories to newspapers in far-off places, could she keep herself sane, for this allowed her to cover all manner of 'forbidden' subjects (contributing to it was, she said, 'like confiding a message to a bottle and casting it out to sea', the stories circumnavigating the world 'without remonstrance'). It was for the foreign press that she wrote of the spellbinding lecture given by the French actor Jean-Louis Barrault, to the students of Oxford University; of Henry Moore's retrospective at the Whitechapel Art Gallery; of the thrilling change Maria Callas had made to her interpretation of Medea between dress rehearsal and premiere.

She sometimes asked herself what her page *did* for women. Was it a morale booster? She hoped so. She deplored the pitiful women in the paintings of John Bratby,* who stared out of his canvases as if through the bars of a prison (they seemed, his defeated females, always to be surrounded by great piles of washing-up). She believed that women would rather learn than go shopping. She wanted her readers to look out to Europe, where life seemed altogether jollier and more enlightened, and it was therefore on their behalf, or so she told herself, that she travelled so much (on freebies, wherever possible; the paper was notoriously parsimonious, at least with her). She went to Paris and Milan, to Genoa and Venice, and even, on one occasion, to Turin, where she wrote about Pier Luigi Nervi's extraordinary modernist exhibition hall of reinforced concrete and ribbed steel: 'awe-inspiring, vast, a summit of engineering'. Her bosses, of course, remained mostly indifferent to 'the innovative genius burgeoning in foreign parts', and had their revenge by insisting that she also write a column about worthy domestic bargains such as rubber-backed carpets and battery chickens: 'Etonian tit-for-tat,' as she called it.

But I don't suppose she was really unhappy. Life was busy and interesting. She had several suitors, and at least one lover – though he was married and often unavailable. She was also in the throes of a heady platonic affair with Irving Davis, who sometimes accompanied her on these press trips. She and Davis, a gnome-like antiquarian book dealer with a shop in Bloomsbury, had met in London shortly after the publication of *Plats du Jour*. Shocked that she had had the temerity to write a cookbook

---

* John Bratby (1928–92) was a leading exponent of what the critic David Sylvester called the 'Kitchen Sink School'. He was married to the painter Jean Cooke, a much more talented artist than him – and, threatened by the competition, he was known to paint over her work when he ran out of canvases of his own. He would also beat her.

before she met him – Davis was a gourmet and a famously good cook – he had quizzed her on fungi, and when she passed this test with flying colours had invited her to dinner at his flat in Brunswick Square. Davis's dinner parties, held in his kitchen, were legendary affairs: best bone china, Venetian glass, fabulous claret. A highly particular cook, if a dish wasn't right he would destroy it altogether. He once threw a duck, imperfectly roasted, out of a window, where it became attached to a drainpipe several stories up; some days later the fire brigade had to be called, it being summer time and his neighbours put out by the smell. Thanks to this, dinner at his place was inevitably served rather late – though as he surely knew, this only heightened the pleasure of his guests, hunger making everything seem the more delicious.

It was at Davis's table that Patience now learned the 'full poetic meaning' of the word 'classical' when it came to cooking. 'His dishes were invocations to the ideal,' she writes in *Honey from a Weed*. 'His method of presenting them a celebration of his Mediterranean past [in 1911, when Davis was twenty-three, he had opened a bookshop in Florence with Giuseppe Orioli, a lover of Norman Douglas]. The effect was a kind of alchemy by which the past became manifest, and made me feel, in knowing him, I held the key to that lost Bohemia where Orioli, Douglas, Lawrence, Furbank, Beerbohm were creatures of substance, not of reminiscence.' The meal would usually begin with something simple: leeks *à la grecque*, sorrel soup or a plate of marinated anchovies. This would be followed by lobster, a *matelote* of eel or, in season, a game bird. Finally, to finish, there would be a salad with an 'admirable' dressing and, if Irving had been in Paris, perhaps some little goat's cheeses. I can't help but wonder whether devouring these feasts ever put the crimp on the success of *Plats du Jour*; the book might have been very different had it been written under Davis's influence. But it must have been wonderful, too: not just the deliciousness, but the feeling that he was a kindred spirit.*

Davis, whose wife Ivy Elstrob had died during the war, was a great womaniser. He and Patience were not lovers but they grew very close very quickly, and it wasn't long before they went travelling together, driving from Naples to Lecce in a tiny Fiat. This journey, made in the footsteps of Norman Douglas, took three weeks and was often arduous: Patience recalled 'tomb-like' hotel rooms and the fact that drinks were sometimes hard to come by ('If you see a bar, however primitive, stop at it – there won't be another for forty miles!'). But there were good olives to be had, and a perfect dish of mussels, cooked in their own juices over a hot fire at the side of the quay in Taranto. She was certainly enjoying herself. The children had joined her on this trip – Nicolas was by now sixteen and Miranda fifteen – but when Irving's stepdaughter Ianthe turned up and expressed surprise at his companions, it wasn't Patience who scarpered. Only the children were expected to disappear. She gave them twenty pounds – it was all she had at the time – and told them to hitchhike back to London. 'We walked along the road to Paestum,' remembers Miranda. 'A lady stopped in a car. She said: I will give you a lift, provided you let me take you to your parents. And we said: it's our mother who sent us off like this.' She and Nicolas made it to Rome and thence to Florence, relying on strangers to take them in. En route to Monaco they stayed at the house of Percy Lubbock, the memoirist and critic, in Lerici, Liguria; an acquaintance both of their mother and of their aunt Tania, they had his

---

* Many people, of course, found this kind of simplicity slightly baffling: the long years of rationing meant that they craved novelty, complexity, colour and the richness of sauces made from eggs and cream. Thanks to this, and to television cooks like Philip Harben and Fanny Cradock, dinner-party food had grown loopily garish. Cherries, angelica and pineapple chunks featured prominently; so too did piped mashed potato and strips of pepper arranged over the top of dishes in complicated geometric patterns.

address and made good use of it. They finally arrived in London three weeks later, where there was still no sign of Patience. 'She wasn't worried about us,' says Miranda. 'That didn't apply. She wasn't like other people's mothers.'

Back at the *Observer* — she made it home in the end — Patience had a new boss, George Seddon. She dropped into his neon-lit cubby hole of an office for a talk. Seddon told her that he had discovered *Observer* readers to be mostly working men living in Victorian back-to-backs in the Midlands. What did she think about this? She remarked that these working men clearly showed great discrimination when it came to their Sunday reading. Seddon, however, was unconvinced. Everything had to change, their needs catered for. As she would put it later, 'Consciences were wrung, *Which?* flourished, advertising perked up, and the paper, heading for Consumerland, began to descend the treacherous slope — to sing the deceptive but seductive joys of acquisition.' For the editor of 'A Woman's Perspective' this was the beginning of the end. In 1962, almost four years after her arrival at the *Observer*, Patience received 'a kind note from David Astor, doubtless on the urgent recommendation of George Seddon'. Time to go. Ah, well. She tried not to mind too much. She had enjoyed a good innings, given that most of her colleagues had never stopped thinking of her as an outsider. 'I think I was regarded as something of an anarchist,' she said, recalling her *Observer* days in 1987. 'I had a phobia about fashion . . . People were *appalled* by my appearance.'

Like many of the women in this book, Patience Gray's professional life had a resounding and singular second act. Hers, however, was an awfully long time coming. The curtain would not go up on it for another twenty-five years.

It happened like this. In 1962, she was at staying at Furlongs, the Sussex home of her friend Peggy Angus, the painter, designer and

Tea at Furlongs by Eric Ravilious

teacher. Furlongs, a former shepherd's cottage near Firle on the South Downs, had been much frequented by artists before the war, Eric Ravilious, Edward Bawden* and John Piper among them. Actually, there is a well-known painting by Ravilious from 1939 called *Tea at Furlongs*, and when I think about Patience at this time in her life it is this that I see in my mind's eye – an image at once both bohemian and intensely domestic, just like her. A table, set with a plate of bread and butter and covered with a strange black parasol stands hard by a low flint wall; beyond it cornfields unfold, yellow and green, like silk handkerchiefs pulled from a magician's hat. For Patience, Furlongs was a refuge, convivial

---

* Patience used to take Miranda to Great Bardfield in Essex to see Edward Bawden at his home there.

and restorative. She and Peggy were cut from the same cloth: passionate, fiery and more interested in creativity than in money.* In 1962, however, Peggy was happily consumed by her latest hand-printed wallpaper designs. Patience, on the other hand, was restless, expectant, waiting for the next thing. Her energy had nowhere to go.

One evening at Furlongs, a splendid sight: in the gloaming, a wild-haired Flemish sculptor called Norman Mommens appeared over the brow of a nearby hill, effigies on sticks in his hands. (Perhaps it was 5 November; there was certainly a bonfire at Furlongs that night, for Miranda, who was there, remembers that Norman put his sheepskin coat around her shoulders as she sat by it.) Had he walked the seven miles to Firle from the house he shared with his wife, the potter Ursula Mommens,† in South Heighton? It seems more than likely; he had about him the air of a man on the run.

By all accounts, Patience should have met Norman years before; he and Ursula had previously earned a living turning out mould-made ceramic heraldic beasts for the Festival of Britain, and they and Patience knew plenty of people in common. But for one reason or another, this was their first collision. Inside the house, they stood by the fireplace and talked: Patience told Norman that she was worried about Nicolas, who was then going through a rebellious phase. Norman told Patience about the difficulties in his marriage.

It wasn't long before Norman was visiting Patience at the Logs. For Miranda, now a student at Chelsea School of Art, this was

---

* Following her resignation from the *Observer*, Patience was working as a textile designer. She had also worked as one of the translators of the 1961 English-language edition of *Larousse Gastronomique*, and had written for *House & Garden* (the Logs even made it to the magazine's pages).

† Ursula Mommens, who died in 2010 at the age of 101, studied pottery with William Staite Murray at the Royal College of Art, and under Michael Cardew. Her first husband was the painter Julian Trevelyan.

delicate. Three was a crowd and so, without telling her mother what she was going to do, she quietly moved in with friends. Patience was upset by this, but perhaps she was relieved too; certainly, it was left to Norman to arrive at Miranda's door with a little bunch of snowdrops and ask her to come home. Norman, you see, was five years Patience's junior, and she was worried that he would run off with someone else – even with her own daughter. Of course, on the surface of it, this was silly. Norman was as devoted to her as she was to him. But you can see how the muddle arose. Of the two of them it was Patience who was the more altered by their relationship. Everyone saw it. She was transfigured; Norman had made her young again. She saw him as her destiny, a man to be followed like a star. No wonder she panicked.

In 1963, in an effort, perhaps, to dispense with these anxieties once and for all, the two of them left for Greece. For their friends and relatives their departure was a great drama. How long had they been planning it? Or were they just acting on a whim? Patience wasn't letting on, and in her book about their subsequent

Norman Mommens in the Fifties; 'Goliath' was made for, or bought by, Leonard Woolf

adventures on Naxos, *Ringdoves and Snakes*,* she gave the gossips short shrift: 'Who cares now whether the departure was contemplated a whole winter from a hammock strung between two beams in a billiard room whose clerestory windows were caked with snow, or whether one morning we woke up to say: we're starting? Why must people know why we went? When we arrive, we leave behind the reasons why we came. We shed a snakeskin of fuss, plans, hesitations and other people's claims.' But if she *had* to answer the questions that assailed them, she would say that it all came down to Norman's appetite for marble, which was rather hefty. Though this might not have been the whole truth, it was no lie. As things turned out, they would spend the next seven years in search of stone, an odyssey that would take them from the Cyclades to Tuscany, from Catalonia to the Veneto and, finally, to Apulia.

They lived hand-to-mouth. Penniless and itinerant, she and Norman existed 'in the wild' and 'on the margins of literacy', an experience that changed the way they thought for ever. They relied on providence and nothing else, and in the process discovered that poverty gave the good things of life 'their proper significance'. At first, Patience would come back to London for visits, putting up with the questions and uncomprehending stares of those who accused her of slumming it. But as the years went by, she became ever more prickly and ever more peculiar-looking – 'a wild-haired, gap-toothed gypsy woman' according to one friend – and in the end it must have seemed easier not to bother; letters would suffice. In 1970 she made the separation permanent when she and Norman moved into the vaulted barn of a ruined sheep farm – a *masseria* – called Spigolizzi in Apulia, in the heel of Italy, and began a rooted new life of making and growing.

---

* This strange book – it has the same paranoid textures as the early novels of Mary Stewart – was written in 1963–4, but she did not find a publisher for it until 1988.

Spigolizzi as it was when Patience and Norman found it

(Patience, inspired by Norman, began to design jewellery.) The house was – it still is – very remote, and it had neither running water nor electricity; she cooked over olive wood in a huge hearth that had once, long ago, been used for smoking cheeses. When Patience's old friend Henrion came to visit he was shocked, appalled: how on earth would they survive the winter? But it was what they wanted. A homely wilderness. As she would write, 'Self-preservation is a poor substitute for an unfettered life.' It was with some reluctance that she finally agreed to have electricity installed in the early Nineties.

It was at Spigolizzi that Patience began working on her second cookbook, a volume that would contain all that she had learned in the marble years, and all that she was learning now, from her peasant neighbours (though it wouldn't be long before they were learning from her). This book, uncanny and deliberate, would celebrate the feasting and the fasting that is the lot of anyone who relies on windfalls. Eat, preserve, wait for the next bounty: where there is subsistence farming and extreme weather, this is how it goes. More particularly, it would eulogise the edible weeds, bitter, abundant and health-giving, in which she had first become interested on Naxos: dandelions and wild chicory; comfrey and sorrel; glasswort and samphire; broom rape, fat hen and tassel hyacinth. There would be recipes for polenta, wild boar and fish soup, but for mischief she would include a recipe for a stew of *la volpe*, given to her by an old anarchist in Carrara. 'A male fox shot in January or February,' begins this alarming recipe. 'Skin it, and keep the carcass in running water for three days, or, otherwise, hang it up outside in a frost.' Beneath it she noted that these preliminaries are vital, since they remove the otherwise rather 'foxy' taste of the meat – and that the procedure works for badger too.

Patience tried for years to get her curious, prescient book published. But no one was interested. This was before the nose-to-tail eating was made fashionable by cooks such as Fergus Henderson;

The kitchen at Spigolizzi; the refrigerator was not installed until 2002

the foraging of Michelin-starred chefs such as Rene Redzepi at
Noma in Copenhagen; the establishment of the Slow Food movement by Carlo Petrini in Bra, in Piedmont; the trend for local
foods, organic foods and something known as 'heritage tomatoes'; the tendency for cookery writers to punctuate their recipes
with scholarship and memoir. It wasn't until 1986 that it was
finally taken on by Alan Davidson, the food historian, who ran a
tiny company called Prospect Books and who also happened to be
a man after Patience's own heart.

Honey from a Weed (the title is from William Cowper*) was not,
and never will be, a best seller. But its reception in food circles
was rhapsodic – in the *London Review of Books* Angela Carter
acclaimed it as a 'unique and pungent book . . . a baroque monument'; Elizabeth David also wrote to its author, congratulating
her on its success – and it has had a cult following ever since,
both in Britain and, more particularly, in America, where its
peculiar syntax and unfamiliar delights are a staple of gastro-
nomic symposia and learned journals. It is a book, never out of
print, that brings forth joy in some, but earnestness in an awful
lot more. It is, you can't help but notice, especially loved by male
cooks, who seem to find its rigour excitingly macho. In Patience's
lifetime it brought to Spigolizzi a steady stream of pilgrims, men
and women she would happily feed and put up for the night.
After all, as she always maintained, one of the purest, most
human delights was the 'disorderly' feel of a successful
lunchtime. But she must also, I think, have enjoyed watching
them watch her, for in old age she made for a remarkable sight.
Physically, she was a paradox: as strong as an ox – she had to be,
living there – but a skinny-limbed brown thing too, a wizened,
witchy-looking woman (she was a passionate smoker) with wild

* Cowper, 'Pine-Apple and Bee': 'They whom Truth and Wisdom lead / Can gather Honey
from a Weed'.

Patience in 1987. The portrait was taken by Jane Bown,
who was one of her contemporaries at the Observer

hair and wide eyes. And always at her side was Norman, aka
the Sculptor, who looked, with his long white hair and beard,
like Abraham or Moses. She rarely disappointed her visitors,
even at her most irascible. Her talk was as sinewy as her prose,
and weeds, whether fresh or bottled, seemed always to be on the
menu. Was she homesick? No, definitely not. 'I wasn't absolutely
mad about English life at all,' she told a (young, male) journalist in 2002.

They were a happy and devoted couple, these two. Every year

Norman would devote the month of October to making a book for Patience, to be given to her on her birthday. She kept these treasures, with their paintings and their poems, each one more precious than the last, in a large wooden chest. While she was alive they were her secret. After she died, Rossella Piccinno and Tommaso Del Signore made a beautiful film about them, *To My Darling*.

Patience finally gave up her long-standing opposition to the institution of marriage in 1994 when, more than thirty years after their first meeting, Norman Mommens became her husband.

When he died six years later she announced his death to friends with a card that read, 'Norman is among the angels.' She lived on in the *masseria*, watched over by the silent sentinels of his sculptures until, in 2005, she went to join him. One assumes that by now the angels have learned how to rustle up a decent bowl of *orecchiette con la rucola*.

The Show Must Go On

Three trouser-wearing characters: Nancy Spain,
writer and personality; Joan Werner Laurie, magazine editor;
Sheila van Damm, rally-car driver and theatre manager

'If you like: ambition'

People curl their lips at celebrity memoirs, and talk of them as a sign of the times. If only they knew. In 1956 Hutchinson & Co. published an autobiography by the well-known personality Nancy Spain.* It was called *Why I'm Not a Millionaire,* because Spain was an incurable spendthrift. 'Here is the book that 11 million people have been waiting for,' boasted the jacket. 'A life story that will make you laugh and cry, all about the good times of Nancy Spain, book critic of the *Daily Express,* gossip writer of *SHE,* and popular panellist of *What's My Line?* Rich with anecdote, thick with a procession of glorious personalities, with Nancy you can meet Noël Coward, Marlene Dietrich, Lord Beaverbrook, [and] the Duke of Windsor, get engaged to Gilbert Harding, ride down the Fosse Way on a milk-cart horse and penetrate behind the scenes at Lime Grove. Crackling with wit, bursting with vitality, this is one of those books that will go straight to your heart. Because every word of it is true.'

Why I'm Not a Millionaire received more than its fair share of publicity. Naturally, it was serialised in Nancy's own paper, the *Daily Express,* which in 1956 had a circulation of more than four million. But its author also had the temerity to review it there herself, amusingly drawing attention to its absurdities – 'As a matter of fact, I don't really believe in this N. SPAIN,' she wrote. 'N. SPAIN is obviously a figment of Lord Beaverbrook's

---

* Before there were celebrities . . . there were personalities.

imagination'* – even as she dropped the big names her fame-hungry fans would find among its pages, if only they would go out and buy it. In the *Evening Standard* her close friend and putative fiancé Gilbert Harding authenticated his praise – 'the best thing that Miss Spain has written ... vastly amusing ... ' – by accompanying it with a typically ill-tempered description of his usual feelings about her work (he did not understand her detective novels; her children's books left him cold; as for her journalism, he could take it or leave it). Elsewhere Spain's swash-buckling social climbing – not for nothing did her friends think of her as a pirate, albeit one with neither cutlass nor eye patch – seemed somehow to have scrambled critical faculties. Even the *Times Literary Supplement* found itself unwilling to state the obvious, which was that her book was as shallow as a puddle. 'Her courage, both on and off the hockey field, is most impressive,' it noted. 'Those who admire the muscular heroines of John Betjeman will find the author of this book no less strongly adorable.'

That word, though: *courage*. In 1956 courage was still very far from being a synonym for gumption, and it was used with rather less abandon than today. For this reason, it catches the eye. Why did the *TLS*'s reviewer use it? It's possible, of course, that he (or she) was simply referring to Spain's experiences during the war, when she had served in the Women's Royal Naval Service as a press officer, a post that kept her in London during the Blitz. Nancy had no choice but to be brave then. 'I never knew if I left someone at Admiralty Arch, say, and walked across St James's

---

* Spain was devoted to Beaverbrook, the owner of the *Daily Express*. 'Five minutes with the Lord and the adrenalin courses through the veins,' she wrote in *Why I'm Not a Millionaire*. 'Fifteen and I can move mountains.' She once asked him if it was true that he received his editors naked and sitting on the lavatory. 'Naked, yes,' came the reply. 'On the lavatory, no.' For a slightly less adulatory view of the press baron and arch manipulator, see Evelyn Waugh's novel *Scoop*, or his biography by Anne Chisholm and Michael Davie.

My copy of Why I'm Not a Millionaire

Park to my office, that there might not come a chuffing noise, a gliding silence, and a crash,' she wrote in her memoir. 'And I might never see or speak to my friend again.' When a V2 landed on the Guards Chapel during the morning service of 18 June 1944 her office in Petty France was all but demolished; unable to open the building's first aid kits, she ripped her shirt tails into bandages for the injured Wrens outside.

But there is another explanation. Perhaps this anonymous critic intended the word 'courage' as covert praise for her book's daring subtext. For beneath all its frivolity, *Why I'm Not a Millionaire* is nothing less than a tightrope walk, an immense and danger-ous gamble. It is as if Spain has made a bet with herself to see how

far she can go, and the danger involved in this – the risk that she
will jeopardise her place in the public's affections, a collective
embrace that has come to define her – seems only to spur her
on. Imagine propriety – the propriety of the Fifties, when homosexuality was illegal and lesbianism apparently not yet invented –
as a line in the sand of a pristine beach. In bare feet, her trousers
rolled up to her knees (like her friend Katharine Hepburn,
Nancy wore trousers most of the time: she was, by her own
description, 'a trouser-wearing character'), she strolls right up to
this line. She never crosses it, not quite. But then she doesn't
need to; the feeling of the cool sand between her toes is quite
bracing enough. She knows that if she keeps this up only the
most wilfully blind of her readers will fail to grasp that the life
of their favourite personality is built entirely around that of
another woman – even if the intimate details of this relationship
must, like the word 'lover', remain for ever unspoken.

Nancy Brooker Spain was born on 13 September 1917 in Jesmond,
Newcastle upon Tyne, the second daughter of Lieutenant-
Colonel George Redesdale Brooker Spain, a land agent and
volunteer soldier, and his wife Norah Elizabeth. Her grandfather
was the Victorian writer Samuel Smiles, and her great aunt was
Isabella Beeton, whose biography she later wrote. Spain loved
Newcastle and remained attached to it for her whole life, though
it was not its middle-class denizens, with their 'pathetic routine
of bridge parties and back-biting, jealousy and keeping up with
the Joneses' that she admired, but its working classes, 'with all
their faults'. What did she know of working class life? Hardly a
thing. But this was typical Nancy: romanticism and rebelliousness
fighting each other to be heard.

In 1931 she was sent to board at Roedean in Sussex. She
loathed Roedean but you feel, somehow, that it forged her. I
don't mean the voice, soon to become so familiar, though its

fruitiness and precision must have owed something to her teachers. Rather, it was that school taught her how to keep a secret, a skill that would later mark her out. There was her diary, which she had to keep hidden from the staff, and there were her daydreams, her best form of escape. Nurturing an inner life – 'my subconscious and unconscious mind was driven underground' – meant she had also to develop a Teflon* confidence, a tough exterior designed to protect the softness within. 'Girls and staff at Roedean were without exception high-minded, pure-souled conformists,' she wrote in *Why I'm Not a Millionaire*. 'Most of the time, they couldn't make out what I was laughing at.'

When she departed Roedean four years later she took with her a poetry prize and a pathological desire to take the mickey out of the school at every opportunity; also, more surprisingly, a determination to dress like a man. According to her biographer Rose Collis, soon after they had left school a friend called Pamela Howley invited Nancy to supper. The other guest was Douglas Fairbanks Jr – Pamela was by this time at RADA – and presumably it was his appearance at the dinner table that was intended to cause the biggest stir of the evening. It was Nancy, however, who made the greater impression, by matching her skirt with a man's jacket, shirt, tie and shoes.

If Pamela made plain her consternation, it had no effect. Spain, handsome and smiling, seemed not to care. In 1942, through a friend, she met Naomi 'Mickie' Jacob, the prolific popular novelist, who lived openly as a lesbian – visitors to her house, Casa Mickie, in Sirmione, Italy, included Radclyffe Hall – and dressed

---

* Incidentally, the first non-stick frying pan made using Teflon (or polytetrafluoroethylene) was manufactured in 1954 by the French engineer Marc Grégoire under the Tefal brand name. Non-stick frying pans were one of a whole range of new products that came on to the market in the Fifties – others were twin-tub washing machines, domestic refrigerators, electric toasters and kitchen mixers – all of which made the life of women unimaginably easier.

mostly in tweed suits and brogues, her sole concession to femininity being to put on a skirt when she attended mass.* At last, Spain had a role model. Jacob was, like her, from the north. She was also moderately well known as an actor, writer and broadcaster, a rackety sort of fame which Spain, a born show-off, hankered after for herself. Most of all, though, Mickie was uncompromising about her appearance. When the war ended, spurred on by her example and an ever-increasing need to save money, Nancy 'threw off for ever the last rags of conventional dress and behaviour . . . I wore dungarees and never went to the hairdresser. I cut my hair myself with a pair of curly nail scissors and washed it every day in the bath . . . I decided then and there that I could never have another job that would demand little black suits and diamond clips . . . I didn't want to meet anyone who would make me put on a skirt.' Some women – especially her sister, Liz, a fashion designer – were horrified by this. 'Darling, must you?' came the plaintive cry. However, as Nancy later noted, only one man ever complained about her style: her friend Noël Coward, the dedicatee of *Why I'm Not a Millionaire*, who would tell her, not without some justification, that she looked like 'a *dégringolee* farmhand'.

But we're getting ahead of ourselves. What was Nancy to do now she had left school? Her mother was keen that she work as a games or domestic science teacher until she married. Nancy, though, was damned if she was going straight back to the kind of establishment from which she'd only recently escaped. Luckily she was saved by her father, who gave her an allowance and told her she could live at home rent-free. Uncertain what to do next,

* My favourite story about the extraordinary Jacob – for more, raid Paul Bailey's superb *Three Queer Lives* – is that during the fight for suffrage she put an alarm clock in a tin box and placed it outside a seaside house Lloyd George was visiting in Selsey, Sussex; believing it to be a bomb, the Liberal leader's bathing companion screwed up all of his courage, raced down the beach and hurled it into the sea.

she began playing lacrosse and hockey for Durham and Northumberland, and this had a happy side-effect. When the editor of the *Newcastle Journal* was casting about for someone to write reports about the exploits of the local women's teams, Nancy was in a position to be chosen (or perhaps she chose herself) for the job. It wasn't long before her reports, under the by-line 'Baseline', were being syndicated to other newspapers, the *Yorkshire Post* among them.*

Spain loved team sports, but her enthusiasm for them soon had a deeper wellspring in the form of twenty-three-year-old Winifred 'Bin' Sargeant, a golden-haired, blue-eyed, middle-class girl from West Hartlepool who drove a green sports car, had a fondness for gin and tonic, and whose proficiency at tennis was such that she had tried, more than once, to qualify for Wimbledon. It was like falling over: no sooner had Nancy clapped eyes on Bin than she was smitten. 'To have seen Bin flash down the left wing and shoot a goal was a sporting experience on a par with Bannister's mile,' she writes in *Why I'm Not a Millionaire*, as if her new friend had strolled straight from the pages of *Bunty*. At first her adoration was a secret, the slushy poems she dedicated to 'WS' carefully secreted in the pages of her diary. But within a year it became clear that her feelings were reciprocated. Soon she and Bin were spending every available moment together, and in the summer of 1939 they holidayed in the south of France, camping in a field near St Tropez.

It was a blissful trip, its pleasures – fresh lobster, warm morning rolls, a beach that seemed to be theirs alone – only heightened by the fact that both girls knew there was trouble ahead. Sure enough, by the time they arrived back in Newcastle Neville

---

* Having auditioned for the BBC Newcastle drama department, she also got work in radio. In *Fell Top*, an adaptation of Winifred Watson's 1935 novel about Weardale, she played the heroine, Anne Mary. One can only imagine the accent she gave her.

Chamberlain was ready to announce that Britain was at war with Germany. The idyll was over, 'the carefree pagan life' Nancy had glimpsed in Provence now ruthlessly snatched away. The war, Nancy said, 'struck my little life a smart blow. It disappeared without trace.' Both women joined up, Bin enlisting with the ATS (Auxiliary Territorial Service), Nancy volunteering as an Air Raid Precautions driver (later, when she grew to feel that the war demanded more of her, she joined the WRNS). But disaster struck even before the fighting had begun. On 22 December Winifred, having fallen ill with encephalitis lethargica, died at the age of just twenty-seven.

Nancy was in shock. How had this happened? She was, she soon found, so paralysed with grief she was unable even to attend Bin's funeral. And the pain would not go away. In the Fifties, by which time she was in love with someone else, she continued to be haunted by her friend. As she wrote in *Why I'm Not a Millionaire*: 'Quite often, I still think I see her, laughing in a crowd; and once I am sure I saw her come into a restaurant. She sat down and ordered, of all things, a Scotch egg. But when I leapt up to say hello she seemed to vanish, leaving a hard clear line for a second, as a piece of paper does when it burns in the fire.' (If this sounds frank, I should point out that she was also careful to give Bin not one but two fiancés in her memoir, and to speculate that had she lived 'she would have married . . . and raised tennis-playing children to the glory of County Durham'.)

The war, though, must have helped. Her tears, like everyone's, had to be dried quickly. In the autumn of 1940 Nancy was ordered to appear before a WRNS selection board for cipher officers, and having passed muster was dispatched to Greenwich for training. In the following January she became Third Officer Spain. There followed a posting to Arbroath, where she was responsible for servicing planes at the base, and then in October she arrived at WRNS HQ to take up a post as a press officer. It was a job that

drove her mad, for all that it brought her closer to her beloved
Fleet Street. Not only did she feel she was playing no part in the
'real' war effort; 'tarting around with journalists' seems to have
stirred up a certain amount of envy. When her frustration boiled
over and she argued with her superiors she was exiled to the
north as a recruiting officer – a relentless role, she found, like
being a 'mad mouse in a wheel'.

But Nancy was ever resourceful: 'I knew I could never go back
to life on the old, pre-war terms, changing library books, playing
a little tennis, helping mother about the house.' Determined to
come out of the war 'big with experience', by the time she was
promoted to Second Officer in 1943 she had already completed
Thank You – Nelson, a personal account of life as a Wren, and though
the rejection letters at first piled up she eventually sold it to
Hutchinson in a two-book deal (she was, she told her publisher,
already hard at work on a detective novel). Whatever she had to
endure until the end of the war would, she thought, now be bear-
able; it was marvellous to have a plan. As things turned out, she
didn't have long to wait. In January 1945, having been struck by
asthma attacks, Spain was officially discharged from the WRNS.
In the same month, something even more wonderful happened:
A. A. Milne wrote a rave review of *Thank You – Nelson* in the *Sunday
Times*. Reading his words over her dried eggs – Pooh's creator mar-
velled at the fact that Nancy had turned out 'a book all about
herself, of which she is neither the heroine nor the stooge' – she
was reduced to grateful tears. Thanks to Milne, the book became
a surprise best seller.

After this, Nancy moved fast. Resting on her laurels would get
her precisely nowhere. *Poison in Play*, her detective novel, was published in 1946, by which time she had already bagged both her first
newspaper job, as a gossip writer on the *Sunday Empire News*, and her
first celebrity friend in the form of the actress Hermione Gingold
(Nancy arranged to interview her, and they fell platonically in

love). 'I love a big name,' she would write in *Why I'm Not a Millionaire*. 'I like to go where they go. I always hope (don't you?) that some of their lustre will rub off on me.' Failing that, it was helpful to know people, and Gingold, whose nickname among the critics was Malice in Wonderland, was nothing if not well connected. It was paradoxical. All around Nancy, London lay in ruins: ducks living on the pools built by fire fighters, pink willow herb growing over the uneven ground where buildings had once stood. But in her private universe it was as if someone had fired a starting gun, and she leapt out of the blocks unhesitatingly.

By 1950 Nancy was well established as a writer of detective stories (her sixth, *Cinderella Goes to the Morgue*, would be published in April that year).* In addition, she had published, to good reviews, a biography of her relative Isabella Beeton. Her new friends included Margery Allingham, Angus Wilson and Elizabeth Bowen.† But she was also, having been sacked by the *Empire News*, stony broke (her

---

* Spain was ultimately the author of ten eccentric and outrageously camp detective novels, most notably *Poison for Teacher* (1949), which is set in Radcliff Hall, a thinly disguised Roedean, and features as its sleuths a revue star called Miriam Birdseye and her chum, the Russian ballerina Natasha Nevkorina. Birdseye was based on Hermione Gingold, who had begged Spain to put her in a book. *Poison for Teacher* received rapturous reviews, including one by Elizabeth Bowen: 'It is to be recommended, albeit recklessly, to girls'-school fiction addicts . . . an inspired craziness rules.' This last point is certainly correct. It is barmy. But it is notable also for its portrayal of gay and lesbian characters – Miss Puke, the classics mistress, yearns hopelessly for Miss Fork-Thomas, who teaches chemistry; not for nothing does Roger Partick-Thistle teach the organ – and for the fact that it is suggested to one character that she have an abortion. Spain's prose, moreover, has great style: when one fellow takes off his shoes his toes uncurl and crimp like 'an oyster in hot milk'. Personally, I find it irresistible, though I do see why an *Observer* critic described Spain as belonging to the 'lunatic fringe' of detective writers.
† Spain attended Bowen's parties in London, where she met writers such as Henry Green and Elizabeth Taylor. She also stayed with the author at Bowen's Court, her home in Ireland. In *Why I'm Not a Millionaire* she describes this visit in some detail. Eudora Welty was another houseguest – she had 'hands like graceful fish' – and to show her gratitude was determined to make Bowen a Mississippi Witch Pie, to be eaten at midnight. On being told there was no oven, Welty simply fashioned one from an old biscuit tin and a frying pan. 'We bolted [the pie] manfully,' writes Spain. '"Creative genius takes us the strangest ways," murmured Miss Bowen mildly, on the stroke of midnight.' Bowen and Spain's friendship was, however, short-lived; the novelist turned cool on Nancy, possibly because she made a pass at her.

naval pension had been withdrawn when her health recovered). She began to think of letters as bombs, to be touched at her own peril: 'I never, never opened the horrible little square buff envelopes from the Income Tax Boys.' Then, out of the blue, salvation: a publisher, T. Werner Laurie, asked her to become the editor of its monthly magazine, *Books of Today*. 'It was,' she wrote, 'as though a man had rushed up to the scaffold on a horse, waving a parchment, crying, "Reprieve! Reprieve!"'

According to Nancy, *Books of Today* was 'a dear little moribund magazine originally published by the firm of Hatchards in Piccadilly as a sort of library list. It was sent out by Hatchards, monthly, to all Duchesses, Marchionesses, Countesses, and other good customers of this famous bookshop.' Not for long, though: 'When I became editor, it had a terrible shock. It burst out into nasty, crude, primary colours on the cover, and it contained some pretty pungent stuff in the shape of book reviews. So all the Duchesses and Marchionesses wrote in and cancelled their subscriptions.' With no budget for editorial Nancy relied on her new literary friends to write for the magazine; it is a measure of her great charm, and perhaps of her pushiness too, that most of them were willing to review books for free. She also made full use of young 'starving poets', not to mention her own hack talents. Every week she would creep along with her typewriter to Hermione Gingold's house in Chelsea, where she would take down the actress's thoughts for a column they'd devised together entitled 'This I Have Loathed' (Gingold had wanted to call it 'Worst Book of the Month', but a libel lawyer put paid to that).

Tottering or not, *Books of Today* changed Nancy's life for ever. In an upstairs room at the office in Piccadilly there lurked the daughter of the firm's founder, a redoubtable creature called Joan Werner Laurie — Jonnie to her friends. Nancy was often urged to go and speak to Miss Laurie, the company's production manager and an expert cost-cutter, about her budget, and when she grew thoroughly sick of hearing such advice, this is what she did. Climbing the stairs, she expected to be bored into submission by an elderly spinster in a high-necked blouse and cameo brooch, but there followed instead a *coup de foudre*. 'She was very full of her love for Joan, and her excitement about it, and how bowling over it was,' her friend the novelist Elizabeth Jane Howard told a Radio 4 documentary in 1993. 'She couldn't stop talking about Jonnie and how immediate the whole thing had been, and how the moment she saw her she was sure, and how amazed she was when Jonnie reciprocated.'

In *Why I'm Not a Millionaire* she was only slightly less circumspect. She describes their first encounter in a girlish rush, unable to resist its drama, but knowing, too, that she must sweep over its central feature: her physical attraction to Jonnie. The result is rather odd: 'You could,' she writes, 'have knocked me down with a little statue by Henry Moore with a hole in its stomach when I walked into her office and found a girl four years younger than me, very good looking with rather a long nose and a very small waist. She was married, she had a little boy called Nicky. All of which gives no idea of Jonnie's excellence. Her friendliness and generosity are such that she is always surrounded by lame ducks and doting boy-friends. And very rapidly, I was a lame duck, too, living in her house, rent-free . . . She had a very small red MG with brakes that seldom worked. Using this splendid vehicle . . . we moved my belongings to 35 Carlyle Square, Chelsea, where Jonnie lived.'

There follows a description of the Sitwells, who lived opposite (Nancy would sometimes spot Sir Osbert creeping slowly down the road), and a mention of Paul Seyler, Jonnie's dead husband, 'who had obviously been a darling'. But soon she is off again, three unstinting pages of praise for the extraordinary Jonnie: 'What a difficult thing to write objectively of a relationship in which I have been happily bound up for five years, and which is still going on! Jonnie is, I think, one of the most remarkable people I have ever met ... She is certainly the only person who has ever let me be myself ... therefore the only person with whom I can cheerfully live in close harmony ... I have no judgement at all. Jonnie has enough for twelve. But when we work together, we are equal to most things. You must have noticed that, although I have only written about the funny bits, until I met Jonnie I was a miserable sort of creature, a failure, hating everybody, living in a sort of ivory tower of work, refusing to allow Real Life in the shape of Family Life to intrude on me at all. I had become a terrible cynic, chiefly because all my boyfriends had darted off and married someone else ... It is impossible for me to take a step without consulting Jonnie ... Oh, how difficult it is to write of gratitude ... My pen dries and my heart spills over and cannot express itself when I think of everything that Jonnie and Nicky have done for me.' The ellipses are mine; Spain, usually wonderfully concise, errs on the side of verbosity here.

Nancy's account of Joan makes her sound a darling, just like her dead husband. But this was not quite the case (and as for the dead husband, he had been about as reliable as quicksand). While people were drawn to Nancy, so warm and funny, Joan kept the world at bay. She was cool and steely and rather humourless. At work she could be terrifying: a stickler, and a martinet. When the internal telephone rang three times – the signal that Miss Laurie was on the line – her staff would shiver inwardly. *What now?* Getting a rocket from Miss Laurie was the worst.

Joan had left home at sixteen after a row with her father. She wanted to be a doctor but she became instead a wife, marrying a man of whom her family did not approve. The marriage was short-lived. Paul Seyler was abroad during the war – Joan meanwhile was, like Nancy, a Wren – and he continued to serve with the Gurkhas after it ended. By the time Jonnie gave birth to her son, Nicholas Laurie Seyler, in March 1946, she was effectively a single parent, and living with a friend, Vivyen Bremner, in Sevenoaks,

Kent. It was Bremner who taught Joan 'how to grow and how to use my grimmer experiences in the process', and it was Bremner who looked after Nicholas when she went back to work in London. Seyler is supposed to have left England for South America in 1948, where he worked as mercenary and a cattle rancher; he died in Argentina two years later. No wonder she was tough.

But however different their personalities, Joan and Nancy were a match. Theirs was not, by any stretch of the imagination, an exclusive relationship. There were times when it seemed to outsiders more like a business partnership than anything else; they pooled their resources and their ideas. But they were extraordinarily close, a reticent intimacy that was sealed for ever by the events of 1952.

In *Why I'm Not a Millionaire* Nancy describes 1952 as a 'vintage year' largely, it would seem, because Fleet Street had finally come calling; she had joined the *Daily Express* as its book critic* and had met Beaverbrook for the first time. And perhaps, looking back, this was the most important thing to happen to her: work was always at the centre of her life. But she also refers, with startling breeziness, to the arrival of one Thomas Bartholomew Laurie Seyler, 'the youngest of Jonnie's responsibilities', making it quite plain

---

* She had left *Books of Today* in 1951 for a job at *Good Housekeeping*, a move she and Jonnie celebrated with a trip to Paris, where they met Colette ('there are people one loves immediately and forever') and Christian Dior ('the flunkeys looked a little bit sideways at us, in our jeans'). At the *Express* she joined another famous woman journalist of the Fifties, Anne Scott-James (1913–2009). 'I did think her clothes were awful by any standard,' Scott-James told Nancy's biographer, Rose Collis. 'She would appear in jeans in the office and then appear at a cocktail party or dinner looking absolutely stunning in a Balmain dress. It was like there were two people.' Scott-James began her career at *Vogue*, a job that later inspired her 1952 novel *In the Mink*, a satire set in the offices of a glossy fashion magazine (for more on *In the Mink* see the Introduction). At the *Express*, she was women's editor, but she also worked, periodically, as a foreign correspondent. Here's a sample: 'I was sitting at my typewriter in my bedroom at the Hotel Metropole in Moscow, wearing nothing but a bra and briefs, for it was boiling hot, when the door burst open and a burly Russian came in without knocking.' In 1964 Scott-James replaced Nancy as a panellist on the BBC show *My Word!* Her son is Max Hastings, the historian and former editor of the *Daily Telegraph*.

that she was present at his birth (strikingly, she uses the word 'damp' to describe his hair the first time she saw it). What would her readers have made of this? She had just told them that Jonnie's husband was dead. Who was supposed to have fathered this new baby, born on 27 August 1952?

Most people must have assumed that the baby was the result of an illicit affair on the part of Jonnie, and that Nancy was merely playing the loyal and devoted 'aunt' when she explained that she loved this boy 'desperately, hopelessly, devotedly'. And perhaps this is what their friends thought too, for almost no one was told the full story at the time. Even those who were in a position to know that Joan had not been pregnant, and that the boy could not therefore be hers, were vague about his parentage. Nick Werner Laurie (he dropped the Seyler as an adult) remembers going to collect his new baby brother in the same red MG as they had picked up Nancy two years before. Where did he think the baby had come from? 'The baby shop.' And when he was older? 'I used to call him my adopted brother.' What did he feel when he finally discovered the truth? 'I thought, Ah, that explains all sorts of things.'

In her memoir Nancy came closer to acknowledging the reason for her devotion to Thomas Bartholomew than she ever did in life. For she was indeed present at his birth; it would have been exceedingly difficult for her to be anywhere else, given that she was his mother. But how had she hidden her pregnancy from her friends? With great difficulty, probably, though since those who knew her were in no doubt about her sexuality they would perhaps have seen only what they expected to see. There is a story that when Angus McBean came to photograph her for the cover of one of her detective novels, her pregnancy was so noticeable that he had to ask her to lie down so he could shoot her from above. Jonnie's brother Dick remembers her squeezing by him one day in the kitchen of Carlyle Square. 'Well, you've probably noticed I'm pregnant,' she said; later he received a letter from Jonnie, informing him that he had a new 'nephew'. Certainly Nancy must have worn something extremely forgiving for her first meeting with Beaverbrook, for she was by then six months pregnant. But in general her condition simply did not register. Years later, when the truth emerged, friends were shaken as much by their failure to notice what should have been obvious as by Nancy's concerted subterfuge.

For all her warmth, Nancy was an expert builder of compartments. Once she and Jonnie had taken the decision that he would be brought up as Nicky's brother – both boys called Nancy 'Tig' – and that Nancy would not acknowledge Thomas as her son, there could be no half measures. If her story was to hold, if she was not ever to slip up, it was vital that she resist telling even her closest friends and family. Her parents never knew they had a grandson, nor was her sister told, or at least not at the time. As Nick Werner Laurie puts it, 'He was there every day: *her son*. She had to go total.'

It was Joan who registered the birth. A copy of the certificate is beside me now as I write. The baby's father was recorded as Paul Clifford Seyler, a cattle rancher of Buenos Aires – a double falsehood, given that the man in question had been dead for two years. The baby's mother was named as Anne Brooker Seyler, formerly Brooker – in other words, a fictitious character with elements of both women's names. The baby was then swiftly handed over to a nanny, that Nancy and Jonnie might return to work. Did this arrangement cause Nancy pain? No. She was not given to backward glances. In time it would be as though she had forgotten the truth herself. Why, though, did she do it? Mostly, she was probably thinking about her career. In 1952 an unmarried mother was unlikely to get work presenting *Woman's Hour* or anything else on the Home Service, opportunities that would soon come her way. She and Jonnie may also have thought it was better for the children to grow up believing themselves to be

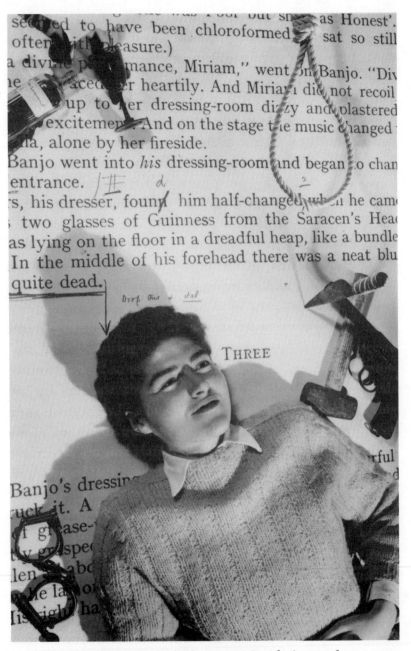

Nancy Spain photographed by Angus McBean for the cover of
Cinderella Goes to the Morgue

brothers. But another school of thought has it that Thomas was her gift to Jonnie: *I love you so much I will give you my child.** What do I think? I think that secrets, even those kept with the best of intentions, can be destructive; and in the fullness of time this one would indeed cause a great deal of collateral damage. For the time being, though, it worked like a spell, binding those who kept it tightly and reassuringly together.

In 1952 Gilbert Harding was as famous as Stephen Fry is today, though somewhat less avuncular. A Cambridge-educated former schoolteacher, he made his name as a regular on *What's My Line?*, a BBC programme in which a panel had to guess the profession of a mystery guest. It sounds laughable now: *'Do you work with your hands? Do you visit people's houses? Are they pleased to see you? Are you a postman?'* But Harding, one of the first household names of the television age, succeeded in making it compelling viewing by dint of the fact that no one knew when he would next explode in frustration: 'He acquired the reputation of being as remorselessly rude as Dr Johnson used to be two hundred years ago,' as Compton Mackenzie once put it. Was his rudeness a put-on job? His contemporaries thought not. Harding never owned a television set himself, and was often unable to hide his contempt for the medium. He was also shy, lonely and thwarted. As a homosexual, his private life was fraught with danger; as a Catholic convert, perhaps it was also the source of self-loathing.

Nancy Spain met Gilbert Harding at a dinner party, four months after the birth of her son. She thought him clever and

---

* We do not know for sure that Nancy deliberately decided to get herself pregnant, but given her sexuality it seems likely. If it had been some kind of accident a woman like Spain – metropolitan, well connected – would have had less difficulty than you might imagine arranging an illegal abortion. See *About Time Too*, a memoir by Penelope Mortimer, in which she describes being taken to a Chelsea abortionist by her future husband, John Mortimer, in 1948 or thereabouts ('he had,' Mortimer writes, 'sophisticated friends').

funny, and instantly became his 'slave for life'. It was a form of slavery that involved an endless round of lunches, teas and telephone calls – and, in 1954, a trip to Jamaica on a banana boat. Harding had trouble with his lungs and his doctors, as they were periodically wont to do, had given him a year to live. He needed rest, fresh air and sunshine. Jonnie and Nancy, meanwhile, had also been coping with illness – abdominal surgery for Jonnie, pneumonia in the case of Nancy – and they had recently moved to a new house in Clareville Grove, Kensington. In addition, both had big new jobs. Nancy had begun presenting a 'Personality Diary' for *Woman's Hour* (a chance to recycle her assignments for the *Daily Express*). She was also enjoying a stint as a film critic for another of Beaverbrook's papers, the *Evening Standard*. Jonnie was busy developing a women's magazine for the National Magazine Company, to be called *SHE,* a title that would cause a revolution in the world of publishing on its launch in 1955. ('On average,' Jonnie said later, 'not more than about twelve [readers] a month cancel their subscriptions because of the horror at my lack of refinement in choosing the contents … *SHE* has dealt in full detail with menstruation, hysterectomy, breast cancer, lung cancer, leprosy, brain tumours. We have even told our readers exactly what a bidet is for.') It was agreed that the two women would join Harding on a ship called *Matina,* which would leave Liverpool in early March.

No sooner had the boat set sail, however, than Nancy was filing copy to the *Express*; copy in which she wrote all about her celebrity travelling companion. One thing led, as it is apt to do, to another. In London the gossip columnists sharpened their pencils. 'Is Gilbert Harding thinking of marrying?' asked the *Daily Sketch*'s writer. 'I hear talk of a romance between the irascible 47-year-old TV bachelor and novelist Nancy Spain, who is 37.' The next day all the national dailies cabled the ship demanding news of the happy couple. Doubtless these journalists did not really believe Gilbert and Nancy to be a couple, but the story was irresistible all the same. Nor did it do Nancy any harm: by the time the *Matina* returned to Southampton she was firmly lodged in the national consciousness as the woman who might be about to usurp Gilbert Harding's housekeeper, Mrs Clarke, in his affections.

Back on dry land, she did nothing to disabuse the public of this idea. The rumours rumbled on into 1955, when Nancy, by now herself a panellist on *What's My Line?*, announced that her remaining ambition in life was to marry Harding. She followed this declaration with the planting of a kiss on his cheek. The trouble was that Nancy knew good publicity when she saw it, and though the friendship with Harding was genuine – he was, it seems, one of the very few people she told about Tom – it would not be unfair to say that she sacrificed a measure of his dignity for her own gain. Her love for her friends was shot through with a pragmatism that could border on the ruthless. The same was true of her relationship with the children. As a boy, Nick ate lunch at the Ivy so often he knew how to make *crêpe suzette* before he was nine. But such treats failed to compensate for the days – weeks, sometimes – when he and Tom saw their mothers not at all; for the fact that they were brought up by a series of nannies, each one more incompetent than the last. When they were older and at boarding school – Tom was sent away at the age of six – the boys were expected to stay put during the holidays if Nancy and Jonnie had something better to do (the 'something better' might involve work, but it could also include renting a villa in Cannes). When Nick was fourteen he blew up the school chemistry lab. During the six weeks he spent in hospital recovering from the accident, he received not a single visit from Jonnie or Nancy.

Was Nancy any more careful of Jonnie's feelings? Hardly. In 1955, shortly after the publication of her final detective novel, *The Kat Strikes*, she was asked to introduce Marlene Dietrich on stage at the Café de Paris in Piccadilly, an event for which she wore a pink silk

Joan with Nick and Tom in Clareville Grove

dress with an ostentatious bow – a frock that wouldn't have deceived 'a drunken child of two and a half', according to Noël Coward. At some point after this she and Dietrich began an affair.* 'Dear me,' she writes in *Why I'm Not a Millionaire*. 'How Marlene mops us all up ... Ageless, genderless, so blazingly attractive that she snuffs out any woman in the room with her as effectively as a searchlight would obliterate a candle flame, Marlene is at her very best when all the props have been thrown away and she stands there in slacks, or an admiral's overcoat, or a simple well-tailored little suit.'

But this dalliance was brief. More serious by far was her relationship with one of Dietrich's lovers, Ginette Spanier, the directrice of Balmain. (Dietrich and Spanier were involved, on and off, for

---

* Nick Werner Laurie has a memory of being taken to Dietrich's London pied-à-terre for tea, whereupon Nancy and Marlene disappeared 'for an hour and a half', leaving him all alone.

some six years.) She and Nancy met in 1956, Noël Coward having played matchmaker. Coward was staying with Spanier and her husband in Paris, during which time he happened to be devouring a proof of *Millionaire*. 'You must read this,' he said. Spanier inquired after the book's author: *Nancy who?* 'I vaguely remembered . . . pictures of a girl in a sweater on the front of buses in London, advertising Basildon Bond writing paper, I think.' So what, she asked, was this Nancy like? 'Tough,' said Coward. 'A duck. Is mad about Beaverbrook, and me.'

Soon after, encouraged by Coward, who informed her that simply everyone stayed with Ginette in Paris, Nancy invited herself to lunch (she was in France to interview the Duke and Duchess of Windsor for the newly launched *SHE*). Ginette was smitten. She describes their first encounter in her 1970 memoir *And Now It's Sables*: 'In my sitting room when I rushed in late I saw a young woman in a navy suit looking up from a book. One of my books, from one of my shelves. Soft eyes. Shy. Why had Noël said she was tough, I thought. How often in the years that followed was I to see Nancy Spain look up from a book to greet me, at airports, in restaurants . . . We laughed right through lunch. We had each found a friend. The quicksilver brain, the instant understanding, the sense of humour, the biting wit; they never lost their fascination for me.' Things Nancy and Ginette both loved: work, the heat of the sun, laughter, music halls, work again. Things they hated: 'what other people think', amateurs, laziness, antiques.

Spanier's outward appearance – elegant, immaculately dressed, never without her crimson lipstick and a string of good pearls – gave no hint of the unconventional, determined character within. She and her husband Paul-Emile, a doctor, had somehow managed to survive in Occupied France in spite of the fact that they were Jewish, an experience that gave her a lifelong hatred of Germans (another thing she and Nancy had in common). She had joined Balmain in 1947, at the invitation of the designer's mother, who had seen her berate the sales staff for trying to sell unsuitable clothes to the daughter of a friend. A born sales-woman, she remained the directrice of the company for the next thirty years, a job she adored – not least because it brought so many glamorous names to her door. In the Fifties guests at her Avenue Marceau apartment, with its fifty-foot drawing room and grand piano, included Laurence Olivier and Vivien Leigh, Judy Garland, Claudette Colbert and Louis Armstrong. Signed pho-tographs of these visitors adorned the walls of her bathroom – caught, as Nancy put it, 'like flies in amber'.

But Ginette was also, Nancy noticed, restless. The 'undiluted couture diet' was beginning to pall; something in her longed for what she later called the 'hammy' side of life. Nancy's response was typically over-the-top. She decided to turn *la directrice* into a

Nancy with Ginette Spanier

personality. First, she interviewed her on the radio. Then she wrote about her in the *Express*. Finally, she helped her to write a memoir. And when *It Isn't All Mink* was published in 1959 she travelled with her to the US to publicise it, ostensibly acting as her secretary. (Thanks to Nancy, Spanier would go on to appear on both *Desert Island Discs* and *This Is Your Life*.)

Nancy's letters home during this book tour are ostentatiously devoted. Jonnie is 'Darling sweet Mrs Bunny' and 'my best beloved little cat', and even as she waits for her plane to New York she makes the time to pick up her pen and say that she is finding 'it all very strange and rather frightening' (though she carefully omits to say precisely what 'it' was). Later she makes a great deal of her homesickness. But there is also a strong element of performance about them, and when she writes that she hopes Jonnie will be 'okay and Sheila [will] look after you very nicely', it sounds like nothing so much as a gentle reminder. *You have your friendships,* she whispers, *and I'll have mine.**

Sheila? Ah, yes. In 1958, or thereabouts, the household at Clareville Grove had gained a new member: Sheila van Damm. Sheila was famous in her own right both as a rally-car driver and as the daughter of Vivian van Damm, the owner of the Windmill Theatre in Soho, an establishment she now helped to run. A stay of a few days while she looked for a new flat had somehow turned into a permanent arrangement, as a result of which she now formed the third side of an increasingly complicated triangle. If, as those who knew them will tell you, Jonnie never grieved over Nancy's affairs, perhaps this was because she already had a stalwart ally of her own.

Sheila van Damm was a small, well-padded woman with a gap-toothed smile and a brisk, no-nonsense manner. In her bulky twin

* From 1957 until 1964 Nancy spent a week of every month, at least, in Paris.

sets and with her hair tightly set she looked, more than anything else, like a maiden aunt. This seemed to surprise people. Strangers expected something wilder, more risqué, though why this should be, Sheila never quite understood. As she noted in her memoir *We Never Closed*, the Windmill Theatre was not the den of iniquity outsiders imagined it to be: 'Our fan dance was usually such a masterpiece of timing it could have been performed at a vicarage fête with scarcely a tut-tut of embarrassment.' Not that Sheila was a dancer, fan or otherwise. Her figure wasn't built 'for terpsichorean fantasies'. In the early days, when she played teenage understudy to the theatre's publicist, she was required to deliver fliers by hand, a job that meant she spent most of every day on foot. Alas, any weight she might have lost was dealt with between calls: 'I had to keep reviving myself by stopping at a milk bar.'

Sheila was born in 1922, the youngest of three sisters. The family was Jewish. There was, as she later put it, 'only one male in the home, and he dominated it completely'. This was her father, Vivian van Damm. A more dynamic man it was hard to imagine, and it took Sheila many years to acknowledge that, just occasionally, he could be wrong. 'He was kind, generous, lovable – and a complete dictator,' she said. 'We regarded him with immense respect, verging on awe, and complete trust. It was not a case of father knows best: father knew everything.' Vivian van Damm had begun his working life in the garage trade, eventually opening the first service station in Britain. By the time Sheila was born he had moved into the cinema business, a world that better suited the showman in him, for he knew instinctively how to pull in the crowds. As manager of the Polytechnic cinema in Piccadilly, he showed a documentary, made originally for soldiers, on the hitherto unmentionable 'perils' of venereal disease. But he had two prints made: one showed certain 'startling' scenes, the other did not. Screened alternately, furious arguments would break out between those who had seen print one, and those who'd seen print two. The only way to resolve such arguments was for customers to pay to see the film again, a ploy so successful the police had to be called in to control the swelling crowd, and two nurses employed, ready to revive swooning patrons.*

In 1931, just as he was about to sign a lucrative contract with Sidney Bernstein, who wanted him to manage his Granada cinemas, van Damm was introduced to a sixty-nine-year-old widow named Laura Henderson, the new owner of a small Soho theatre, the Windmill. It's hard to say now who fell harder for whom. Certainly Mrs Henderson, whose first show *Inquest!* had lost her a great deal of money, was badly in need of someone like Vivian. But something in her must have spoken to him too. After all, she was offering him a salary of just eight pounds a week to take care of her theatre; Sidney Bernstein had agreed to pay him ten times that. Perhaps it was her pluck he admired. When, at the end of a difficult first year, van Damm wondered aloud if they shouldn't simply cut their losses and close the Windmill, Mrs Henderson told him that he had 'no courage'.†

Vivian van Damm's solution to the Windmill's financial problems was, famously, for it to stage a continuous variety show every day from 2.30 p.m. until 11 p.m.; each of the four daily performances would last two hours. When this failed to increase the theatre's pitiful takings he added nude women to the mix, something the Lord Chamberlain's office allowed provided they did not move. (The *London Evening Star* ran a reader competition to find a name for the new show, which was won by Mr Arnold Kite of Ellen Street, E1, for Revudeville.) So the girls stood there like classical statues in

---

* When he screened the silent film *The Four Horsemen of the Apocalypse*, he employed thirty men backstage to imitate the sound of galloping horses and gunfire. The film ran for eight months, and was seen by Queen Mary and the Prince of Wales.
† Henderson, who wore a diamond tiara to dinner every night, was a noted eccentric. She would sometimes arrive at the theatre in disguise and, on occasion, auditioned as a novelty act: dressed in an animal skin, she pretended to be a polar bear, which danced ponderously about the stage on its hind legs.

Sheila at the Windmill

strange tableaux, their limbs posed for up to twelve minutes at a time. This rule was broken only once, when a V1 exploded fifty yards from the theatre (the Windmill remained open throughout the Blitz, the only West End venue to do so – hence the title of Sheila's memoir): 'After the shattering crash had subsided, the nude in the Spanish tableau, wearing nothing but a large hat, slowly, very slowly, raised a hand and thumbed her nose upwards, in the direction from which the bomb had come.'*

Sheila loved the Windmill. 'It wasn't just the glamour and the glitter that drew me, but the strange, homelike atmosphere behind the stage. To me, it was another home – another family,

* Van Damm's first few (non-nude) acts were terrible: a man who juggled apples at the same time as eating one; a violinist from Huddersfield who played while knotting his arms and legs into extraordinary contortions. But van Damm also went on to discover many future stars, among them Bruce Forsyth, Tony Hancock and Peter Sellers.

with the same head ... When I was not at school, I haunted the place.'* She began working there at sixteen, a few months before the outbreak of war. Like Nancy, she found that the fighting opened more doors than it closed. As the men began to disappear, opportunities increased. Within months she had been promoted first to assistant stage manager, then to head of publicity. When the Blitz began she moved into the theatre full time. She and her father slept, like the rest of the staff, on mattresses on the floor. This was clearly the practical thing to do, but it was also a matter of solidarity, for to read about the Windmill in wartime is to marvel at the courage and good humour at those who worked there. Gas-mask drills were held in the stalls; tin helmets hung on the back of dressing-room doors; many of the dancers became ARP wardens. Should the theatre receive a direct hit, it was agreed that the show would simply move to the Comedy Theatre near by. One girl, having left the theatre at night, was so badly injured by shrapnel it was thought she would not dance again. Three months later, however, she was back, worrying like all the other girls about whether her costume would survive the rigours of the show — it was vital that girls did not get carried away and burst out of their outfits; thanks to clothes rationing, they were now impossible to replace.

* Some Windmill facts — which Sheila knew by heart. In the course of an average year a Windmill Girl would walk thirty-five miles on the stairs between her dressing room and the stage. She would change costume five thousand times, perform seventy-five thousand high kicks and wear out seventy-five pairs of dancing shoes. These girls were well cared for: the theatre had a doctor and a subsidised canteen, and in summer a miniature lido was installed on the roof, complete with deck chairs and flowering plants. They were also well paid. Strange as it may sound, the ethos of the theatre was curiously feminist. 'It was totally liberating working there,' says Iris Chapple, a former Windmill Girl. 'It was tough, but it made us free. You were earning and it gave you self-esteem, and you improved and improved. We felt powerful; we felt women could do anything they wanted. If we have a get-together now, you'll find only about five out of twenty of us married. We travelled, we made loads of money and we blew it, we met interesting people. You never even thought about getting your pinny on.' Sheila van Damm paid for Iris Chapple to have a breast reduction. Iris, who hated her breasts, was thrilled. Afterwards, Joan ran a feature about the operation in *SHE*.

On Sundays the cast gave free shows for servicemen at stations, camps and gun-sites. The theatre itself became a favourite haunt for servicemen on leave. As Sheila put it, 'Revudeville fortified London in a way which sandbags and gun-sites could not.' She was determined to be a part of this morale boost, and doggedly remained at the Windmill until 1942 when, having been conscripted into the WAAF, she was posted to Weeton, near Blackpool, for a ten-week driving course, and thence to Fighter Command in Stanmore. She spent the rest of the war whizzing through an empty London, driving officers 'from one party to another'.

In 1946 she handed in her stripes – she had been promoted to corporal shortly after VE Day – and returned to the theatre only to find her father had replaced her as publicity manager. It seems she had no complaint about this – the new man was, she thought, much better at the job than she'd been – but having been so long away from Vivian she now found herself unable to remain silent when she disagreed with him. 'The first time I did it, he was too dazed to speak,' she wrote in her autobiography *No Excuses*. 'The second time he told me to shut up. The third time he told me to get out, and I landed in Shaftesbury Avenue with a resounding thud.' She was still brushing herself down when he sent for her again. 'I'm thinking of starting an air charter company,' Vivian said, so casually he might have been talking about mowing the lawn. 'Go and learn to fly.'

Sheila learned to fly. She didn't want to; she longed only to work at the Windmill. But pride dictated that she had no choice but to do otherwise. And if she was going to do this she would do it well. Her instructor was the formidable Joan Hughes,* the

---

* Hughes (1918–93) served in the ATA for six years, never losing an aircraft – though on one occasion she was forced to land a Hurricane whose undercarriage she was unable to lower. The only damage was a bent propeller (a relief, since the first Hurricane flights by women had attracted much attention, on the grounds that female pilots might not be physically strong enough). It was Joan who coached Kenneth More, another famous graduate of the Windmill, for his role as Douglas Bader in *Reach for the Sky* (1956).

Sheila with Joan Hughes

youngest of the first eight women to join the Air Transport Auxiliary in 1940. Eleven hours by Joan's side and Sheila was able to land her Hornet Moth alone.

Vivian duly bought himself a plane, but his charter business died before it was born; Sheila joined the RAF Volunteer Reserve instead, where she learnt acrobatics and formation flying. She hoped for a commission, but this was futile: in the late Forties there was no place for a woman in civil aviation. What to do? In *No Excuses* she tells the reader that around this time she nearly got married: 'Only one thing stopped me – he went off and married someone else.' This seems unlikely: no one who knew Sheila van Damm was ever in any doubt about her sexuality. But there was a new relationship on the horizon – with cars. In September 1950 her father's personal pilot, Zita Irwin, told her that Vivian had entered Sheila and her sister Nona in the *Daily Express* rally, the first such race in Britain since the war. Sheila was astonished. Her father had written her off – entirely without justification – as a poor pilot, so why would he suddenly put so much faith in her driving skills?

She did not tell the family dictator that she disliked the idea of driving a car with the words 'Windmill Girl' painted on its side.

Nor did she express her desire to be known as a competitor in her own right, rather than as the daughter of the more famous Vivian. She simply got on with the job. The rally involved driving a thousand miles in forty-eight hours, a feat she would pull off with the help of what she chirpily called 'wakey-wakey pills' (in the days before dope tests, amphetamines were used widely and unabashedly). Sheila would be part of the Rootes team, in a Sunbeam Talbot. In theory, all she had to do was follow George Hartwell, her fellow team member, which is pretty much what she did, a gold St Christopher in her pocket for luck. But if Sheila did not expect to do well in the rally – she hoped only to finish – her father's expectations were even lower. On a rest break she rang him from her hotel; when she told him she was in bed, he asked, 'Which hospital?'

It came as a surprise to both of them, then, when she learned that she and Nona had come third in the women's competition. Even more startling, Rootes wanted to know if she was interested in competing in further rallies. Her father was delighted by this: her first drive had brought the Windmill a ton of publicity. Sheila, though, was more ambivalent – or at least, that was the impression she was careful to give. In *No Excuses* she describes her subsequent invitation to join Elsie 'Bill' Wisdom's team as third driver of a Hillman Minx in the 1951 Monte Carlo Rally only as rather 'lucky' (they came fifth in the coupe des dames), and even at the height of career she tended to downplay her talent. In part, this was another way of pleasing her father, who worried she would get 'exaggerated ideas' about herself. But it was also a smokescreen, lest the men start regarding her as a threat. Any remark that came within a mile of what we would regard as a feminist statement had always to be undercut with studied deprecation. Women, she notes in *No Excuses*, have more stamina than men. On the other hand, 'men do most things better than women. I think it is a good thing they do, although it would do them no harm to be beaten once in a while ... meanwhile the rally girls have done a lot to destroy the regrettable idea that all women are bad drivers (which is not half so regrettable as the idea that all men are good).' Unpick this, and you'll notice that it is not what it seems.

But such tactics could not entirely camouflage her competitive spirit: she won too often for that. Her first major success was the 1952 Motor Cycling Club Rally, when she bagged the ladies' prize in a Sunbeam Talbot. At the 1953 Monte Carlo Rally she was unsuccessful – too many punctures – but nevertheless she entered the record books when she outpaced her team mate Stirling Moss to set a class record for 2–3litre cars, driving the pro-totype Sunbeam Alpine sports car at an average of 120 mph at Jabbeke in Belgium ('The Fastest Woman in Europe,' said the newspaper headlines). At the 1953 Alpine Rally she and her co-driver Anne Hall won the coupe des dames and a coupe des alpes (for finishing the event without time penalties). In 1954 she and Hall won a coupe des dames at the Tulip rally in Holland, a per-formance that also saw her winning the climactic ten-lap race around the Zandvoort circuit; she finished seven and a half sec-onds ahead of the second-placed driver, a man. A further ladies' prize in the 1954 Viking rally in Norway meant that she and Hall clinched the Ladies' European Championship, a feat they repeated in 1955 when they began the season by winning – at last – a coupe des dames at Monte Carlo.

It wasn't only rallying at which Sheila excelled. She was a capa-ble road racer too, and in 1956 partnered the Le Mans driver Peter Harper at the wheel of a Sunbeam Rapier for the Mille Miglia in Italy, the most dangerous motor race in the world. (An endurance test of one thousand miles, it was finally banned in 1957 after a crash killed the Spanish driver Alfonso de Portago, his nav-igator Edmund Nelson and nine spectators, five of whom were children.) The going was extremely tough: in the Futa Pass they

Monte Carlo, 1952

dealt with driving rain, wind, flooded roads and icy surfaces; con-
ditions were so perilous Stirling Moss and his car slid down a
mountainside, their progress to a drop of three hundred feet
impeded only by a lone tree. But she completed the race all the
same, and thus maintained her record of finishing every event she
started. She and Harper also won their class, having somehow
managed to average 66.37 mph.

Rally cars were far heavier then than now, and their brakes
and tyres much less efficient. Road surfaces were often poor.
Sheila must have been very strong. And brave. Not for nothing
did bloodthirsty crowds gather at the worst bends during races
like the Alpine Rally. But she was not without fear. During her
pilot training at White Waltham she had seen a man whose head
had been shaved after he had suffered a serious head injury, and
his alabaster skull came back to haunt her before every race. Nor
could she ignore the headlines. In 1955 eighty-five spectators
and a driver, Pierre Levegh, were killed at Le Mans following a

catastrophic accident; the spectators were killed mostly by fire, but some were decapitated by flying debris. The risks were huge. The more she raced, the more she felt she was tempting fate. Once she had proved herself, it wasn't her competitive spirit that kept her going so much as her conviction that there was something liberating about the camaraderie of the road. This was what pulled her on, in spite of the risks, for in what other realm would a man like Stirling Moss offer to wash a girl's 'smalls'? She relished the good-luck telegrams that flooded in before every race, and came from as many male colleagues as female; she adored the cheering and the fan mail; and she took pride in her unique status. 'On a rally, you have to forget the eye-black and lipstick,' she wrote. 'But if the going is reasonably good, I like to arrive at the end looking as fresh as I can.'

In 1955, though, she decided to retire. Her father, now in his sixties, was unwell; there was the question of the Windmill. She would clearly be taking over from him at some point in the not-too-distant future and the staff, she felt, would never treat her as the boss so long as she was always jumping in and out of motor cars. The people at Rootes, however, begged her to enter the 1956 Monte Carlo Rally, and she agreed out of 'friendship'. This race was not to be among her successes. Even before it began she was convinced she was about to run out of luck: 'I had a premonition . . . There had been a lot of hoo-ha in the Press about this being my Swan Song, and for the first time in my life I was really superstitious.' Worse, she discovered that she had somehow contrived to lose the St Christopher, a present from Joan Hughes, that she had sewn inside her jacket pocket two years before. In the end she was not even among the top ninety drivers. Sheila blamed herself for this – faced with thick fog on the Col du Granier, she had driven far too cautiously – but she had no regrets. 'I was sure that I had finished what would prove to be the best five years of my life,' she wrote later. 'But it was lovely to wake up in the morning and find I had nothing to worry about.'

Naturally, no sooner had Sheila's driving career come to an end than her father miraculously recovered. This was entirely predictable – but she stubbornly shadowed him all the same, finally taking her first rehearsal in 1957. Her judgement, though, had been correct: his health could not last, and in December 1960 he died. His devoted daughter withheld this news from the newspapers until five minutes before the Windmill's final curtain call. Inside the theatre she pinned up a note. 'I am with you all here today,' it said. 'The show must go on exactly as usual. No one is to behave differently in any way. This was VD's last wish. There must be no mourning. You can show your love and respect in the way which would have made him happy: go out on that stage, and give it all you have got.' In her theatre diary she wrote: 'December 14. Father died in the clinic this evening after weeks of hell. God bless him. He is now at peace.' Her loss was hard to believe. She kept imagining she had made some kind of mistake. *'He'll walk in the door. Or I'll hear his voice. Or I'll suddenly meet him in one of the corridors.* Then I snapped back to reality. To face facts. To push on.' Two days later she was calm enough to set about improving Revudeville. 'This is the first speeded-up show,' she wrote in the diary. 'Three good acts, including Ray Allen. Comic very good.' Even in the depths of her grief, she could feel it turning inside. Ambition. At last, she was the Windmill's manager.

So, Nancy loved Jonnie, Sheila loved Jonnie, Jonnie loved them both and they all three, in their different ways, loved Nick and Tom. Is this right? I think so, though I'm mindful that two people can gaze on the same photograph and each see completely different things. On Nancy and Joan's side, everyone will tell you that Sheila was just a sympathetic friend. But talk to Sheila's people and they are quite certain that it was Sheila and Joan who were the couple, and Nancy the interloper. Not that they felt protective of the relationship. Sheila, it was generally agreed, had awful taste in women, and Joan was just the latest manifestation of this. Sheila didn't suffer fools, but Joan was absolutely terrifying. Sometimes Sheila would bring Joan home to her parents' house in Angmering, Sussex, for the weekend. On other occasions, she would bring Joan *and* Nancy. On Saturday mornings these working girls were not to be woken up early. Whispering was the order of the day: they were entitled to lie in. What did Sheila's mother feel about all this? It wasn't easy, having a daughter like Sheila, not in the Fifties. On the other hand, this was a theatrical family. Everyone was accepted, everyone was welcome.

Sheila and Joan

But these relationships were about more than physical attraction. The three women formed a mutual support system. By the time the Fifties ended they were each at the height of their careers, and though they loved their work – they lived for it – the pressures were mounting. Joan had to feed the ravenous maw of *SHE*. Nancy was on the radio and the television, and was shortly to join the *News of the World* as a columnist.* Sheila was running a theatre that was by now in serious financial trouble (with the advent of the strip club, the Windmill had begun to seem unfashionably respectable).

Nancy was also increasingly concerned for her reputation. Was her sleight of hand about to be revealed? Would someone voice what had been hitherto unspoken? It was possible. The era of the Fleet Street sex scandal was beginning; Christine Keeler would soon be, for her sins, a household name. Nancy heard talk, some of it spiteful, and it rocked her faith in her public image sufficiently to provoke her into wearing a frock more regularly.† Her friends found this terribly sad. 'It was like a bad female impersonation,' said Tony Warren, the creator of *Coronation Street* and a particularly close pal. 'It was eerie.' At an awards ceremony, he recalled, his mother was moved to advise an awkward-looking Nancy that it was 'okay to put her bag down'. It is impossible not to notice that one of the first features she produced for the *News of the World* saw her

---

* She also continued to write books, among them the *Nancy Spain Colour Cookery Book*. I have not been able to discover the name of the home economist who helped her with this volume (knowing Nancy – 'I am an impromptu cook,' she writes in her foreword, with some understatement – she couldn't possibly have written it herself). Among its pages, you will find recipes for such delights as jockey club salad (pineapple in gelatin, set in moulds so it resembles a jockey's cap, and served on a lettuce leaf) and French egg casserole (hard-boiled eggs in white sauce).

† Peter Sellers sent up Nancy – he called her Nancy Lisbon – in a sketch on his 1957 album *Songs for Swingin' Sellers*, in which she was sent to interview Major Rafe Ralph, a horse dealer turned rock-star manager, at his home in Mount Street, Mayfair. The sketch was written by Frank Muir and Denis Norden, and Sellers played all the parts. With its hints about double lives, it was quite close to the bone.

registering with the Golden Key Marriage Bureau. She also, according to Rose Collis, began to toy seriously with the idea of making a 'lavender' marriage (Gilbert Harding died from an asthma attack in 1960, but there were, Nancy thought, several other men who would oblige).

At home, the women could be themselves. Drink, gossip, listen to records. Sheila was happy to act as 'mission control' and take care of the children if Joan was working late or Nancy was abroad.* But crucially, they weren't afraid to criticise one another – or at least, Joan wasn't. When Nancy embarked on her second volume of autobiography, *A Funny Thing Happened*, Joan told her she would have to re-write at least the first thirty thousand words. It was Joan, too, who in 1961 persuaded Sheila that to close the Windmill would be an admission of defeat: 'For two solid hours she tore into me. She told me that I was gutless; that I hadn't any fight. She went on and on and on ... How had I won the Monte Carlo Rally? How had I won the Tulip Rally? Was I really so spineless?' It was a pep talk that saved her, or so Sheila later insisted, from a 'nervous breakdown'. The next morning she scrapped the first house, sacked twelve girls and asked her executive staff to take a pay cut. For the time being, the show would go on.

In late 1963 Nancy and Joan bought a house in Clapham, south London. It had five bedrooms, one of which was designated for Sheila (Nancy and Joan still shared a bedroom, for all that Nancy had by now taken, in addition to Ginette Spanier, another lover, Dolly Goodman). The house would give the women the space to remain together – the complicated nature of their triumvirate did not lend itself to small rooms and narrow hallways† – and to warm it they threw a New Year's Eve party. It will give you some

---

* Sheila did a lot of childcare. 'She was one of the family quite quickly,' says Nick Werner Laurie. 'And she was the one who was there most often.'
† In a letter to Beaverbrook at this time, Nancy also refers to needing more space, and a garden, for 'her' – i.e. Joan's – children.

idea of Nancy's fame at this point to know that among the 150
guests was Paul McCartney.

The Grand National, 1964. Nancy's latest wheeze.

She was going to cover the race for the *News of the World*. But
why shouldn't she turn the assignment into a family day out? She
and Joan would fly to Aintree with their guests, Dolly Goodman
and her husband Leon. They would bring with them a Fortnum's
hamper and some champagne, a little of which they would drink
high in the sky. Meanwhile, Sheila and her sister Nona would
drive at least part of the way, a picnic prepared by Mrs O'Dea, the
Windmill's cook, safely stowed in the boot of their car.

It all happened so quickly.

Sheila and Nona arrived at Aintree shortly before three o'clock
and began to look for Nancy and Joan. 'Nona [had] heard
rumours that there had been an air crash,' Sheila wrote later. 'But
it was said to be a Dove from Scotland. Jonnie and Nancy, I knew,
were flying in a Piper Apache from Luton.'

The sisters went to their stand so they could watch the next
race. 'At 3 p.m., something – I don't know what – made me
switch on my portable radio, and I heard the terrible news. I
exclaimed: "My God, it's them!" My immediate reaction was to
want to sink into the ground and let the shock wash over me.
Then I heard: "Sheila, pull yourself together!" Nona, instinctively,
had jumped down from the tier above me and landed by my side.'

The plane had gone down at about half past eleven in a cabbage
field close to the racecourse. There were no survivors.

A police patrol car passed them. Sheila told its occupants who
she was. Would she come and identify the bodies? Of course. 'They
drove me to the mortuary, a low brick building adjoining
Ormskirk hospital.' As she looked on the broken bodies of her
dear friends she held a policeman's hand, and 'nearly broke it'.

At school in Derbyshire, Nick heard about the crash on the

The wreckage of Nancy and Joan's chartered plane in a cabbage field near Aintree

radio, whereupon he rang the *News of the World*, just to be sure. At school in North Wales, Tom was asked to see the headmaster. 'Your mother has been killed,' he was told. 'What about Nancy?' he asked. 'Yes, she was involved, too,' said the headmaster. In Trouville, France, Ginette Spanier's husband, Paul-Emile took a telephone call from Marlene Dietrich. 'She had taken the telephone book and rung every hotel in alphabetical order until she found us.'* Outside the house in Clapham, Nancy and Joan's lawyer, David Jacobs,† knowing the press would soon arrive, had a policeman installed.

The following morning Joan's brother Dick travelled up to Liverpool with Jacobs. On the train they had gin and kippers for

---

* This quotation is taken from Ginette's memoir *And Now It's Sables*. Ginette does not mention that Joan had also died. In fact, Joan is not mentioned anywhere in the book.
† Jacobs, who was gay, is best known as the lawyer of the Beatles and Brian Epstein. He also represented Marlene Dietrich, Judy Garland and Liberace. He hanged himself in 1968.

breakfast. Jacobs wept so hard his mascara ran. Sheila van Damm
met them at the other end. She had organised everything. When
the police tried to show Dick photographs of the bodies in the
wreckage of the aircraft she said, with a certain fierceness, 'You
don't look at this. I'll look at this.'

It was Sheila, too, who arranged the funerals, which took place
one after the other at Golder's Green Crematorium. These funerals, which were private, were attended by Nick but not Tom
(amazingly, the boys had still not seen one another since the accident; no one seemed to think this was necessary). Two women in
dungarees were also present, friends of Nancy's who seemed to
Dick to be 'sort of hiding behind the columns outside'.

The aftermath of any sudden death is horribly painful for those
left behind. But there is sometimes a kind of comfort to be found
in practicalities, in the cumbersome paperwork of an estate. Not
in the case of Nancy and Joan. The latter's will consisted of a tiny
scrap of paper hidden away in her wallet. She left everything to
Nancy, to distribute as she thought fit. Nancy's will, made only a
month before the accident, left everything to Joan. Neither had
ever stopped to consider what would happen if they died together.

When two people with interchangeable wills die at the same
time, the law decrees that whoever was the oldest at the moment
of their deaths died first. Nancy, then, had died first. Her estate
had therefore passed to Joan, with the result that it would now
pass to Nick as Joan's eldest child. Tom would get nothing, nor
had any provision been made for his guardianship. In the end the
question of money was fairly easily resolved – Nick was prevailed
upon to share, and two separate trust funds were established –
though the situation was complicated somewhat when various
women came out of the woodwork to ask if they might sell the
properties they co-owned with Nancy. (Dick Laurie remembers
at least two such women.) By the time of her death, it seems,
Nancy had a small portfolio of secret love nests. The question of

who would look after Tom, however, was more vexed. No one in the family offered to keep him, perhaps because no one knew exactly whose responsibility he was. It had taken Nancy's death for her sister Liz to discover she was an aunt.

In the end, it was agreed that Tom's headteacher and his wife would give him a home, 'and that was rather uneasy because his [the headteacher's] rages used to go on and on'.

Did he know, yet, that Nancy was his mother? No. This was something he wouldn't find out until he was nineteen, when a trustee of the estate suddenly corrected his 'misapprehension' that Joan was his mother. But Nick knew. In the days after the crash Dick told him, thinking the truth had better emerge sooner than later. How did he react? With deadly silence at first. He was hurt that Nancy and Joan hadn't trusted him enough to tell him. Then things began to make sense. Only much later – many years later – did anger set in.

For Tom, it was something of a relief to find out that Nancy was his mother rather than Joan. Like Nick, it was Nancy he had loved the most, and her loss he felt most keenly. Both boys had been rather afraid of Joan. But who was his father? Someone – Dick, perhaps – advised him to go and see Nancy's doctor, Nelly Newman, and it was Newman who sent him in the right direction. He had no name, but he was certain that the man in question had been married to Nancy's friend Margery Allingham. Tom looked up Allingham in *Who's Who*, where he read that the detective novelist had been married to a man called Pip Youngman Carter. He rang Nelly back. Was this the right name? Yes, came the reply. Carter had died in 1969, three years after Allingham. Soon after this Tom changed his name from Seyler to Carter.

Oh, the layers of misery that are here. Allingham had always longed for children. Her husband, however, had always refused to give them to her, and though there is no evidence that either one of them knew of Tom's existence you can't help but wonder how she would have felt had she ever been made aware of the truth.* The pain of it. An ache that would only have been made worse by the fact that her friend had carried out the deception with such astonishing sangfroid. In 1954, when Tom was only two years old, Nancy breezily interviewed Allingham for *Woman's Hour*. Two years later Allingham made it to the pages of *Why I'm Not a Millionaire*. 'Marge sees everything in gigantic terms,' Nancy wrote. 'Life, parties, dinner, conversation, literature. That's why she, too, is on such a grand scale, mentally and physically. When I first met her, I was knocked down by the weight of her thought, the living profusion of her ideas, the glory of her language.' *Marge!* It's tempting to see this as brazen, or even cruel, but more likely it was simply the result of Nancy's willed absent-mindedness. By 1956 it's quite possible that she would only have been able to remember the name of the father of her child if you had put a gun to her head.

As for Tom, his life was not easy. After university he had a series of breakdowns and spent the rest of his life struggling with mental illness. He died in 2012, in the bathroom of the psychiatric wing of Yeovil District Hospital.

And Sheila? She had now been running the Windmill alone for four years. In that time it had made a profit only once. In the early summer of 1964 she took the painful decision to close it. Revudeville had by then run for longer than any show on earth, at some sixty thousand performances; though the theatre had only 320 seats, more than ten million people had seen it. Nonetheless, the moment had come. When the news broke Fleet Street descended, and *Panorama* too. Among the letters of condolence was one from the Lord Chancellor's office. It was the end of an era.

The final show took place at 10 p.m. on 31 October 1964. Both companies gave her presents: a table lighter from A company, a

* See *The Adventures of Margery Allingham*, a biography by Julia Jones.

gold windmill charm for her bracelet from B company. Among those who attended the final show were Dick Emery and Harry Secombe. Bruce Forsyth, another Windmill alumnus, sent a telegram: 'DO WISH I COULD BE WITH YOU AS I AM SO GRATEFUL TO THE MILL FOR SO MANY THINGS STOP GIVE EVERYONE MY FONDEST LOVE LITTLE ME – BRUCE'. Afterwards, Sheila had five hundred bottles of champagne waiting for her guests. 'I was determined that this last night should not be a wake, and that we would go out with our heads held high.' The curtain, she decided, would not come down that evening. 'The curtain never came down.' The party went on for hours. When she slipped out, at a quarter past two in the morning, she was the first to go.

Sheila went to live with her sister Nona in deepest Sussex, where they had bought a small farm and stables. She took comfort from a letter she received from a spiritualist, who told her that Jonnie and Nancy were with her father, and that they were fine. She believed in the afterlife. But the crash, the loss of Joan and Nancy, had changed her. In the years following she had a nervous breakdown, suffered from a depression bad enough to be treated with electro-convulsive therapy, and grew reclusive. She would see members of her own family: her mother, sister and nieces. But people from the old life were reminders of all that she had lost, and she would always put them off.

She died of cancer at the London Clinic on 23 August 1987, an illness she kept from her family until two days before her death. There was no funeral.

Sheila didn't want a fuss.

A Monumental Ambition

Alison Smithson, architect

Alison working at the Solar Pavilion, otherwise known as Upper Lawn

'Mies is great, but Corb communicates'

It's not hard to find a good photograph of Alison Smithson. She was a striking woman who knew precisely how she wanted to present herself to the world; the camera loved her Russian-doll face and avant-garde clothes. But the picture that perhaps captures her best was taken in 1964, by which time she was the most well known and controversial female architect in Britain. Not that there was much competition. In 1964 you could count the number of women architects who'd had even one major project built on the fingers of your right hand. Alison Smithson, however, could already put her name to two.*

The photograph was taken at the Solar Pavilion (otherwise known as Upper Lawn), which was where Alison and her husband Peter spent their weekends. The Pavilion was little more than a cube – a 'camping box', they liked to call it, for they thought of it as a kind of permanent tent – built on the site of a labourer's cottage on the Fonthill Estate in Tisbury, Wiltshire. It consisted of two rooms on two floors, connected by a steep wooden ladder. Downstairs was the kitchen, if that is the right

---

* Of the several hundred post-war buildings listed since 1987, only a handful were designed (in fact, co-designed) by women. By 2003 there were, according to my calculations, just eight. Two were domestic houses: 3 Church Walk in Aldeburgh, Suffolk (1963–4), which was designed by H. T. and Elizabeth Cadbury-Brown, and Creekvean in Feock, Cornwall (1964–7), which was designed by Team 4 (Richard and Su Rogers, Norman and Wendy Foster). The Pilkington offices in St Helens and the Passfields Estate in Catford, London were designed by Fry, Drew and Partners (Maxwell Fry and his wife Jane Drew). The four remaining buildings, and by far the most important on such a list, were designed by Alison and Peter Smithson.

word: the house had no fridge, and cooking was done on a rudimentary stove powered by bottled gas. Upstairs were the sleeping
quarters, though there were no beds: the Smithsons slept on
mats, which were rolled up during the day. It was often cold – the
Pavilion had no central heating, and only one fireplace – and it
was always uncomfortable, there being neither armchairs nor sofa
(Peter Smithson despised the sofa as a symbol of all that he and
Alison wished to change about the world; unlike a good chair,
which, done right, could be classed as architecture, a sofa was
always just a soggy, bourgeois mess). But the almost 360-degree
views were exhilarating, the changing seasons as integral to the
building's design as its flat roof, its lean wooden beams and its zinc
cladding.

It is high summer. Alison is sitting at a rickety table on the
Pavilion's terrace, her face in shade, her back warmed by the sun.
She is wearing dark glasses and a striped jumpsuit; she looks Left
Bank-ish and cool. Her self-conscious style, though, is at odds
with her pose, which is utterly unselfconscious: oblivious, transported, sealed off. If she is aware that someone is taking her
picture she gives no outward sign of it. One hand supports her
chin, the other clutches a pen; she is gazing down at a sheaf of
papers. You might take her for a student: selectively deaf, self-
absorbed, a long vacation stretching ahead of her.

But in 1964, Alison was thirty-six years old. Look closer. Over
her right shoulder a small boy can be seen, climbing on a wall.
And what's this? On the floor beside the table is an oblong box
with long handles, and now it comes to you: this isn't a box at all,
but a bassinet, and of a kind only big enough to contain a tiny
baby. Alison is working – and by the look of her working quite
hard – while one of her children plays and another sleeps (and
there was a third child, somewhere off camera). Suddenly her
modishness seems almost incidental, her clothes rather less
modern than her conviction that work was as important to her

as it was to any man. Some women, trying to wrestle papers over the course of a hot weekend, would find themselves distracted by their children. Here things have been turned on their head. Work is the distraction; it's her drawings that lasso her attention.

Even in the Sixties Alison never described herself as a feminist; she had, perhaps, ploughed too lonely a furrow for too long to join that particular club. The building with which she had made her name – a ruthlessly spare secondary school, built of steel and glass, in the seaside town of Hunstanton in Norfolk – had been completed a full decade earlier, in 1954. But still, her example was plain for all to see. She was a mother and she was a famous architect. How, you might ask, did she do both, and without even employing the services of a nanny? For Alison, a Calvinist creature who disliked fuss, this wasn't complicated. Mostly it came down to the fact that she simply could not abide waste. The hours were there to be snatched, to be made use of like the crab-apples she turned into jelly, the mattress ticking she made into dresses. The two things – work and home – were also intimately connected. Designing a space wasn't the only job of an architect. A more interesting question was, how might the space be inhabited? A sleeping baby was both an excuse to start sketching and a means of tethering her immaculate, improbable drawings to her lodestar, the idea of home.

At the Solar Pavilion the idea of home could be elusive – or that was how it felt to visitors, told they would be spending the night in a sleeping bag on the floor. Its clattery emptiness provided a bracing slap, not a warm embrace. In London, though, where the Smithsons lived in Cato Lodge, a tall Kensington villa built in 1851, visitors saw a different side of them: a collection of teapots, a battered Persian rug, a couple of Eames chairs covered wittily in chintz. The ground-floor studio, where the Smithsons worked together, their drawing boards barely a foot apart, had a crowded mantelpiece on which sat a bust of their early hero, Mies van der

Rohe, the great German-American architect,* a fez pulled comically over his head. And close by, cast in plaster of Paris, two more unlikely sources of inspiration: Peter Rabbit and Benjamin Bunny.

Was this a private joke? No. Alison was deadly serious when it came to Beatrix Potter. In Potter's world, objects and utensils hang on hooks and nails, and they are all the decoration her spaces need. The bare necessities are raised to a kind of poetry, just as they had been by Alvar Aalto,† Le Corbusier and the other guiding spirits of the modern movement. To Alison, the home Potter created for Mrs Tittlemouse was not so very different from the house Corb designed for Mr Shodhan in Ahmedabad.‡ Both were tailored to the individual needs of their inhabitants; both used materials 'as found'; both spoke eloquently of the 'simple life, well done'.

In low moments – and she would have more than a few of these in the course of her career – Alison would gaze at Peter Rabbit and Benjamin Bunny, and despair at the short-sightedness of those who seemed to have made it their business never to give planning permission to a Smithson design. It was a source of disappointment to her that a man who would no doubt have smiled indulgently at the frontispiece of *The Tale of Two Bad Mice* or *The*

* Mies van der Rohe (1886–1969), last director of the Bauhaus, emigrated to America in 1937, after the Nazis declared his work un-German. In the US he was appointed the head of architecture at the Illinois Institute of Technology, where he designed many campus buildings, most notably Crown Hall. His other great works are the Villa Tugendhat at Brno in the Czech Republic (1930), and the Farnsworth House at Plano in Illinois (1951). Mies's less-is-more style utilises minimal framework and the idea of free-flowing space. He was a glass and steel man, and a bona fide architectural genius.

† Alvar Aalto, the Finnish architect (1898–1976). Mrs Tittlemouse is the proud owner of a bentwood rocker that Aalto, a keen designer of chairs and stools, would have admired for its clean lines.

‡ The Villa Shodhan was built between 1951 and 1956 for Shyamubhai Shodhan, an Indian mill owner. Usually when discussing the work of Le Corbusier, the Swiss-born architect who was the Smithsons' major influence, people talk about such things as pilotis (stilts) and plasticity, but the Villa does indeed resemble a home an animal might build, albeit on a giant scale. Side on, its rooms look like a warren or a nest – a feeling its roof garden only emphasises. Other Tittlemousian features include the ramps that lead to the main and mezzanine levels; its natural climate control system; and the connectivity of its inner spaces.

'A camping box': the Solar Pavilion, otherwise known as Upper Lawn

Tailor of Gloucester would only curl his lip at a scheme for a new apartment building. 'It would still be a brave architect who would submit a white house to a County Planning Authority,' she wrote in the magazine *Architectural Design* in 1967. 'Even though it was suspected that the officers and the lay committee in question had read *Jemima Puddleduck*.' She never quite shook off the habit of being amazed by this collective failure of imagination (the cottage outside which Jemima Puddleduck waddles is white, as I'm sure you know). On a good day, bolstered by her innate self-belief, Alison could brush it off, even laugh at it. But on a bad day, when the books were bare and bills demanded to be paid, it made her feel misunderstood and, sometimes, just a little lonely.

Alison Smithson grew up in South Shields, where her father, Ernest Gill, was the principal of the School of Art. No one seems to know why she wanted to be an architect – it wasn't an ordinary kind of ambition, not even for the only child of a draughtsman so accomplished as Ernest – but no doubt the war played its part. Made vulnerable by its shipyards, South Shields was continually under attack. The worst air raids took place in October 1941 and involved some fifty bombers (the teenage Alison could identify planes the way other people could identify butterflies); sixty-eight people were killed and two thousand lost their homes. Many of the Gills' neighbours, meanwhile, were in the merchant navy. 'My parents could count the chimneys of twelve houses where captains or chief engineers had gone down with their ships,' Alison wrote in an unpublished memoir. When the bombings were at their height she was evacuated, albeit briefly, to Edinburgh, the home of her grandparents. It isn't difficult to see how the contrasting cityscapes of South Shields and Edinburgh – the piles of rubble and the mighty Mound, the yawning craters and the ordered New Town – might have worked on the imagination of a restless and precociously clever teenage girl. But whatever her motivation, she was nothing if not determined, taking up her place at the King's College School of Architecture at the University of Durham in Newcastle upon Tyne in 1944, when she was just sixteen. (The war, of course, may also have spurred her on to apply to university early: the fear was that when the men came back from the fighting there might be rather fewer places available to women undergraduates.) She arrived at university, moreover, fully formed: preternaturally self-possessed and with a look that was all her own. Unlike most undergraduates, who were in old knits, tweed and ugly Utility clothing, she favoured – who knows how she came by these things – flowing chiffon, printed silks and Liberty prints. 'It was obvious she was interesting,' remembers a contemporary. And Alison's outward exuberance was matched by an inward energy. In classes she expressed her views forcibly. Her sketches, though deft, were only just the right side of fanciful.

Alison heard about the man she would marry long before she

Alison, aged sixteen

clapped eyes on him. Peter Smithson, the only child of a travelling salesman from Stockton-on-Tees, had joined the School of Architecture in 1939, but in 1942 had left Newcastle to serve with the Royal Engineers and Queen Victoria's Own Madras Sappers and Miners in Burma. Most of the architecture students, however, already knew of him by reputation as a group of them had found some models in a storeroom: cardboard constructions of extremely white, extremely modern buildings in the style of Le Corbusier, whose name was then something of a dirty word. Who had made these models? They asked Gordon Ryder,* their tutor, who told them that they were by Peter Smithson. It was clear from the look on his face that he couldn't wait for the model-builder's return.

In 1945 Smithson did return, first as a student and then, after he had completed his degree, as a studio assistant. Like many of those who had served in the war, he took his studies more seriously

---

* Gordon Ryder was excused war service thanks to a climbing accident. He left his teaching post in 1948 to work with Berthold Lubetkin on the first plans for the new town of Peterlee, and later became famous as half of the Ryder & Yates partnership, designers of outstanding modernist architecture in the north-east and elsewhere.

second time around, and was struck both by what he thought of as the élan of the younger students and their determination to enjoy themselves. What drew him to Alison? 'She was a one-off,' he said later. 'Like many of the girls at university she was original in a way that the boys just weren't.' He, too, was struck by her clothes – her long coats especially. Thanks to the wartime diet she was also extremely skinny: 'She looked like Popeye's girlfriend. Her nickname was Chippendale because her legs were so thin.'

But it was Alison who made all the running. She seems to have decided that Peter was what she wanted, and when she graduated in 1949 she followed him to London, where they joined the schools division of the London County Council Architects' Department and lived in a Bloomsbury flat – two rooms, kitchen, shared bathroom – which they rented from Theo Crosby, the architectural writer, who lived upstairs.* They were married, to the surprise of many of their friends, in August of the same year, in Regent Square, St Pancras; Alison wore a home-made dress and carried a bouquet of wax orange blossom. No doubt they chose the Presbyterian church for its convenience rather than its symbolism (they would eat their wedding breakfast at home in Doughty Street), but the imagery cannot have been lost on them. On the afternoon of 9 February 1945 it had been hit by a German bomb, and though it still stood, or just about, the structure was deemed

---

* Before Alison's arrival in London, Peter and Crosby, a South African émigré, enjoyed an 'intense dialogue' about the future of architecture. It came to an end, however, when Peter married. Afterwards, Peter said, he felt he didn't 'necessarily need anyone else', but Crosby would be influential on the Smithsons' careers and was probably more responsive than his peers when it came to the idea of a female architect. He had begun his career in the office of Maxwell Fry and Jane Drew, a place he described as 'a hopeful, laughing place, a nest of eaglets'. Drew (1911–96) was so determinedly feminist that in the early years of her practice, when Fry was on overseas service with the Royal Engineers, she only employed women. In 1953 Crosby became technical editor of *Architectural Design* under Monica Pidgeon. Pidgeon's appointment as editor in 1946 had made the magazine's owners so nervous they insisted that male names – Erno Goldfinger, Denys Lasdun – sit beside hers on the masthead as consultants, the better to reassure advertisers and readers.

18 August 1949

unsafe and services had to be conducted in a nearby lecture hall. They were a young couple who wanted to build the future. Where better to seal their union than amid the wreckage of the past?

Newly married couples have a certain energy, and the Smithsons were no exception. They began working together immediately, entering a competition to design a new secondary modern in Hunstanton, and to general amazement – Peter was still only twenty-six, and Alison just twenty-one – they won it. Most architects then, as now, expected to wait for middle age before getting a break; it's for this reason that the epithet 'young' is habitually applied to any architect under fifty. But the Smithsons had got lucky. The competition had just one assessor: Denis Clark Hall, an architect who specialised in school design and who had himself won a major competition at the age of just twenty. The commission would prove to be a significant one: on the back of it, they would be able to set up their own practice. But it would be life-changing in another way too. There was a severe shortage of materials in post-war Britain. In most instances, prefabrication was the order of the day and would be for years to come. The Smithsons, though, were blessed with a contractor, F. W. Shanks, who seemed not to care about profit – perhaps because (this was Peter's theory) the company was in effect building the school for the children of its workmen. From the outset, it was clear to its architects that no corners would be cut: they could have all the glass and steel they required – the school would utilise the county's entire allocation of steel until 1953. Even better, the Education Committee was taking strangely little interest in the plans. Their design, so radical it would in time join the beach and the pier on postcards of Sunny Hunny's meagre attractions, would not be compromised. It would win them a place in architectural history.

Pevsner calls the school, which is now Grade II* listed, 'the paramount example among the innumerable interesting post-war schools of England of a rigidly formal, symmetrical layout', and it's certainly the case that the building's arrangement is easily described, consisting as it does of a single oblong with three internal courtyards – the middle of which is roofed so as to provide the school with a hall – and ten open staircases rising to the classrooms, which are arranged in pairs on the first floor. To twenty-first-century eyes, a first glimpse brings some disappointment: for a modernist masterpiece, it is surprisingly dinky.*

---

* I first visited Smithdon High School on a trip organised by the Twentieth Century Society, which campaigns to safeguard the heritage of British architecture from 1914 onwards. As our coach pulled up I was listening to a conversation between two professors of architecture, one British (let us call him Tweed), the other American (Seersucker). 'Oh,' said Seersucker, gazing out of the window. 'I always forget how small it is. Gosh. I mean, it isn't even remotely on the same scale as Mies.' Poor Tweed was crushed.

Smithdon High School

Move closer, though, and you will find that its precision beats a contemplative rhythm: the tick of the glazed panels, the tock of the gyratory corridors. And there is something at once triumphant and tongue-in-cheek about its Braithwaite water tank, raised high on an open frame so that it resembles, especially at dusk, the pit-head machinery that both Alison and Peter would have known from their childhoods. It is this tower, asymmetric and industrial, that gives the school its distinctive silhouette. Like a fading scar on a beautiful face, it is a flaw, deliberate and brazen, that only accentuates its abiding grace.

It took four long years to build what is now known as Smithdon High School, and when the scaffolding finally came down, there was the most tremendous fuss. Local people hated it. They worried that passers-by would be able to see up the skirts of female students, and there were concerns – these, admittedly, were more well-founded – about how cold the building, a veritable greenhouse, would be in winter, and how hot in summer.* Mostly, though, it was the building's appearance that was disliked. It wasn't only the feeling that this gleaming edifice had been beamed down from another planet; inside, its exposed ceilings and drainage pipes – the architectural 'honesty' to which the Smithsons would adhere for the rest of their working lives – seemed cold and standoffish, as if its architects had entirely forgotten that it would be inhabited mainly by children.

Was this unfair? Not entirely. Of course the Smithsons didn't forget who the building was for. They gave it the requisite cloak-rooms, hall, craft room and, in a separate block, gymnasium. But

---

* In the Eighties, the lower panes of each window were changed to black sandwich panels. This certainly ensures no knickers can be seen, but it also ruins the building's careful symmetry. Smithdon was originally heated by under-floor coils, but they were slow-responding. As Pevsner explains, they 'could not compete with the cold of the exposed N side, but roasted the greenhouse-like S classrooms when the sun shone, even in winter. A temperature gradient of up to 30 degrees C could exist in any season across the width, and the frame distorted the more.' Conventional heating was installed in 1990–1.

there must have been moments when they wished their school could be allowed just to stand among its playing fields, pristine and untouched. Alison, who was responsible for Hunstanton's landscaping, gave the grounds a ha-ha, a detail strongly suggestive of a certain kind of isolated splendour, and when the time came for the building to be photographed for the architectural journals she and Peter removed every last stick of furniture from its interior, thus returning it, in the words of one architectural writer, to a 'protean, didactic state'.* Peter wrote of it insistently as a building that had 'two lives'. The first, by day, was bustling and noisy, a scramble of scuffed shoes and satchels. The second, entirely nocturnal, was almost silent, when the structure became once again an idea.

Naturally, there was an entirely different kind of fuss in the architectural press. Alison and Peter were careful, in their own accounts of their design, to emphasise the school's Palladian formality. Yes, they had built what was 'probably the most truly modern building in Britain',† but it also had 'a clear English precedent' in the form of Hardwick Hall in Derbyshire, the magnificent Elizabethan country house designed by their namesake Robert Smythson. Others begged to differ, most notably Philip Johnson, the man who had been instrumental in bringing Mies van der Rohe to America, and who is probably most famous for his Glass House in New Canaan, Connecticut, a brief but endlessly

---

* The school was photographed by Reginald Hugo de Burgh Galwey for *Architectural Review* and *Architects' Journal*. He gave it a 'noir' feel, holding his camera close to the floor, the better to emphasise the height of the interior. It was also shot by the Smithsons' friend Nigel Henderson, with the architects themselves – and Ronald Jenkins of Ove Arup and Partners (the building's engineer) – arranged in and around it. These photographs anticipate the album covers of the Sixties. Photographs were vital to architects in post-war Britain because it was so difficult to travel. Peter Smithson first encountered the work of Mies van der Rohe at the Illinois Institute of Technology Campus – Smithdon High School's chief influence – in *Architectural Journal* in 1946, 'an act of publication that completely changed my life'.

† Alison was not shy when it came to proclaiming the building's greatness. On a trip to see the school with the architect Trevor Dannatt, she claimed, 'There's been nothing like it since Inigo Jones.' John Winter, another distinguished architect of the period, told me: 'She used to say: "We're the best architects in the world." It wasn't very English at all.'

beguiling essay in minimalism. In *Architectural Review*, Johnson saluted the Smithsons for mastering the language of Mies and praised their building's engineering for its amazing lightness. It was true that in using a frame system the architects had given themselves a problem where the frames met at right angles – 'definitely not elegant!' – but overall he was reluctant to 'cavil in the face of so much distinction'. This must have been thrilling for the Smithsons, whatever they said about its Englishness. They feared and loathed the parochial – in the summer of 1951 they had gone on holiday to Greece with the sole aim of avoiding the Festival of Britain, the architecture of which they considered singularly provincial* – and now here was a famous American architect speaking of them as the children of Mies, a titan of modernism in Europe and America. Englishness be damned!

But in another sense such an anointment, however glorious, had come too late. Even as their school was being built the Smithsons were in the process of forsaking Mies for an altogether sterner master; in 1951, they had attended a meeting of the Congrès International d'Architecture Moderne (CIAM) in Hoddesdon, Hertfordshire, at which Le Corbusier had spoken, and it was his theories that excited them now. As Johnson mournfully acknowledged in his review, these two young architects had become part of the movement 'they call the New Brutalism', – a phrase that was 'already being picked up by the Smithsons' contemporaries to defend atrocities'. The 'inherent elegance' of their school was, he hinted, unlikely to be on display in their next work. For the rage now was not for

---

* The general public thought the Skylon and the Dome of Discovery terribly exciting and modern, but most young architects were rather less impressed. Peter Smithson disliked its 'dowdy English jokiness . . . [the work of] *Punch* cartoonists made solid'. Trevor Dannatt says: 'As young bloods of a Corbusian persuasion, we were critical. We felt it was full of whimsy. I liked the Lansbury Estate, but even at the time, we thought it was retro.' (The Lansbury Estate was, and still is, to be found at Poplar in the East End; it was built on a bomb site and includes Britain's first purpose-built pedestrianised shopping area, Chrisp Street Market.)

steel and glass. The rage now was for brick and concrete and timber.

Brutalism. What a word. Unlovely and unloved, it began its life as a bilingual pun on the English word 'brutal' and the French *'beton brut'*, a term used to described the coarse, irregular concrete finish of Le Corbusier's Unité d'Habitation in Marseilles (it has an echo, too, of *art brut*, Jean Dubuffet's term for what has come to be known as outsider art) – and its coinage is most often attributed to the critic Reyner Banham, whose essay on the New Brutalism appeared in *Architectural Review* in 1955. Banham, invitations to whose Sunday morning 'at homes' in Primrose Hill were much sought after in London design circles, was the nearest thing architecture then had to a hipster. He was also, alas, an almost unreadably bad writer. But we can sum up his arguments thus: a Brutalist building is a straightforward, bloody-minded building, whose form and function can be understood by the passer-by in little more than a single glance.*

Except that it wasn't Banham who first used the word in print, for all that it reeks of testosterone. It was Alison and Peter Smithson. In 1953 they wrote a short piece about a house that they had planned to construct on a bomb site in Soho (it had not happened because they had been unable to buy the plot of land), which was published alongside their original drawings in *Architectural Design*. This house, which would have had a flat corrugated-iron roof, was intended, wherever practicable, to have no internal finishes whatsoever. The concrete beams that

---

* As Jonathan Meades points out, Banham had an embarrassing fondness for 'both beardie hep-cat jazz talk and after-dinner speaker's bumptious archaisms, *hath wrought*, etc'. Incidentally, I agree with Meades when he argues that, had Banham not written his essay, or had he at least dreamt up a less loaded-sounding term for this new aesthetic than Brutalism, 'the fate of buildings in this idiom might have been happier, for their opponents ... would not have had the ammunition of what seems like a nomenclatural admission of culpable aggression'. Banham went on to devote an entire book to the New Brutalism. Don't, whatever you do, try reading it.

comprised its structure, moreover, would be incorporated uncompromisingly into its façade. Highlighting a specification that Alison and Peter had written – 'The Constructor should aim at a high standard of basic construction as in a small warehouse' – they added, almost casually: 'Had this been built, it would have been the first exponent of the "new brutalism" in England.' (There was perhaps an in-joke at play here too: Peter had christened himself Brutus at college, a name Alison always loathed.)

By 1955, then, the Smithsons were in an enviable position: whether by accident or design, they were at the forefront of a nascent movement. Their school was much debated, their ideas much talked about (architecture does love theory; therein lies its downfall). They were increasingly well-connected. Thanks to their involvement with Team X, an off-shoot of CIAM,* they had struck up friendships with several European architects. At the Central School of Art and Design, where he was teaching, Peter had met the sculptor Eduardo Paolozzi and the photographer Nigel Henderson, who were both members of the Independent Group, a coalition of artists whose interests lay in the relationship between modernism and mass culture. The Smithsons duly joined them, with the result that they were among the contributors to *Parallel of Life and Art*, a 1953 exhibition at the Institute of Contemporary Arts of images from ordinary life, nature, art and architecture that was designed to make people look again at the everyday. In short, the Smithsons could not have been more fashionable if they had tried.

And yet, none of this helped them to get anything built. Hunstanton soon began to look like a one-off, a false dawn. Over

---

* They were active in Team X, which began its life in 1953 as a group that hoped to reform CIAM by challenging its doctrinaire approach to town planning (Corbusier held that cities should be zoned into separate areas for work and leisure; the Smithsons and others disagreed). It was Alison who organised Team X meetings, during which, predictably, she also took the minutes.

and over, they had failed to win the competitions they entered: for a new cathedral for Coventry; for new buildings at Sheffield University; for new housing – it would incorporate, famously, the idea of 'streets in the sky' – in Golden Lane in the City of London.*

Luck played its part in this, of course – and sometimes it was simply the case that another architect came up with a better design; Basil Spence deserved to win the competition to rebuild Coventry Cathedral for the simple reason that he was the only entrant of two hundred to grasp the importance of keeping the ruins of the old cathedral intact (the fragment symbolising sacrifice, the new building, resurrection). There was also the matter of logistics. Alison had her first baby, a son called Simon, in 1955, and she was determined to keep the office manageably small, the better that she might combine work and motherhood; she had returned to her desk a week after giving birth, periodically dashing upstairs to breastfeed (a series of lodgers did all the baby-sitting). But she and Peter were increasingly convinced that, at bottom, the drought was personal – that competition judges and planning officers had only to see their names on a drawing to lose interest. It had been a political statement, of sorts, to call their partnership 'Alison and Peter Smithson', and Alison now suggested, only half-jokingly, that they should start using only Peter's name, or even a pseudonym.

This dry spell would continue for the rest of the Fifties. But it wasn't only their designs that caused people to baulk. Somewhere

* They spent a year working on a design for Coventry. Their design had a cantilevered concrete shell roof, resembling a giant clam – but the moderators chose instead Basil Spence's more traditional basilica. Peter later dismissed Graham Sutherland's altar tapestry and John Piper's window – both commissioned by Spence – as 'Festival of Britain trivia', though he never saw either of them in the flesh. In their designs for Sheffield University, the Smithsons put lecture halls away from faculty buildings and linked them with a raised walkway, a feature that would become commonplace in British universities in the Sixties. The idea of 'streets in the sky', inspired by Nigel Henderson's photographs of the East End, first became reality at Park Hill in Sheffield (Jack Lynn and Ivor Smith, 1957–61).

along the way the Smithsons gained a reputation for being difficult. Specifically, Alison gained a reputation for being difficult.
'The problem was that she could upset clients,' says a former assistant. 'It wasn't just the case that she thought she was right; the
client should do what she said too. That didn't go down well.'
Another architect: 'Alison whined. She was relentless. Her voice
was relentless. She had a chip on her shoulder.' And another: 'I
found her difficult. She had a beastly temper, and she could be
horrid to people.' And here is Jane Drew: 'I thought her voice
always had a moan in it somewhere.' I take all of these comments
with a pinch of salt; visible women in male-dominated professions
are often characterised as shrill, bossy, chippy, stubborn and com-
plaining, even by other visible women. On the other hand, Alison
could be exasperating. Even those who loved her will tell you so.

Excluded from the work of rebuilding Britain, the Smithsons
began to turn their ambition inwards, their projects tending now
to be private rather than public, domestic rather than commercial – something which may have suited Alison (though she would
sooner have shopped for a set of antimacassars than admitted this
in public). After all, home was her great preoccupation: its
rhythms and its rituals. Sunday colour supplements were still some
years in the future – the *Sunday Times* would not launch its magazine until 1962 – and yet her lifestyle could have come straight from
the pages of one. It wasn't only her furniture, though that was
plenty striking enough in the days when most modern people
longed for nothing more than an Ercol dining table. (The
Smithsons' sitting room was a museum of modern chairs: Thonet
rocker, Bertoia wire chair, Rietvald Zig-Zag chair, several alu-
minium chairs by the Eames, and not a cushion in sight.) It was in
the food she cooked, the clothes she wore, even the way her marriage worked. She and Peter had a determinedly egalitarian
relationship, with the exception of the car, which he always drove
(they owned a Citroën DS, a vehicle that fascinated them so much

Alison went on to write a book about it).* In the office, their thinking went along the lines that 'an experience shared was an
experience solidified'. It was the Smithsons 'versus the world ...
impossible to have a conspiracy of one'. This doesn't mean every
aspect of every design was a total collaboration. The vast Smithson
archive makes it fairly clear who sketched what, and sometimes it's
only Alison's name (or Peter's) on a drawing. But it was as complete
a partnership as it is possible to imagine; the Smithsons were like
Charles and Ray Eames without the jokes and the home movies.

Away from the studio, they took turns when it came to cooking, and Peter did most of the shopping. Their kitchen staples
included olive oil, vine leaves and feta cheese (purchased at a
Greek shop near Hyde Park), and the still wildly exotic aubergines
and avocados. They drank strong black coffee and red wine rather
than tea and beer. Alison, maker extraordinaire, sewed most of
her own clothes and Peter's too – and they were, everyone agreed,
startling. His shirts were stitched in Liberty lawn, with a kind of
built-in cravat (beautifully cut, they would become his trade-
mark); she even made him a pair of swimming trunks, fashioned
entirely from diamond-shaped offcuts of leatherette. Her dresses
were copied from *Vogue*; one of the most memorable was covered
in what looked like Formica samples, arranged like the scales of
a fish. Later, when money allowed, there would be pinafores from
Mary Quant, kaftans by Marimekko.† The Smithsons were frugal;

* The book, published in 1983, was called *AS in DS: An Eye on the Road* and was shaped like a DS.
Roland Barthes wrote an ode to the Citroën DS in his 1957 book, *Mythologies*: 'I think that cars
today are almost the exact equivalent of the great Gothic cathedrals: I mean the supreme creation of an era, conceived with passion by unknown artists, and consumed in image if not in
usage by a whole population which appropriates them as a purely magical object.'
† Alison once threw a glass of red wine over the architect James Stirling when he poked fun
at one outfit by unrolling its exaggerated collar and tying it on top of her head. After her
death some of her clothes were donated to the Fashion Museum, Bath, by her daughter
Soraya. Among the items in this collection is Mary Quant's famous hessian pinafore; two
brightly coloured harlequin-style unitards (these were much clearly much worn; their heels
have even been darned); a silver dress with cut-outs in the torso, à la Bodymap; and a silver
polyurethane trouser suit with matching boots. Not bad for a mother of three.

they had to be. But they also knew exactly how they wanted to live. 'Most architects are happy if they do a pretty elevation,' says one of their contemporaries, 'but it was a total experience for them; it was a way of life.' According to Tim Tinker, who worked as their assistant, life and art overlapped: 'They were in the business of acting out the life of a modern person.' Another friend remembers, as if it were yesterday, a pair of curtains Alison made. They were covered with the shards of Delftware she had found while digging over her flowerbeds, and must have jangled merrily whenever they were drawn.

Nineteen fifty-six. Britain was changing. John Osborne's play *Look Back in Anger* had its premiere at the Royal Court, and in doing so practically ended the career of Terence Rattigan and all who sailed in him; Colin Wilson published *The Outsider*, a book about social alienation in the work of Camus, Sartre and others, and it became a best-seller; and Samuel Beckett's *Waiting for Godot* began a somewhat tricky tour of the provinces (it even took in Blackpool, where it competed for ticket sales with the likes of Ken Dodd and Jimmy Clitheroe). Meanwhile, the urban environment was undergoing its own existential crisis. The Clean Air Act had finally come into force, four years after the smog that had paralysed London and killed thousands, transforming many landscapes simply by dint of restoring the view; in Manchester, winter sunshine doubled as a result. Just as dramatic in its effect, the Housing Subsidies Act now made it financially advantageous for local authorities engaged in slum clearance to build high-rise blocks rather than houses (the subsidy for a flat in a fifteen-storey tower was three times that for a house). After a slow start – for years after the war, people had wondered aloud why bomb sites continued to stand empty – great swathes of cities such as Glasgow, Liverpool, London and Newcastle were now in the process of being demolished, a programme of 'improvement' that provoked high praise in some quarters and extreme horror in others.*

In March the *Daily Mail* staged its Ideal Home Exhibition at Olympia, an annual event that was covered by every newspaper in the land and almost every magazine. Among the commissions for the Jubilee edition of the show, which would be attended by more than a million wide-eyed visitors, was a design by the Smithsons entitled the House of the Future. From the outside, this house – its name, projected on one side, flashed on and off, Piccadilly Circus-style – appeared to be little more than a large white box tacked on to the end of a small 'street' of prefabs. It had an opening at one end, and inside was another slightly smaller box, its exterior wall forming a rectangular corridor with the interior walls of its larger partner. There were two ways to see the contents of this second container: visitors could either peek in through a series of small windows at ground level, or they could ascend to an upper level where a viewing platform provided a bird's-eye view. Outside, queues soon formed. For a new generation of new and wannabe home-owners, aspirational and optimistic, the House of the Future's flashing sign announced a must-see attraction. This was the era of the New Town, of open-plan living rooms, of DIY, Formica and gleaming, seductively advertised appliances.

It was Alison who designed the interior of the House of the Future (Peter restricted himself to the external structure), and it was a remarkable thing: 'a Wellsian fantasy in plastic' according to the magazine *House Beautiful*. Cross Jules Verne's submarine, *Nautilus*, with the Jetsons' apartment in Orbit City (though, of

* In the former camp was Brendan Behan, who visited Leeds and 'saw, with interest as a former slum dweller and building worker, the beautiful flats at Quarry Hill estate'. In the latter was John Betjeman, a founding member of the Victorian Society, who spoke out against the proposed demolition of the City of London's 'impressive, vast and exquisitely detailed' Coal Exchange to make way for the widening of Lower Thames Street.

course, *The Jetsons* was a creation of the early Sixties), and you're still only about halfway there. For its influences did not stop at sci-fi. According to Peter, Alison was also inspired by *The Garden of Paradise*, a fifteenth-century German panel painting by the Master of the Middle Rhine, and by the ancient cave dwellings at Les Baux in Provence. Perhaps, too, she had in mind the air-raid shelters she'd known as a teenager in South Shields. Part touring caravan, part nuclear bunker and part space station, her home of the future (of 1981, to be exact) was an antiseptic, airless, hermetic pod where the tasks to which housewives had previously devoted themselves with such fervour – the laying of fires, the dusting of skirting boards, the scrubbing of floors – had been firmly consigned to the (shiny, plastic) swing bin of the past.

Although it was little more than a stage set – the *Daily Mail*'s

House of the Future

contractors built it in just ten days, mostly of plywood – to the naked eye the House of the Future's interior was all of piece: curvy, smooth, unbroken. And no wonder: in the first instance it was a paean to synthetic materials in all their various guises. The kitchen sink, sunken bath (with automatic rinsing system) and shower cubicle (also a dryer, thus dispensing with the need for germ-ridden towels) were made of a Bakelite polyester/fibreglass moulding in pimento red. The mattresses and 'headrests' – no unhygienic pillows here – were of latex foam. The bedclothes consisted of a single nylon fitted sheet as, naturally, the House of the Future was climate controlled. The kitchen cupboards and work surfaces were made of something called Pitch Pine Warerite. Alison had designed four chairs for the house and these, too, were experiments in plastic. The folding Pogo was made of steel and Perspex, the Egg, Tulip and Saddle of moulded polyester resin.

The space-age theme was explicit. In the kitchen were eggs without shells, their contents – separated into yolk and white – instead packed in polythene sachets. Among the list of objects the Smithsons wanted to be included in the house was a book, open at a page featuring an image of a spaceman, and a film still of someone on Mars in a silver frame (such a picture proved difficult to find). The house's survivalist undertones were easy to spot too. Rainwater was collected from the roof and all the food in its store cupboards had been bombarded, visitors were told, with gamma rays 'to kill bacteria'. The design included hatches where delivery men might leave their parcels, and a series of air locks. In the centre of the house was a garden so tiny and protected it was really little more than the memory of a garden: a fragment of a once verdant past, to be gazed on like a photograph in an album.

Who occupied this house? A cast of actors, whose presence was designed to turn visitors into unwitting voyeurs (the House of the Future reminds me, strongly, of the *Big Brother* house). These men and women wore clothes by Teddy Tinling, a sportswear designer who had designed outfits for Wimbledon – though the Smithsons had strong ideas about what they were expecting from him (they wanted gear that reflected the 'atmosphere' of the house, its 'glamour'). The *News Chronicle* described the result, somewhat wryly, as: 'FOR HIM: A Superman space outfit of nylon sweats and tights with foam rubber fitted soles. FOR HER: The Pixie look – a sort of nylon skirt with a scalloped edge, and tights with high-heeled fitted soles.' To the Smithsons' horror, these costumes sometimes reduced the crowd on the viewing platform to helpless giggles – though when Peter looked at his own photographs of the actors and the visitors side by side forty years later, it was, he thought, those dressed in the fashions of 1956 who looked the more ridiculous.

In May, the Smithsons took part in an even more significant cultural event when their installation *Patio & Pavilion* was included in *This Is Tomorrow*, an exhibition at the Whitechapel Art Gallery. *This Is Tomorrow*, conceived by their friend Theo Crosby, was a quasi-anthropological, semi-ironic look at the imagery of the post-war mass market and is remembered mostly for Richard Hamilton's collage *Just What Is It That Makes Today's Homes So Different, So Appealing?* This piece, which appeared on the exhibition poster and is now considered to be one of the earliest examples of what came to be known as pop art, features a naked woman with a lampshade on her head and a muscled man holding a large lollipop in a living room scattered with emblems of the new affluence: a tinned ham, a reel-to-reel tape recorder, a vacuum cleaner. But the Smithsons' installation must have struck contemporary visitors just as forcefully. The words 'patio' and 'pavilion' – so suburban, so genteel – were a kind of horrible joke in this instance. In fact, the pavilion was a rudimentary shelter of wood and corrugated plastic furnished with the kind of basic objects (a wheel, a fishing net) a human being might need to survive *in extremis*; the patio, meanwhile, was little more

This Is Tomorrow (left to right): Peter, Eduardo Paolozzi, Alison, Nigel Henderson —
plus iconic chairs

than a sand pit. Nowhere did it say so explicitly, but the installation neatly encapsulated the fears of an age. This was what life
might look like after the Bomb.

The novelist J. G. Ballard, shortly to become a popular poet of
the post-apocalypse, considered *This Is Tomorrow* to be the defining
event of 1956. 'I thought: here is fiction for the present day,' he
recalled in 2008. 'I wasn't interested in the far future, spaceships and
all that. Forget it. I was interested in the evolving world, the world
of hidden persuaders, of the communications landscape developing, of mass tourism, of the vast conformist suburbs dominated by
television — that was a form of science fiction, and it was already
here.' And he wasn't alone. The exhibition thrilled many of those
who saw it, and it made Richard Hamilton famous. It also
marked — as Ballard noted — the final dethroning of the establishment avant-garde as represented by the likes of Henry Moore and
Graham Sutherland. What did the Smithsons feel about it? This is

more complicated. Their picture in the exhibition catalogue – they were photographed with Paolozzi and Henderson, who showed in the same room – looks like nothing so much as an album cover. Taken in a Chelsea street, and featuring several pieces from their collection of iconic chairs, they look arrogant, proud, painfully cool. Alison is dressed like a French resistance fighter, or perhaps a car mechanic. Peter is wearing desert boots and a frown. But when, a year later, Hamilton sent them a letter in which he tentatively felt his way towards a definition of pop art,* he received no reply (and, according to Hamilton, Peter later denied ever having received it). Collaboration, you feel, did not come naturally to them. And perhaps, too, they were wary of being identified with yet another *movement*. To be associated with one may be regarded as misfortune. To be associated with two begins to look like carelessness.

Nineteen fifty-six was also the year the Smithsons finally managed to get another of their designs realised: the Sugden House, in Watford, Hertfordshire. This modest, undramatic home – only the slightest of tweaks distinguish its exterior from the rows of semis near by – is not generally considered to be a masterpiece; it was not even listed until 2012. But in truth, it is among the most elegant of all their built designs for the simple reason that it is wholly successful. It works.

Derek Sugden, who commissioned it, worked as an engineer at Arup, which was how he knew Alison and Peter. He had long dreamed of building his own place and, having bought a plot of land, thought he would have a go at drawing up the plans himself. After all, he had designed sheds and even a factory. How difficult could it be? Unfortunately, the answer was: extremely

---

* 'Pop art,' he wrote, 'is Popular (designed for a Mass Audience), Transient (short-term solution), Expendable (easily forgotten, Low Cost, Mass Produced, Young (aimed at youth), Wicked, Sexy, Gimmicky, Glamorous, Big Business.'

difficult. After working on the project for a month, he realised it was beyond him. He would need an architect.

Sugden mentioned this problem, in passing, to Peter, and to his amazement – the budget was only £2500 and Sugden and his wife Jean were adamant that they did not want a house that could be described as 'contemporary' – Peter suggested that he and Alison do the job. 'Oh, Peter,' said Derek, embarrassed. 'You can't do it. You're famous.' But Peter was insistent. Why not? They'd be happy to take it on. After all, they had nothing else on the books.

It was Alison who drew up the first scheme, and it was a disaster. 'She gave us . . . *this thing!*' recalls Derek Sugden. Yes, she had raised the house up, on a man-made platform at one end of the site, which seemed absolutely right: the view would take in the extent of the long garden. But in every other respect her drawings felt completely wrong. In particular, Derek and Jean hated the windows, which were little more than 'arrow-slits'. The Sugdens associated the modern movement with big windows. They wanted air and light.

A meeting was called. The two couples went laboriously through the plans (baby Simon was in some kind of hammock beneath Alison's drawing board) until – at last – Derek just came out with it. 'Actually, we don't like it,' he said. Alison was furious and told him, 'Well, you'd better find another architect, then.' She seemed to be on the point of walking out. It was left to Peter to save the day. 'If we can't design something for the Sugdens, we may as well pack up now,' he said. He would do a new set of drawings.

Three weeks later a second set of sketches arrived. This time, everyone was happy. The house would be built of brick (second hand, to keep down costs); it would have a saddle roof and no dreaded valley gutter (the first design had incorporated three roofs, each of a different height); and it would have lots of regular-sized windows in a uniform steel-framed Critall system, slender and durable. Alison, it was agreed, would do all the interior detailing. It was Alison, then, who designed the house's fitted cupboards, including their wooden handles; it was Alison who elected to make the kitchen counter open to the dining room, and to give it a floor of black-and-white vinyl, inspired by the Dutch interiors of Vermeer and de Hooch; it was Alison who chose the elegant Troughton & Young wall lights. The only splash of colour would be provided by the anthracite boiler, which would be a striking purple, an idea the Sugdens loved.

But, still. The difficulties continued. When Alison and Peter came to the see the house shortly before it was due to be finished, Peter rubbed his face, and emitted a moan – a sign, as Derek knew very well by now, that he was about to raise something his client might not agree to. On this occasion, it seemed that the Smithsons wanted to dye the wooden door frames and staircase green and purple. When Derek queried this – wasn't the idea to use materials 'as found'? – Alison told him this was already '*passe*'. (He stuck to his guns and, in the end, the wood was merely sealed.) And what were the Sugdens' thoughts regarding curtains? Alison thought they should be white. When Jean demurred – the idea was impractical with three children in the house – Alison announced, 'There is enough colour with your shirt and those books.' (Derek was wearing a red shirt, and owned a lot of orange-spined Penguins.) By way of concession, Jean and Derek did allow their architects to paint each window's opening light a different colour, but at the first opportunity they had them repainted in white.

Were the Smithsons pleased with how the house looked once it was inhabited? Not exactly. Alison disliked the Sugdens' new furniture, some of which they had bought from Heals, and said so. When Jean asked Alison what she thought of her curtains (black, not white), she affected not to have noticed them. But they appreciated the way the Sugdens took care of the house – its

The Sugden House, with its Vermeer-inspired floor and Troughton & Young wall lights

comfortable spaces are unchanged, even today – and it pleased
them that the family was clearly happy there.*

The two couples never became friends. While Peter was always
genial, Alison did not invite closeness. Some time later, Derek
Sugden introduced her to two young colleagues in the hope that
they might be able to help her with an engineering problem. The
encounter was a disaster. They were terrified. 'We can't work with
her!' they told him. 'You'll have to do it.' Years of experience
meant that he knew how they felt. Was this forbidding exterior
a carapace, a defensive shell? Or did it run deeper than that? Derek
believes it was both: 'Nature *and* nurture. Her experiences – she

---

* How did the Sugdens whizzy modern house go down with friends and family? 'It's nobbut
a West Riding weaving shed,' said Derek's father-in-law, a Yorkshireman. 'It's the ugliest house
you've ever seen!' said his mother-in-law.

was unusual, and she must have felt it – magnified that side of her character.'

Alison gave birth to her second child, a daughter called Samantha, the next year; once again, she returned to work after only a week. Her marriage to Peter was happy, but the couple were prone to 'fantastic quarrels', rows whose source was partly 'sexual . . . each desires not to submit'. Did Alison 'submit' to Peter? *Never.* She had, he thought, a certain 'intactness', and though he admired it hugely, it was also infuriating. The children (Soraya would arrive in 1964) were Alison's idea – Peter would have been content not to have any – and though he loved them he felt himself to be a slightly inadequate father, perhaps because he was so dazzled by his young wife's metamorphosis into motherhood: 'This weird business of a transformation of a girl into a mother . . . One is astounded by their competence. Men are shits . . . [I was] thoughtless, taking her for granted, just not thinking about it . . . [that she was] bringing up children, and doing a job.' It was Alison who was the disciplinarian; she ran the family on Edwardian lines. The children were given defined slots in the day and knew better than to interrupt their parents, even when, as they grew older, they arrived home from school. The Smithsons did not down pencils until 6.45 p.m., and that was that.*

---

* Here is Simon Smithson, now a distinguished architect himself, on life with his parents: 'We would come back from school, poke our noses round the door of the studio and then go upstairs and make ourselves some toast. At 6.45 they would come up and make dinner, and afterwards they would read or go back to work. Up until I was about eleven there was a level of ignorance [on my part]. After that, it was traumatic because they were wildly different to other parents: the food we ate, the fact we didn't get a telly until very late, even the fact we had a dishwasher and central heating. They were architecturally politicised: they believed in the idea that architecture could improve society. So they sent me to Holland Park, the first custom-built comprehensive [designed by Leslie Martin for the LCC, Holland Park opened in 1958]. For them, it must have been a pleasure to go there. But I was very marked by it, aesthetically and culturally. It was chaos, and I was bullied. All my neighbourhood friends went to public school. Your objective [when young] is to be normal. You become very conscious of the differences. Only when you're older do you say: "That was amazing."'

At last it seemed that the Smithsons' luck might finally change. In 1958, when they entered a competition to design new buildings for Churchill College, Cambridge. They did not win it, but their involvement led to a major commission from the chairman of *The Economist*, Sir Geoffrey Crowther, who wanted to build a penthouse for himself and a new home for his magazine's office on a tight three-sided site in the heart of London clubland (the Smithsons were selected for the job from among those who'd entered the Churchill College competition). And this time, it was love all the way between client and architect. Sir Geoffrey said that *The Economist*'s staff had felt 'trepidation' on first meeting the Smithsons, but took leave of them 'with awe and affection', while the Smithsons thought their client brave and generous. '*The Economist* was a wonderful client,' they wrote. 'They had the nerve to commission and to build their own building, without any previous experience of how to do such a thing; allowing their architects to shape their work space from its presence in St James's Street, Piccadilly, to its filing systems and taps in the lavatories.' The buildings they designed for this space – a more than usually complex land deal meant that they needed to accommodate not only *The Economist*, but a bank and serviced flats for Boodle's next door – is considered by many to be their masterpiece.

At first sight, it's difficult to see why. The development comprises a family of three towers grouped around a plaza. The largest of these towers feels too tall, and all three are clad in dreary roach-bed Portland stone, which looks just like concrete to the untutored eye. The Smithsons called their design 'didactic ... dry' and, though they certainly didn't mean this as an apology the buildings can feel, even on a bright spring morning, more of a study than a habitat, for all that they are very definitely occupied. Part of their brief was to provide a public open space that might become part of a wider network of pedestrian routes. But since this never really happened – you can catch a glimpse of Bury

The Economist building

Street at its far side, but the courtyard is not much in use as a short-cut – the plaza feels curiously dead: a destination rather than a thoroughfare, and definitely not one that invites you to linger outdoors. Hardly surprising, then, that in 1992 someone had the bright idea of sticking a water sculpture in the middle of it.

But a second visit makes things clearer. It's pleasing that the shortest of the three towers – the one on the all-important street side – doesn't try to compete with the older, fancier buildings that surround it, and the neat, chamfered corners of all three towers, designed so as not to steal light from adjoining buildings, have a softening effect on the group as a whole. The Smithsons anticipated and managed the weathering of their cladding, preventing the formation of the stains – like mascara that has run – that ruin the appearance of other modern stone-clad London buildings. Most admirable of all is the scheme's attitude. I won't call it unapologetic; that makes it sound like it's waving two fingers at snooty St James's, and this is not the case. But it isn't tentative. It doesn't tremble and quail in the face of what Alison called 'a street and a district densely suffused with historical fact and accumulated meanings'. Nor is it overly fussy, as if to compensate for its status as upstart. The client, wary of 'salaried teamwork', was loathed to commission a large firm, choosing instead a pair of architects who represented themselves rather than an office, and this proved to be the right decision. The Economist group is what it is. The critic Kenneth Frampton is right when he says that it has withstood the flow of time, the quality of the work appearing to improve rather than fade. There is something peevish about the argument, periodically raised, that it should be delisted (it was listed at Grade II* in 1988).

But if only the office's interior had survived its 1988 refurbishment. This was again Alison's realm, and included a filing system in the form of a series of glorious Japanese-inspired lacquer boxes. Pillar-box red and silk-smooth to the touch, these tactile caskets seem to capture her essence in a way no building does; it's hardly surprising to discover that she kept a couple back for her own use (one was used as a kind of vanity case, a home for a string of beads, and a comb, hairbrush and mirror*). A woman who understood more than most the power and comfort of work, she could have paid *The Economist*'s harried secretaries and journalists no greater compliment than to imbue their daily rituals with beauty, and just a hint of the clandestine. These are repositories for treasure, for secrets, for time bombs.

Speaking of time bombs . . .

With the exception of the Economist group, which was completed in 1962, the Sixties brought only more disappointment.† In

---

* Her daughter Samantha now uses another of these red boxes as a drinks cabinet. Samantha also owns two of Alison's sculptures: a world made entirely of coral; and an island crafted from a tree stump.

† Simon Smithson: 'I don't know how they kept going, emotionally. [Alison] was enormously confident about her own abilities. But going through long periods without work, you saw occasional bouts of crisis – though she had a game face because it was important not to show the chink in your armour.'

1966 the Smithsons designed an accommodation block for St Hilda's College, Oxford, a tower (now Grade II listed) that they swathed in wooden screens 'like a yashmak' to create 'a girl's place'; also, perhaps, to nod in the direction of Britain's half-timbered heritage, Tudor and Tudorbethan alike. (In the same year, as if to underline how little practice work they had going on, Alison published a stream-of-consciousness novel, *Portrait of the Artist as a Young Girl*.) But they lost two important jobs, turning down a commission for offices of *The Times* so that they could concentrate instead on designing a new British embassy for Brasilia, which, thanks to government cuts, was never built. This seems to have limited their careers decisively. The only other design they realised in this period was an extension to the Bayswater home of Wayland Young, the writer and politician: a chilly, single-storey pavilion built round an old tree, whose trunk burst exuberantly through its roof.

Then, just as the decade was about to end, Alison and Peter finally got the chance to design, as they had long dreamed of doing, a vast social-housing project in Poplar, east London. (The LCC still had fifty-two thousand people on its waiting list; something had to be done). Here they would build the 'streets in the sky' they had proposed for Golden Lane almost twenty years before. Here they would build their answer to Le Corbusier's Unité d'Habitation. And on this project Alison would be the lead designer, working on every detail, right down to the mural in the old people's social centre (she made it herself, each tile comprising a collage of broken pottery unearthed during the excavation of the site).

The scheme had a pretty name: Robin Hood Gardens. But though it looked fabulously arresting in photographs, as such egg boxes always do, it was not pretty at all in the flesh. It consisted of two non-identical slab blocks of pre-cast concrete, 'split like a kipper' as Peter put it, and bent around a green mound made with the spoil of the buildings it replaced. There were 213 flats in all, access to which was provided by lifts at the end of every block and continuous decks that ran their full length.*

Robin Hood Gardens was occupied in 1971, and completed in 1972, at a cost of £1,845,585. Vandals began their angry work soon after the first residents moved in. The facilities at the base of the building – the social centre and the launderette among them – closed just weeks later.

Afterwards, Alison and Peter turned to teaching and writing. In the Eighties they designed several buildings for the University of Bath, where Peter lectured, and they worked on a house and small museum for Axel Buruchhäuser, the manager of Tecta, a furniture manufacturer in Bad Karlshafen, Germany.

Alison died of breast cancer at the Royal Marsden Hospital in Chelsea, London, on 14 August 1993. Before her death she wrote a last letter to Peter, in which she told him she could not have imagined a better life. At the end, Peter felt, their disappointments faded from view. The period from Golden Lane to Robin Hood Gardens had been a long haul; trying and failing to get things built had, he admitted, made them 'lugubrious'. But as she lay dying, her work was only a comfort.

No one knows how Peter got through the days at his drawing board after her death. It must have been agony; they had worked opposite each other every day for more than four decades. But somehow, he did. He compiled two volumes of their work, published as *The Charged Void*, and every year on Alison's birthday he would whittle a small wooden memorial. He died, of a stroke, on 3 March 2003.

Of all the women in this book, it is Alison Smithson whose legacy is the most visible. It is also, as a consequence, the most tattered. Robin Hood Gardens is in a terrible state: shabby, depressing,

---

* Access to the flats in Corb's monsterwork is provided by a dark, internal corridor: fine for the sunny Mediterranean, but not so great for gloomy Blighty.

fortress-like and cut off, as if by a hedge of thorns, from all that surrounds it. Tower Hamlets, the council that manages it, would like to knock it down and start all over again, but the architectural community continues to push for its listing.* Who will win? The smart money must be on Tower Hamlets. Only rarely do Brutalist buildings escape the wrecking ball once a campaign against them begins. Owen Luder's Trinity Square in Gateshead – the car park in *Get Carter* – has already gone; so too has his Tricorn Centre in Portsmouth. Preston's bus station may soon follow. Park Hill in Sheffield has been saved, it's true, though you have to ask, at what cost? So much has been lost following its whizz-bang refurbishment by Urban Splash. But whether it stays or it goes, Robin Hood Gardens will never not be a symbol, now, of the modernists' desire to realise a theoretical position at any price: the theory is that people can just as well live in a street in the sky as at ground level; the price is that unless they are rich and out at work all day, doing so makes them miserable and isolated. And this has fatally damaged the reputation of the woman who co-designed it.

You might say: serves her right. But you might also think, what a pity, to be remembered only for this. Alison wasn't easy. Her ego was as big as the more ambitious of her ideas. But she was clever, principled and fearless at a time when it was difficult for women to be any of these things. At Hunstanton she made an extraordinary building that changed the way many people thought about architecture, and which endures to this day. And her example gave permission to the women architects who came after her – step forward Zaha Hadid, with your socking great rings, your Comme des Garçons coats and your conviction that Robin Hood Gardens is your favourite London building – to be at all times wholly themselves.

---

* In 2009, English Heritage ignored the advice of its commissioners and refused to recommend such a proposal. The then culture secretary also issued a certificate of immunity, which means it cannot be considered for listing again until 2014.

In the Garden with . . .

Margery Fish

'Dead nettles can be quite decorative . . .'

In 1956 Vita Sackville-West reviewed a new gardening book for the *Observer*. All stirred up, she was unstinting in her praise. 'It is,' she said, 'by a woman who, with her husband, created out of nothing the sort of garden we should all like to have: a cottage garden on a slightly larger scale . . . Crammed with good advice . . . I defy any amateur gardener not to find pleasure, encouragement and profit from [it].'

This was quite something. Sackville-West, then the most famous plantswoman in Britain, had created a ravishing and much-photographed garden at Sissinghurst Castle, and yet here she was sounding halfway to envious of someone else's rather more modest plot; if the publisher had written the review himself he could not have made the book sound any more appealing. But it was also a little misleading. *We Made a Garden* — its author went by the somewhat unprepossessing name of Margery Fish — was more memoir than manual, a collection of reminiscences rather than a step-by-step guide. Readers in search of hints for mulching their roses were going to be severely disappointed.

Sackville-West was only half right when she wrote that the book tells the story of how Margery and her husband, Walter, built a garden from scratch. In truth, it tells two stories. First, there is the garden that Walter wanted: a regimented suburban parade of paths and lawns and dahlias; and then there is the garden that Margery longed for, and did in fact successfully create in the years following his death in 1947: a harmonious, informal,

WE MADE
A GARDEN

MARGERY FISH

frothing sort of a garden, its borders filled with 'green' flowers, its shady corners crammed with hellebores, primroses, epimediums and, most important of all, her beloved snowdrops. Until her publisher put a stop to the idea Margery had wanted to call her book, which was her first, *Gardening with Walter*. But if she thought she'd produced a tribute to her husband she was surely deluding herself. A more honest title might have been *A Gardener's Revenge*. Impossible to imagine for a moment that she would, or could, have written it when he was alive.

When the book begins, it is 1937. Walter, a former editor of the *Daily Mail* who is eighteen years his wife's senior, is convinced that war is coming, and that it would be wise for them to leave London. So they begin looking for a house in the country. This takes a while: Walter is, shall we say, difficult to please. Early on they see a place – long and low and built of honey-coloured hamstone, it comes with a malthouse and a barton (the Somerset word for farmyard) – at East Lambrook, near Yeovil, on which Margery, though she doesn't dare say so out loud, is quietly keen. But Walter takes one look, shouts, 'Not at any price!' and promptly turns on his heel. Three months pass. They argue bitterly and fail to find anything at all worth buying, at which point, on a whim, they return to the first place they saw. This time it looks a little happier. Tiles have been replaced and the walls repainted, and Walter is now rather taken with its flag floors and wardrobe-sized fireplaces. Even so, you sense Margery's amazement when he agrees that, yes, this will do. All their friends had thought they'd choose a house in good repair with a garden all 'nicely laid out and ready to walk into', but now the opposite is about to happen and Margery and Walter – metropolitan flat-dwellers who haven't a pair of secateurs between them – will somehow have to create a garden 'from a farmyard and a rubbish tip'.

Where to start? Walter's approach to the initial work is typically bullish. What he can't burn he buries; poor Margery, out and

about with her trowel, will regularly stumble on 'grisly memen-
toes' of this time for many years to come. And once the old beds,
rusty oil stoves and ancient corsets have all been cleared, the ide-
ological battle must commence. In the red (and yellow and
orange) corner is Walter, with his Tudorbethan ideas about tidi-
ness and colour. In the green corner is Margery, all sculptural
seed pods and luxuriant foliage. Walter is alarmed. He hadn't
taken his wife for a modernist.

So he goes on the attack, arguing for, and winning, his much-
desired lawn, a province with which he is soon quite obsessed.
'Walter would no more have left his grass uncut or the edges
untrimmed than he would have neglected to shave,' writes
Margery, who at this stage in the book is still doing her best
impression of a loyal wife. It is deliberately, aggressively vast, this
lawn, and it is only grudgingly that Walter makes space at its edge
for a very narrow flowerbed in which Margery is allowed to plant
a few perennials *so long as they don't encroach on the grass*. In another concession, he gives her permission to build a dry-stone wall. She
does this very ably, tucking alpine plants into the crevices as she
goes along, and Walter likes the result: he feels the same way
about walls as he does about hedges. But if only she hadn't spent
so much time 'poking belly-crawlers into rat holes'.

And so it continues, like a bad sitcom (the fact that it began its
life as an article for *Punch* may go some way to explaining this) –
except that with every chapter Margery seems to grow more confident: no, she was obviously telling herself, Walter's ghost, pale
and pugnacious, is really *not* about to burst in through the French
windows. Her courage blooms. She couldn't tell Walter at the
time what she thought of him, but she can say whatever the hell
she likes now. She attacks his dahlias ('the most flashy collection
I have ever seen, only fit for a circus'). She repudiates his paths
(since his death she has loosened the cement between the stones
with a crowbar). She admits to her deceit in the matter of such

things as manure (she used to steal it from around his roses, remembering as she did his oft-repeated comment that 'women have no sense of honesty!'). What a fuss-pot he was, always counting the leaves on his clematis, and what a bore, droning on and on about the gardener he used to have in Sydenham, where he lived with his first wife before she died.

And the sheer barminess of some of his schemes!

At one point he and Margery agreed to train some red roses up the mellow walls of their house. Walter, though, was not known for his patience, and he knew it would be some time before the plants would make much of an impact. So he devised a plan. 'One day, without telling me, he bought a collection of stuffed heads and mounted horns at a London sale room. Very soon heads, antlers and horns sprouted from every available wall, inside and out. The malthouse received the most imposing pieces from the collection, and very soon our house wasn't known as "the one with the lovely blue clematis on the front" but as "the house with all the heads on the outbuildings".' Happily, those he stuck outside didn't last long: 'Not being intended to withstand rain and snow the skin soon came apart and flapped open before falling in the drive, the fillings disintegrated, the painted mouths and red nostrils were washed away and before long all that was left were the horns ... When they got to this stage I was allowed to put them on the bonfire, but I am still occasionally reminded of them when I am digging and see a large liquid brown eye gazing up at me.' This thought leads her to a quieter rebuke: 'Walter could never be persuaded to have a wisteria because he said they would take too long to flower. Now I have two, and both flowered about two years after I planted them.'

We Made a Garden does contain some advice, if that is what you're after. By the time she wrote it Margery had become an instinctive and highly original gardener; she knew what she was talking about. But its chief pleasure lies in watching its author emerge from an exhausting, all-consuming relationship – a union in which she was expected to defer to her husband, a man who was never wrong – and become a person in her own right. This is *my* taste, she says; this is *my* opinion; and this beautiful garden (the reader flips again to the book's black-and-white plates of East Lambrook and its gorgeous, verdant vistas) is *my* victory. Not only did I beat the seasons, the Somerset clay and the confusing, unpredictable temperaments of my plants; I overcame Walter's dogged campaign to reign me in, to fetter my unexpected, late-flowering creativity. She describes all this with mounting glee: it rises, like sap. A tiny part of you begins to wonder if she didn't, in the end, bump him off, burying him in dead of night beneath the nearest holly bush.*

In 1956 Margery was sixty-four years old. She had begun her first job before women had the vote. Only now, in late middle age, was she approaching fulfilment. In the weeks after *We Made a Garden* appeared in Britain's bookshops something remarkable hap-pened: a future suddenly opened out before her – and to her astonishment and clear delight, it was more expansive even than her husband's precious lawn.

Margery Fish was born in 1892 at Stamford Hill, London, the second of the four daughters of Florence Buttfield and Ernest Townshend, who made his living as a tea broker. Hers was a conventional, middle-class childhood – Florence was rather straitlaced, and Ernest was the first of a series of difficult men in Margery's life – but the Townshend girls were known both for their cleverness and

---

* Walter's garden does rather lend itself to Agatha Christie-style fantasies. But there is also something elemental about the battle of the Fishes; a Freudian would say they were about rather more than mere taste. In *We Made a Garden*, Margery compares plants to babies – 'they know when an amateur is handling them' – and described how she would look after ailing specimens out of sight of Walter, knowing that otherwise he would pull them up: 'Often I would go out and find a row of sick-looking plants laid out like a lot of dead rats.' Walter had two daughters from his first marriage, but Margery was childless.

Margery with her mother and two sisters

for their liveliness: at the Friends' School in Saffron Walden, they did well academically, and the three eldest all served as head girl.

Her schooling over, Margery decided that she would attend secretarial college. This was controversial – she had to battle Ernest for his permission, but she had a helpful precedent in the form of her older sister, Dora, who was already working for a goldsmith in Hatton Garden. The college Margery chose was Clark's in Chancery Lane, which advertised itself as an establishment that would prepare its students for the civil service, 'the professions and business', and she did predictably well; she left in the summer of 1911 with a glowing reference. 'It is a pleasure to recommend Miss Margery Townshend to any employer who requires a sensible, well-educated and smart citizen,' read this prophetic document. 'She has a wonderful capacity for work; she applies herself diligently and zealously to everything she takes up. She has a good command of English which makes her a good correspondent. It rarely falls to my lot to recommend so excellent a student and one who has reached such a high mark in all the subjects of our curriculum. I am certain of her success.'

But not for Margery the quiet rhythms of a suburban solicitor's office. Instead, she made a beeline for Fleet Street where, after a short stint as secretary to the editor at the Country Gentleman's Publishing Company, she joined the *Daily Mail*. For a girl from Stamford Hill – then an affluent, Pooterish sort of place – this must have been a revelation: the noise, the dirt, the pace; all those men shouting. But if she was shocked she didn't show it. As usual, she simply got on with the job – she was secretary to the advertisement manager – and it wasn't long before her smooth efficiency was recognised: within months she was promoted to the office of Tommy Marlowe, who had been the *Mail*'s editor since 1899.

The *Mail*, 'the busy man's paper', had been founded in 1896 by Alfred Harmsworth, later Lord Northcliffe, and it was by 1911 Britain's biggest-selling daily. Northcliffe – aka the Chief – was a bona fide newspaper genius, but he was also vain (he liked to style himself 'N', the better to signify his position as the Napoleon of Fleet Street), temperamental and fearsomely energetic: when he took up golf on doctor's orders in 1910 he made 284 drives from a single tee before collapsing of exhaustion. He had edited the *Mail* himself in the early years, and in 1912 he was still apt to interfere, sending memos to his editor and other staff at least once a day. As a result the atmosphere on the paper was oppressive: people never smiled, and only rarely did they manage to leave their desks to eat, 'gobbling up' their supper when and where they could. Marlowe and Northcliffe seem to have had a particularly sticky relationship. On the morning that Britain entered the war in 1914, they had a row so violent their staff 'wanted nothing less than to fall through the floor to escape seeing any more'.

What Margery made of all this is not recorded, though it's possible that he was much kinder to her. Female staff were generally devoted to the Chief: Northcliffe, if not exactly a feminist, had realised early on how important it was for newspapers to appeal to women readers, and he was genuinely anxious to hear their opinions. When he launched the *Daily Mirror* in 1903 it was as a newspaper for women, by women. 'I intend it to be really a mirror of feminine

Margery's passport

life as well on its grave as on its lighter sides,' he said. (Sadly, this plan was not a success.) He paid his girls unusually well, handed out bonuses at holiday time and would often give them gifts too: when his private secretary, Louise Owen, complained that her watch was not keeping time he unhooked his gold repeater from its chain and handed it to her. But whatever the tenor of their relationship, he certainly noticed Margery. In 1917, when he agreed to Lloyd George's request that he head a British Mission to the United States, he asked if she would be part of his team there.*

---

* This was one of Lloyd George's several efforts to neutralise Northcliffe, whose newspapers were then so powerful they could bring down governments. Northcliffe was agreeable because, like the prime minister, he believed it was vital that the US join the war on the side of the Allies; he also hoped to ensure that the supply of munitions and goods from America would be stepped up.

Playing deck quoits

Margery agreed to go straight away. For all that she knew that the Atlantic crossing would be extremely dangerous, that there was every chance their ship would be hit by a torpedo from a U-boat,* she wanted to have an adventure and she had Buttfield relations in America whom she longed to meet. Doubtless it was also made clear to her that she would be well looked after. According to the journalist Hamilton Fyfe, a Northcliffe employee and one of his earliest biographers, the Chief was extremely solicitous of the secretaries and stenographers who made the trip. 'For their comfort he was as careful as for his own,' he wrote. 'He gave the girls grants of money to buy suitable clothes for the hot weather in New York. He took trouble to find out how they were boarded and lodged. He arranged little jaunts and excursions for them. One of them said to him, "You are like a fairy uncle to us, Lord Northcliffe." He beamed and answered: "Well, my dear, I've brought you a long

---

* To give just one example: on 7 May 1915 the *Lusitania*, a ship that had briefly been the largest passenger ship in the world, was sunk by a U-boat with the loss of 1195 lives.

way from your home. The least I can do is to see that you get a little enjoyment.'

Nevertheless, Margery's time in the US can't have been easy. She adored America – this would be the first of several visits – and she enjoyed meeting her relations, but her new boss was under pressure and it showed. The British ambassador to the US, Cecil Spring-Rice, his nose out of joint, had proved obstructive, failing even to arrange for an embassy representative to meet Northcliffe when his ship docked. Northcliffe's staff were all watched; his mail was pilfered and his car followed; his schedule – he found himself criss-crossing America at the height of summer – was exhausting even for a man of his energies. He began to unravel. At his home near Broadstairs for a short rest by the sea, he startled Hamilton Fyfe by picking up a heavy stick and striking a seagull. Having stunned the bird, he then proceeded to beat it to death in front of his colleague's 'disbelieving' eyes. His health was failing physically, too. It was at about this time that Northcliffe began writing his 'throat diary', a journal in which he carefully recorded every coughing fit, and the number of times a day that he brought up phlegm.

The war over, Margery returned to Britain, where she was awarded the MBE for her service overseas. It isn't clear what precisely she did next, but in May 1921 Northcliffe wrote to her, asking her to come and see him; word had clearly reached him that she was looking for a new position. 'I am sorry to hear that you are unhappy in Liverpool,' said his note. 'I have been there for nearly a week and had I known you were there, I would have seen you. It is difficult to find appointments just now, but yours is an exceptional case. You crossed the Atlantic when the submarines were at their worst and I have always given special treatment to those of my staff who took the risk. I will do my utmost.' Soon after this she was appointed personal assistant to the *Daily Mail*'s new editor, Walter Fish.

Fish, who came from a newspaper background (his father had been a reporter on the *Preston Herald*), had joined the *Mail* in 1904 and served as its news editor between 1906 and 1919. A Northcliffe discovery – the paper's proprietor referred to him as 'the man with Brixton mind', which was just about the greatest compliment he could pay an employee – Fish was an instinctive and wily newspaperman. It was thanks to his contacts that *Daily Mail* readers were the first to read of Dr Crippen's capture during his attempted escape to Canada in 1910; and it was Fish, too, who had spotted the potential of a small story about what the Connaught Rangers were singing as they marched to war in 1914 and put the piece on the front page of the paper, with the result that the music-hall song 'It's a Long Way to Tipperary' soon became the unofficial anthem of the British Expeditionary Force. But his relationship with Northcliffe was even stormier than Marlowe's had been. In 1922 things got so bad that he started libel proceedings against Northcliffe.* There was also, according to Margery's nephew, a falling out when Fish took exception to a comment Northcliffe made about the way 'Miss Townshend's breasts' looked in a rather daring dress. His colleagues believed that he never really understood Northcliffe.

In the tradition of *Mail* editors, Fish was a difficult boss. Dapper and precise, he was a stickler for correct dress and he expected his subordinates to work as hard he did, which was very hard indeed; his memory was prodigious, which meant that he was always catching people out. Margery, however, must have got along just fine with him because when he retired in 1930 she sent him a note

---

* Northcliffe had objected to Fish's decision – made at the behest of the Newspaper Proprietors Association – to cut the wages of newspaper compositors. He then wrote a piece in the *Mail* about this, in which he referred to Walter as 'the mysterious Mr Fish' and complained that he had not been informed of the decision, which would involve the 'welfare of hundreds of families'. He also noted that Walter was young, and had not yet travelled much. It was these remarks that prompted Walter to sue. In the end, egos were soothed, the suit was dropped and Fish remained in his job until 1930.

in which she offered to continue helping him with his letters. 'My dear Miss Townshend,' he wrote back, 'I was more pleased than I can say to receive your letter. It has always been a very great pleasure to work with you, and I shall miss our happy association very much indeed. But I am looking forward to seeing you frequently as I shall come to the office fairly often. It is very nice of you to offer to help me with my correspondence, but that does not surprise me as I have always found you the most willing girl in the world. Ever yours, sincerely, Walter Fish.'

It seems clear that at this point his relationship with Margery was barely flirtatious, let alone romantic. Then, suddenly, everything changed. Three months later Walter wrote to Margery again, and this time his note was warmer: 'Although we have seen each other for years it is strange how little time we have ever had to talk,' he said. 'That is why it was so jolly to be able to talk to you the other evening apart from business concerns.' I do not know if this letter marks the beginning of their romance; Walter's wife, Nellie, the mother of his two grown-up daughters, Muriel and Frieda,* did not die until 1932. But two years later, on 2 March 1933, Walter and Margery were married at Marylebone Register Office. Margery, at forty-one an extremely handsome, sensual-looking woman with heavy-lidded eyes, wore a fur coat and carried a dainty clutch; Walter, a veritable parody of a Fleet Street editor, wore a bowler hat and spats. At their wedding breakfast, which was held at the Dorchester Hotel in Mayfair, guests were served caviar or oysters, fillet of sole 'Galieni', *supreme de volaille* Maryland, *pêche pompadour* and *patisseries*, all of which was washed down with Pol Roger 1921. In the photographs they appear happy, but somehow *organised* too, as if the wedding were just another professional engagement.

---

* Frieda, incidentally, was married to the proprietor of El Vino, the legendary Fleet Street watering hole.

Wedding day: 2 March 1933

Was this a love match? Not exactly. Margery was certainly fond of Walter, but she was also impressed by him; something in her enjoyed being dominated, at least at first. And she loved the life he was able to give her. They bought a smart new mansion flat in Kensington, with a porter and lifts and polished wooden floors, and when Walter wasn't working – he remained on the board of Associated Newspapers, and would be made an honorary advisor to the Ministry of Information with the outbreak of the Second World War – they gave themselves up to their hobbies and to their diaries, which bulged so very pleasingly. They played a great deal of golf. They motored across Europe – they had a (possibly slightly alarming) passion for Germany. They entertained. They went to the theatre and the opera. Walter was well connected, and Margery had a thirst for novelty and intellectual companionship; in this sense, he suited her perfectly.

They thought of themselves as city people, and doubtless this is what they would have remained for the rest of their marriage had it not been for the threat of war. By 1937, however, Walter was growing increasingly anxious that they find themselves a country home: although he had remained in London throughout the last war, nobly battling the censor on behalf of the *Mail*'s readers, he thought the city would be badly bombed this time. They would hang on to their flat in town, of course: he knew Margery couldn't imagine life without Foyles bookshop in Charing Cross Road, in which she could spend hours at a time. (She loved reading, and would one day introduce her adored nephew Henry to Zola and D. H. Lawrence; he remembers that the copy of *Lady Chatterley's Lover* she gave him was 'well-thumbed'.) But it would be sensible to begin the search now, before it was too late. Margery took this plan in her stride, receiving her marital orders with her usual calmness and efficiency. It would, though, be a mistake to think she was secretly hankering for open spaces, or even for a garden; two of her sisters had recently taken up gardening and had tried in vain to interest her in their new hobby. Asked to choose between gardening and golf, Margery would choose golf every time.

She must have been surprised, then, when she glimpsed the shivering leaves of a variegated sycamore through the open door of a house she and Walter saw at East Lambrook – and found that they lodged in her brain. (Not, of course, that the building itself had much to recommend it: on the occasion of their first visit, the roof was patched with corrugated iron, the front garden was a jungle of rusty laurels and the interior smelt musty and dank.) But surprised or not, this garden – or the idea of this garden – somehow wheedled its way into her affections, where it remained, illicit and unspoken, until they returned three months later. This time – I don't believe for a minute their second visit was the result of a 'whim' – she was ready. Margery, one gathers, was an expert strategist. The thing to do was to coax Walter upstairs where (this is how I picture it) she would throw open a mullioned window and casually offer him the view.

Done! She and Walter got the house for a thousand pounds and spent the next two years travelling back and forth from London while builders set about making it habitable. (The Old Manor, which dates from the fifteenth century, had been a bakery, a post office, and a slaughterhouse; it was uninhabited when the Fishes bought it.) Margery was quietly thrilled. She knew exactly how she wanted to decorate it once it was ready: 'Colours in an old house have to be soft and mellow, no bright blues and hard dark greens, and reds should be faded to the colour of old brick. The only green I use is as light and silvery as the moss that grows under the beech trees.' And with every journey west she fell further in love with Somerset – a county which, though not so spectacular as some, she thought of as 'smiling' and unspoilt: 'Willows are everywhere. Their fluttering leaves are cool in summer and in winter the shoots from the pollarded heads take on a tinge of red. Corot could have painted his pictures here, for the whole scene is one of tender loveliness, with softly luminous skies against blue mists in the distance.'

The Fishes moved into the manor in the summer of 1939, and we already know what happened next: having quickly furnished the house with saleroom bargains, our novice gardeners embarked on remodelling the two acres of land that came with it. Margery and Walter were in firm agreement on some matters. Both believed, for instance, that the garden should be as much a part of the house as possible, and made an early decision to pave the area between the lawn and the door leading into their hall, the main room in the house; when the door was open this space would then merge with the flagstones indoors (they were ahead of their time in wanting 'to bring the outside in'). They also needed its design to be manageable, given that they would still be spending a lot of time in London. They did not realise at this point what a gardening fanatic Margery would become, and a spirit of compromise prevailed at first. But still, the difference in their tastes – a schism neither one of them had expected – soon became apparent, and had it not been both for Margery's supreme diplomacy and for petrol rationing, which limited their trips to nurseries and other gardens, and thus restricted what was available to them to plant, they might have found themselves in a state of open warfare.

There was also the matter of Walter's increasingly poor health. By 1945 he was suffering from high blood pressure and able to perform only the lightest of tasks in the garden. In a way this made life a little easier: when he was resting, Margery was able to garden in peace. But he was a difficult invalid, and more crotchety than ever. How to keep him occupied? She was grateful to old Fleet Street friends who made the journey to see him, though it must have been humiliating for him when he was too unwell to get up. 'I remember that . . . he would thump on the bedroom floor three times, and that would produce Margery with a round of gin and French,' recalled Wilson Stephen, the editor of the *Field*. In the mornings she had to take his toast up to him piece by piece to ensure each one would arrive fully warm. She felt relieved when the newspapers arrived; even in Somerset he still had every paper delivered every day. 'He would read them from cover to cover, criticising and discussing as he went,' she said. 'I used to dread bank holidays when there were no papers, for I knew the lack would make Walter irritable. Newspapers were a lifeline to him.'

She would escape completely whenever she could. In 1943 Lanning Roper, who would later become famous as the designer of Prince Charles's garden at Highgrove and of the woodland walk at Mies van der Rohe's Farnsworth House in Plano, Illinois, had turned up at her door in the uniform of the US navy, clutching a letter of introduction from Bruce Buttfield, one of her American cousins. Margery took to him immediately, and thereafter Roper spent all his leaves at East Lambrook, during which, petrol allowing, they would go off to see local gardens such as Barrington Court and Montacute House. She was also friendly with two other well-known local gardeners. Violet Clive was a disciple of Gertrude Jekyll who lived at Brympton d'Evercy, an estate described by *Country Life* as 'the most incomparable house in Britain'. An eccentric in the grand manner, she wore voluminous black frocks and a huge hat that she skewered to her hair with a large diamond brooch. Visitors sometimes mistook her for a vagrant. Phyllis Reiss lived at Tintinhull, whose garden, with its exquisite compartments and its tranquil mood, Margery admired above all others, for all that their styles were so very different. 'I always felt that Phyllis gardened like a man,' recalled Margery. 'She had the much more direct approach of a man, and less of the sentiment which seems to hamper many women ... Though she preferred to call herself "the Groupist", and me, "the Plantist".' Both Clive and Reiss were her companions on regular plant-hunting trips. If Clive was her companion for the day the women would travel by chauffeur-driven car; otherwise, Margery would take her huge Standard Vanguard out for a run. She was a rotten driver, and an exceedingly fast one.

Walter died on 21 December 1947 of a heart attack, the Sunday newspaper he had been reading only a few minutes earlier still beside him. A part of Margery had long been expecting this, but nevertheless she found herself in a state of shock. Thanks to the fact that he had always been so 'vigorous in mind', he had never seemed his age to her (he was seventy-three). Longevity ran in his family; neither of them had taken his heart condition seriously. 'I found it hard to believe that the scattering of a few ashes in a windswept [crematorium] garden in Weymouth one wintry morning could be the end of such an outstanding figure,' she wrote later, in notes for the biography of Walter that she tried three times to write. 'He was so different from the ordinary run of people that I could not believe anything so ordinary as death could happen to him.'

All the same, she did not grieve for long. It was Christmas time and she was determined that nothing ruin the holiday for her nephew Henry, to whom she was devoted. (Henry's mother was her youngest sister, Nina; she and Margery spoke every day at 6 p.m.). As ever she was determined to be practical, to soldier on just as Walter would have done. 'Self-reliance was the key note of his character,' she wrote. 'Once, for fun, he had a coat of arms painted, and for it he chose the words: Trust thyself. Nothing could have illuminated him better. Now I, too, learnt that in the ultimate resort you have to rely on yourself.' How would she remember Walter? Kindly. Theirs had been a love-hate relationship, but Walter had had his qualities: '[They] came out in everything he did, and I shall always be grateful to him for what he taught me.' The only other fragment of biography that remains is a cryptic list of her first thoughts, and though it reads like a line from T. S. Eliot —

'women, nice young; jewellery; knew it was something you didn't do;* kindness to old; stuffy Victorians; devotion to mother; eye for line; dislike of bad fit; let's go and see, sweetie' – it makes him sound decent, and surprisingly generous.

In early January 1948 there was a memorial service for Walter at St Dunstan-in-the-West, Fleet Street. A few months later Margery went to Plainfields in New Jersey to see her Buttfield cousins, the first of three trips she would make before 1950. She and Lanning Roper went garden-visiting on his home turf, which was unexpectedly eye-opening,† and she returned to Britain with a new wardrobe – her uncle sent her shopping at his expense, knowing how weary she was of coupons – and a fad for raw bran, a bag of which she would take with her wherever she went. Back at home, many of her friends believed that Margery would now return to London, but to their surprise it seemed that she would not contemplate selling East Lambrook: 'It always welcomes me home,' she said. What did she see when she looked out on Walter's garden? Did her fingertips tingle? Did she long to get out there and scatter seeds wildly? Perhaps. But if this was how she felt, she did nothing about it. For the next two years the garden remained just as it had been in Walter's day, as neatly trimmed as his moustache, as tightly buttoned as his waistcoat.

Nineteen-fifty. As if stirring from a long sleep, Margery now began to make changes. First, the house. Out went the mahogany tallboys, the gilded lamps, the detested French bedroom suite

---

* 'Knew it was something you didn't do . . .' Does this refer to their affair? I don't know, but I can't help but wonder.
† They saw the Brooklyn Botanical Garden, the Arnold Arboretum at Harvard, the home of the eighteenth-century botanist John Bartram in Philadelphia, the Thomas Jefferson gardens at Monticello, Virginia and many more. She was also introduced to the work of Beatrix Farrand, a niece of Edith Wharton, through a visit to the garden at Dunbarton Oaks in Washington. Margery had not realised before how much English gardens had been Americanised: she was very struck by the fact that the mop-headed crimson bergamot that grew so casually at East Lambrook had once provided a campfire brew for the Oswego; by the fact that the forebears of her beloved asters grew wild in parts of the US.

which, to her, had always looked so at odds with its surroundings. In came simpler pieces of oak and elm: gate-legged tables and Windsor chairs. In the dining room she banished silverware, replacing it with pewter, which was polished only rarely. Oil paintings in heavy gilt frames gave way to maps, mirrors, etchings and prints by Corot, an artist she adored. She employed a house-keeper and let out the west wing; her home was too big for one, and having two staircases unsettled her. Finally, she changed the name of the house from Old Manor, East Lambrook to East Lambrook Manor, so it would take up two rather than three lines on her printed letterhead. Always a prolific letter-writer – friends used to joke that her (famously hilarious) letters were so long they took two days to read – it was almost as if she knew that her correspondence was soon to quadruple.

The garden at East Lambrook: Margery planted the avenue of evergreen 'Fletcheri'

Next, she turned her attention to the garden. She and Walter had laid some fine foundations: a terraced garden for bulbs and shrubs, and the low stone walls for plants that liked to have their roots restricted; a ditch garden for species needing damp and shade (Margery called it the Lido); and an unorthodox rockery for alpines in the form of a series of half moon-shaped steps, which she referred to, mock grandly, as the Colosseum. (She was wary of traditional rockeries: 'There is nothing more depressing than a few stones rising self-consciously from a suburban lawn.') Gazing out at all this she realised with mounting excitement that she would be free to concentrate – at last – solely on plants.

And so it began: the collection that would one day comprise some two thousand varieties. At first she was casual. She banned Walter's hoe and did all her weeding by hand so she could carefully examine any seedlings. Her favourite tool was her Guernsey hand fork, three tined with a hickory wood handle bent at an angle of almost eighty degrees to enable tomato growers to lift plants without damaging their roots; it came back into the house with her every evening. This fork had previously belonged to her uncle Marsom Buttfield, aka Uncle Marzipan, another tea broker and a disciple of both the 'wild gardener' William Robinson and of Gertrude Jekyll; Marsom, having eschewed the laurels and rhododendrons beloved of most Victorians, had instead planted his carriage drive at Enfield with a double hedge of sweet briar roses and was thus a formative influence on Margery, though she did not grasp this fact until relatively late in life. But she soon realised that it wasn't going to be enough simply to let things self-seed. She was acquisitive in the best sense of the word. If she admired a plant she longed to have it in as many different forms as possible; and she wanted, too, to save those varieties which were rapidly disappearing. She thought of herself as a soppy, 'sentimentalist' gardener. Her two acres would be a safe haven, a place where no plant was ever deemed too small or too insignificant to merit a little tender care.

Some plants – a very few – she bought from nurseries and cata-
logues. Most, though, came as cuttings from friends – or strangers,
if she happened to spy something lovely billowing over a garden
wall. Geraniums, hellebores, rodgersias, scillas, penstemons, irises,
ferns, bluebells, cyclamen, silver-leafed plants of all types, hostas,
bergenias, snowdrops and primroses: she collected all of these and
more (this list is not, I fear, even halfway to being exhaustive). It was,
however, the two last that she loved the best. Snowdrops she adored
for their 'aloofness and purity', and for their plucky earliness which,
for her, made winter almost as exciting as late spring; she grew them
on the banks of her ditch garden, where they were at eye level and
could be properly admired. Primroses she liked for their long
history and, in some cases, for their rarity. The double white primrose – one of her favourite plants in the world – she would later
incorporate into a small 'white garden', a corner that would lead to
several friendly disagreements with Vita Sackville-West, who had
begun developing her own white garden in about 1950.

Margery now became a full-blown advocate of 'jungle' planting, welcoming into her garden even hedgerow species such as
thrift, sweet woodruff ('the scent of new-mown hay is delicious')
and pink cow parsley, a plant whose 'old-world dowdiness' would
have driven Walter quite mad. This was primarily an aesthetic
decision; in Walter's day the garden put on a show for just a few
scant summer weeks, whereas she wanted it, teeming and replete,
to look lovely all year round. But it was a practical move too. It
was supposed to make life easier: the more crowded the scheme,
the fewer the opportunities for weeds. No one had staff any more;
the war had changed that.* A full-time gardener was out of the

* Margery describes these social changes vividly in *We Made a Garden*. When she and Walter first
bought their house, the pantry window was frosted so no one could see the maid washing
up. 'It never occurred to us, the architect or the builder how dull it was for the poor girl to
be shut off like that. When the war came and I spent hours at the sink, I adopted my sister's
suggestion and had clear glass put in that window.'

question. Except that in Margery's case this remained little more than a theory: weeds or no weeds, she was unable, or unwilling, ever to let up. A twelve-hour day was standard; visitors who rose for breakfast at 8.30 a.m. would inevitably find their hostess outside, trug in hand. In the summer she would garden after supper too. Luckily she no longer felt the need to change for dinner; in Walter's day she had sometimes found herself watering in the gloaming, standing there in the flower beds in her satin slippers and a hazardously long gown.

Unimaginable as it sounds, during the war years flowers had all but disappeared from view: urged on by government pamphlets with titles like *Cloches v. Hitler*, and by Mr Middleton of the radio programme *In Your Garden*, Britain's gardeners had dutifully given over their plots to vegetables.* Now, though, they were back: the roses and the dahlias, the geraniums and the begonias – and the brighter the better. With post-war austerity came a new lust for colour. 'We can't buy new clothes, we can't get new curtains, we can't paint our house, we've got nothing . . . except flowers!' said Julia Clements, flower 'decorator' extraordinaire to members of the Women's Institute. Thanks, moreover, to a national house-building programme, some people now had a garden of their own for the first time. It occurred to Margery, journalist *manqué* – while working for Walter she had somehow found the time to write the occasional piece for the women's page of the *Mail* – that she might be in a position to advise all these eager new gardeners, and in 1951 she wrote her first article, for the *Field*.

She was perfectly right, of course: people were ready to listen,

---

* The dig for victory. People missed their flowers almost as passionately as they missed oranges, sugar and bacon. When the government banned the movement of flowers by rail in 1943, there was even an outbreak of smuggling. According to Tim Richardson, in *English Gardens in the Twentieth Century*, flowers were transported in suitcases and even coffins; and cauliflowers had their hearts ripped out, after which they were filled with anemones.

and in the years that followed she would become ever more prolific, writing for *Punch*, *Amateur Gardening*, *Popular Gardening*, *Homes &
Gardens* and the journal of the Royal Horticultural Society. As she
soon discovered, her effervescent plot had the virtue of being somewhat smaller than the great pre-war gardens people were now
visiting in ever larger numbers (after the reclusive Lawrence
Johnston* left it Hidcote Manor in 1947, the National Trust, which
had previously only taken on houses, began accepting gardens,
too); Gertrude Jekyll's 'small' garden at Munstead Wood was fifteen
acres to her two, and while Jekyll had employed a team of some
fourteen gardeners, Margery still got by mostly on her own. Her
readers could relate to her garden; it didn't intimidate. The ideas she
had deployed could very easily be replicated in a smaller space with
just as effective results. When she wrote about East Lambrook she
gave her readers a sense of possibility – and in this sense, she provided a bridge between gardening's high-maintenance past and its
low-maintenance future.

Margery didn't need to work; Walter had left her well provided
for. But she wanted to. It was exciting to see her name in print
again after all these years, and her writing, together with her
growing renown as a plantswoman, had the curious effect of
making her feel almost youthful; in 1952 she turned sixty and yet
here she was, an unlikely pioneer, keeping company with a whole
new generation of professional gardening women. It's true that
the Royal Horticultural Society was a bastion of male activity and
would remain so for another decade. At botanic gardens and
stately homes, head gardeners were still mostly men. But elsewhere women were quietly building their reputations: Alice
Coates, crippled by arthritis and unable to continue as secretary
to the Birmingham Group of artists, was furiously researching old
plant varieties (her pioneering *Flowers and Their Histories* would be

* Johnston, an American by birth, was later one of Margery's many correspondents.

published in 1956); Frances Perry, author of *Herbaceous Borders* and *Colour in the Garden*, would shortly be appointed principal of the Norwood Hall Institute and College of Horticulture;* and Xenia Field, the daughter of a society rhododendron collector, had recently begun a gardening column for the *Daily Mirror*, which then had some five million readers.

And then there were the two women who were making strides in the relatively new field of landscape architecture. Brenda Colvin and Sylvia Crowe were graduates of Swanley Horticultural College and started their professional careers as domestic garden designers, Crowe for William Cutbush & Son's nurseries in Barnet, Colvin for a variety of private clients. The going was tough – their fees, Colvin complained, were too low to provide for anything other than the smallest of livings – but the work was satisfying and it brought with it invaluable experience. By 1939 Colvin, the older of the two, had acted as adviser on some three hundred gardens, including one for Archduke Charles Albert Habsburg at his summer palace at Żywiec in Poland.† Crowe, meanwhile, had a won a gold medal at the Chelsea Flower Show for a design featuring a contoured wood out of which a stream flowed into a naturalistic pond.

During the war Crowe, elfin of face and a born diplomat,

---

* In 1968, Perry was the first woman to join the RHS Council. As Catherine Horwood points out in *Gardening Women*, even in the late Sixties, when women were winning many prestigious RHS medals, the concept of female representation on its council continued to be controversial. The subject was raised at its AGM and members were told that 'at present' the available women did not have 'as useful experience' as the available men. When Enid Bagnold, the author of *National Velvet*, wrote to *The Times* about this, saying Gertrude Jekyll would be rolling in her grave, Lord Aberconway, the president of the RHS, described the ensuing fuss as 'a little storm in ladies' teacups'. Even now, the RHS has a tendency to be male-dominated: in 2011, for instance, the garden judges at the RHS Chelsea Flower Show were all men.

† Returning from her final visit to Żywiec in 1939 – she and a friend had driven there in her Wolseley – she only just managed to miss the German invasion of Poland. '*Wo sind die Männer?* [Where are the men?]' asked the German border guards, unable to believe two women would travel alone. Convinced they must be involved in spying, they then confiscated Colvin's camera.

served with the Polish army in France as a volunteer ambulance driver and then as a sergeant in the ATS (Auxiliary Territorial Service); Colvin, tall and gaunt and notoriously bad tempered, worked for the Women's Farm and Garden Association, organising a training scheme for women gardeners in wartime, and as an Air Raid Precautions warden. Between shifts, they continued to attend meetings of the Institute of Landscape Design at its offices in Gower Street* (its secretary Gwen Browne, they noted, was now sometimes to be observed performing her duties in a tin hat.) 'One got away from the grind of seeing things through and thought about the future,' said Crowe. 'One's creative energies had had a stopper put on them and they came bubbling up.' Having been involved with the Institute since its birth in 1929, they were not about to abandon it for the sake of a few bombs and, as a result, were able to play a role in the organisation's crucial wartime decision not to merge with the Institute of Architects. In 1951 Colvin would be elected the Institute's president, the first women to head any of the bodies that represented engineering or environmental professionals. Crowe would take up the same office in 1957.

For Colvin and Crowe, the war changed everything: the turmoil brought with it opportunity, expectation, even hope. Not only would people's sense of the meaning and reach of landscape architecture expand once the work of rebuilding Britain's cities began, its practitioners would be able to influence the reconstruction from the very earliest stage. Colvin agreed with Clough Williams-Ellis, the architect of Portmeirion and the author of the anti-sprawl polemic *England and the Octopus*, when he said, 'We are now in for a new and splendid age, or else for chaos, and we cannot plan for chaos; so let us work for splendour, especially as

---

* Another regular at these meetings was Marjory Allen, a landscape architect who, in 1954, published an influential volume on adventure playgrounds for children.

by doing so we promote its likelihood.' Speaking at a conference in 1943 Colvin argued that town planners needed to see landscape not as a kind of 'ornament' to be applied only when architects and engineers had finished their work, but as integral to the entire process.

In 1945 Colvin and Crowe, by now close friends and holiday companions, began sharing a cramped office in Gloucester Place, near Baker Street. They also set to work on the fraught business of trying to influence post-war planning. Colvin contributed to a book, *Bombed Churches as War Memorials*, with a planting scheme for Christ Church, Newgate Street – it had an area devoted to the 'veterans of 1940', the self-sown flowers of the Blitz – and she published two texts, *Trees for Town and Country* and *Land and Landscape*, both of which would go on to become standard reference works. She also gave the Ministry of Transport advice on roads and how they might be made more attractive. Much more importantly, both women presented evidence to the New Towns Committee of 1946, which was chaired by Lord Reith.

Such deep thinking and careful positioning paid off when they were duly appointed to senior roles at New Towns. In 1948 Crowe was made the consultant on landscape design at Harlow, Essex, where her job would be to bring to life the green spaces of Frederick Gibberd's masterplan. Two years later Colvin was appointed to a similar job at East Kilbride in Scotland. Britain's New Towns were a giant and slightly mad compromise: a third way between the pressures for new housing and the expansion of the suburbs, and the assiduous campaigning of organisations such as the Town and Country Planning Association, a conservative body that favoured low-density schemes. Throw into this mix the modernist ambitions of the architects employed on these projects – the majority were in thrall to Le Corbusier – and you have a recipe for muddle and disaster. They didn't want to create ersatz market towns, they wanted to build boxes on stilts. Even so, it

Harlow water gardens

must have been exciting to be involved. At Harlow, for instance, Gibberd (now best known for Liverpool's Catholic Cathedral and the Regent's Park Mosque) was employing some of the grooviest names of the day: Philip Powell and Hidalgo Moya, Maxwell Fry and Jane Drew, William Crabtree and H. T. Cadbury-Brown. He was also, as a friend and travelling companion of Geoffrey Jellicoe, the wartime president of the Institute of Landscape Design, a man known to be hugely sympathetic to landscape: for Crowe, Gibberd was pretty much the ideal collaborator.

Like Margery, Colvin and Crowe looked to the past for inspiration for the future. But in their case it was to the open, sweeping style of Capability Brown rather than the thronged charm of the cottage garden; the idea was to combine nature with the freedom and calm afforded by twentieth-century abstraction. Their hallmarks were smooth vistas of bare grass, delicate glades of trees and an intuitive feeling for shape; when it came to large-scale projects they disliked 'small, scattered spaces' squeezed in willy-nilly – such miserly pockets of green were more dead than alive. 'No one uses the odd grass corner,' said Crowe. 'Except to throw bus tickets on it; no one wants to sit midway between a bus route and a terrace of houses.'

At Harlow Crowe was determined to make the most of the understated Essex landscape; her design kept the existing streams and trees of its shallow valleys and she linked areas of housing using old lanes that were turned into cycle tracks. The town park was planned with no hard boundaries cutting it off from the town centre, which itself featured a terraced water garden and, eventually, a fine collection of modern sculpture (Moore, Hepworth, Frink). At East Kilbride Colvin's task was more difficult: the site was bleaker and more windswept than Harlow and she had to work on a massive scale, creating 'a continuous forest belt round the south and west of the built-up area'. Ultimately, she would resign before her job was complete, feeling that the project's general manager was interfering too much. But her trees framed the town beautifully, and her decision to take footpaths off the side of the main roads, putting them above cuttings or below embankments instead, was both forward-thinking and successful. Most are still in use today.

At home in Somerset, Margery must have read about the New Towns and their development in the newspapers. It seems unlikely that they were her cup of tea – it was city or country for her, not the burgeoning subtopia* between – but she would doubtless have been reassured by the fact that it was Crowe and Colvin who were responsible for the landscaping of these slightly forlorn new Jerusalems. She had met Crowe, a friend of Phyllis Reiss, and she certainly knew of Colvin, some of whose post-war gardens for private clients could be seen in the new wave of gardening books (for instance, *Modern Gardens* by Peter Shepheard, which was published in 1953). In particular Margery would have been aware of Colvin's recent 'alterations' to Norah Lindsay's garden at the Manor House at Sutton Courtenay, Oxfordshire, a gorgeous creation whose

---

* Coined in 1955 by the architectural writer Ian Nairn for the areas on the edges of cities that had been failed by urban planning. By 1959 many of the New Towns were deemed to be failures.

influence may be seen today at both Sissinghurst and Hidcote. Margery knew Sutton Courtenay well: Lindsay's plant-hunter daughter Nancy, who lived in a cottage near by, was among her ever-growing band of gardening correspondents.

The garden at Sutton Courtenay was similar in spirit to Margery's – a place of 'thoughtless abundance' with 'an air of spontaneity in the planting, as if the flowers and the trees had chosen their own positions and, like the house, been overlooked by the rushing tide of men'. But its new owner, the newspaper proprietor David Astor, wanted something that was easier to maintain, especially now its presiding genius (Norah) was no longer there to enforce her vision. Colvin's response was a series of lawns and winding paths; *objets trouvés*, sculpture and the few fine old yews that had survived Lindsay's passing provided further focal points. It was, however, a project that she would work on for some two decades, and it tells you everything you need to know about Colvin's sensibility that when the cooling towers of Didcot Power Station – another of Frederick Gibberd's projects – rose in the sky in the late Sixties she refused to screen them from the house with a new planting of trees. They were, she felt, a part of the landscape and could not simply be ignored: 'Our power stations, oil refineries, factories and water works must take their place, in time, with the pyramids, castles and temples of the past.'*

I suspect that Margery would have agreed with the passer-by who told Colvin's assistant that his boss had made Norah Lindsay's lovely, old garden 'look like a public park'; she would have

---

* And no wonder: in 1959 she had been appointed landscaper at Drakelow C Power Station in Staffordshire. Her award-winning design included a wildfowl nature reserve on lakes created by gravel excavation. In the same year Sylvia Crowe was commissioned to do the same job at Transfyndd in Snowdonia. Working alongside the power station's architect Basil Spence, she built an outdoor rest area for staff; it comprises a series of curving dry-stone terraces that feel like the ruins of some ancient building – appropriate given that Spence thought of his design as resembling a castle.

mourned the loss of its dreamy, absent-minded maturity. But she
would also have understood that things move on. After all, wasn't
that the story of East Lambrook? And as it happened, things there
were about to change again. Her career as a journalist now firmly
established, Margery daringly began work on *We Made a Garden*.
How did this feel? Writing such a book wasn't a betrayal, exactly,
but it was certainly an act of domestic insurrection, albeit a post-
dated one – and she must have worried, just a little, about how it
would be received (our own, more confessional age takes memoir
in its stride). Once it was done, though, and she saw how well the
book was received, there was no stopping her. For wasn't this the
great advantage of having dispatched one's most-tricky-to-write
volume first? Whatever followed would be easy in comparison.
Over the course of the next thirteen years she would write another
seven books, perhaps the best of which – it is widely considered a
classic – is *Gardening in the Shade*. To the infuriation of her neighbours
Margery wrote to loud music: Wagner, preferably.* He urged her
on. There was, after all, an awful lot that she needed to get down.
In 1990 some poor fool made a database of every plant she ever
mentioned in print: it comprised some 6500 names, including over
two hundred single-snowdrop varieties.

Then there was the garden itself. Increasingly in demand as a
lecturer – friends remember that she had a clear, low voice, one
she was well able 'to chuck across a room' – and with so much
writing to do, Margery finally took on some proper help. She also
decided to open a nursery. Any money she made could go towards
the salaries of her new staff – though this wasn't its main purpose;
the truth was that only by propagating plants in an organised way
would she be able to replace all those she gave away. The garden,
in its pomp, was now open to visitors one afternoon a week (the

* She loved opera and was a regular at Glyndebourne, for which she used to wear a kimono
that was rather too tight, forcing her to take comically diminutive steps.

Margery working near her beloved 'pudding trees' in the garden at East Lambrook

money went to the Red Cross, one of the many good causes with which Margery was involved locally). Coach parties would book themselves in and – so long as they weren't late – Margery would go to the gate to meet them, offering herself up as tour guide. Those she thought truly interested – she liked young, male horticultural students the best – would inevitably go home with an armful of cuttings. It was a compulsion; she just couldn't resist.

Slowly, her team grew. And yet having these young men and women about the place did nothing to change her own routine. When she was at home she was in the garden, whatever the weather. In summer she wore a cotton dress, the edge of her petticoat trailing below it. In winter, a faded corduroy skirt, its hem drooping at the rear, with a matching jacket, a tweed hat perched on her grey hair, her legs encased in thick lisle stockings (sometimes these didn't match, though no one ever had the courage to tell her so). On her feet, which were big, were her ancient clogs. If it was raining she simply pulled on a long mackintosh. Her days were as full as ever; once it was dark she would return to her desk, where she would remain, head bowed, until one or two o'clock in the morning. Her staff sometimes found her abrupt, and she could be a slave driver; there is a story that one gardener resigned after developing frostbite. But she also knew, in most cases, just how far she could go. When she sensed people were fed up she would turn on the charm, telling her staff how wonderful they were, how appreciated. At bottom, she was warm-hearted. The only thing that truly made her snort was the word 'ladies'. To Margery, women were only ever women.

Life ticked on. In 1963 the RHS awarded her a silver Veitch Memorial Medal in recognition of her work. She began to make regular appearances on the radio. She continued with her various columns. Gardeners, though, have a more than usually keen sense of time passing, and while this is an essential part of the pleasure their plots bring them, nature's metronome is unrelenting.

Groundsel waits for no one. As she grew older and her health became less robust, Margery was increasingly crotchety; there was so much that she wanted to *do*. This is not to say she was ever depressed. She was – here's another trait common to gardeners – an exceptionally content person, and right until the end she always had the energy for a fight. When the celebrated Christopher Lloyd of Great Dixter – *The Mixed Border* was published a year after *We Made a Garden* – came to stay, bringing with him both his irascible dachshunds and his famously autocratic manner, she always gave as good as she got. Why should he have the last word?

Margery's final illness lasted only a week. She died in 1969, at South Petherton Hospital in Somerset, at the age of seventy-seven. When her extended family heard her fulsome obituary on the radio they were agog. They had never taken her gardening seriously – and she, alas, had never troubled to put them right.

Margery lives on in the plants she loved. *Artemisia absinthium* 'Lambrook Silver', a fernlike wormwood, remains a popular variety of one of her favourite silver plants, and she made a special selection of another cherished cultivar, *Euphorbia characias ssp. wulfenii* 'Lambrook Gold'. *Santonlina chamaecyparissus* 'Lambrook Silver', an exceptionally pretty cotton lavender, and *Polemonium* 'Lambrook Mauve', delicate as a butterfly's wings, were also introduced by her. Since her death varieties of penstemon, bergenia, dicentra, hebe and hemerocallis have all been named after her. She is also credited with having given the astrantia 'Shaggy' its delightfully appropriate name.

Her influence lives on, too, in gardens everywhere. Visitors sigh at Sissinghurst, Hidcote and the rest, but they know they cannot ever hope to compete, as you may tell from the consoling way they attack their slices of lemon drizzle cake in the café afterwards. They owe what they do in their own back yards – assuming they're not going the banana-plant route, or importing spindly olive trees in the misguided hope that they will look out of their windows and see Tuscany rather than South London – not to Vita Sackville-West and Lawrence Johnston, but to the altogether less well-known Margery Fish. What a bountiful legacy she left them. Hardy geraniums? It was her who made them fashionable (though she preferred the old name, cranesbill). Hostas and bergenias?* Ditto. Jacob's ladder? Same again.

As for her own garden, it's still there.

When Margery died she left East Lambrook to her nephew Henry Boyd-Carpenter; he installed his parents as his tenants and they looked after it until the house was sold in 1985. Since then, it has had three different sets of owners. In 1992 the garden was listed at Grade I by English Heritage, which is good news in the sense that no one will ever be able to build a bungalow on it. Quite what else this status involves, however, is moot. Will every owner for the next hundred years be under an obligation to grow an avenue of *chamacyparis lawsonia fletcheri* on Margery's terraces?† I don't know. A garden, as some of us sometimes want to shout at our more fussy neighbours, is in a constant state of flux. And so it should be. If it were ever to stop changing it wouldn't be a garden at all.

I went to see East Lambrook Manor one cold, bright morning in March. There is a tea room in the malthouse now, and a too-big car park over the road, its expanse of tarmac as black and as shiny as liquorice. The latest owners, who arrived in 2008 and are extremely welcoming, have big plans, but perhaps they are also just a little overwhelmed by the scale of what they have taken on. The garden's restoration, which began about a decade ago, still has a way to go.

All the same, it is an enchanting place: so much more restful

---

* To be truthful, in the case of bergenias, all leathery and vulgar, I wish she hadn't bothered. I look at them and shudder.

† Margery used to call these sculpted green blobs her 'pudding trees'. The current avenue is not the one she planted; in 2001 a new set of trees were put in, Margery's having been on their last legs.

East Lambrook Manor, veiled in shades of mauve; in Walter's day,
wisteria was strictly forbidden

than those gardens that have been manicured to within an inch
of their lives by massed ranks of National Trust professionals. Its
beauty is quotidian, and therein lies its charm. There are weeds.
There is disorder. It asks for your attention. Even for such a desultory gardener as me, the temptation to fall to my knees and work
for an hour or two is powerfully strong.

My first visit, but I knew my way around. I could have done it
blindfold; thanks to Margery, it was all mapped out in my head.
First the Lido, low and mossy. Then the Colosseum, whose
bathetic scale made me smile. The woodland garden felt, that particular morning, as if it was on tenterhooks, the annual arrival of
a delicate flurry of scillas suddenly imminent. Finally, I went in
search of Margery's first long border. It's still there, that hard-won
husbandly concession with which, in the end, she was never quite
able to fall completely in love. The euphorbias were already well
on their way to being quite magnificent.

The Brontës of Shepherd's Bush

Muriel Box, director, and Betty Box, producer

'I want to go on the films'

Until recently, anyone who wanted to see the film *To Dorothy a Son* had to lock themselves deep in the bowels of the British Film Institute off Tottenham Court Road and watch it on an old Steenbeck editing machine, a cumbersome mechanical beast that would whirr and click fretfully, as if even it was irritated to be involved with such a non-entity of a picture. A little-known comedy from 1954, *To Dorothy* is no one's idea of a classic. It has an infuriating star in the form of Shelley Winters, a creaky screenplay by Peter Rogers (later to become famous as the producer of the *Carry On* series) and a set that looks as if it is on loan from a local amateur dramatics society.

Most of the action takes place in the home of Tony (John Gregson, then a huge star) and his baby-faced wife Dorothy (Peggy Cummins). Dorothy is heavily pregnant and confined to bed. Tony, charming but woefully disorganised, is a composer with a deadline to meet, bailiffs to keep at bay and, thanks to the condition of his wife, a home to run. The house, a picture-postcard cottage, is a mess: washing hangs from an indoor line, and when the telephone rings it can't be found beneath piles of paper. Its proportions are all wrong too; as if doing the ironing wasn't humiliating enough, Tony keeps banging his head on the ceiling. Then, just to make things even more chaotic, his brassy American ex-wife Myrtle (Shelley Winters) turns up, bearing the news that she will inherit her uncle's two-million-dollar fortune if, by a certain date and time, her former husband has not yet produced a son. There follows, as the film's poster had it, 'a riot'. Myrtle is desperate that Dorothy does not give birth until her legacy is safe. Tony, meanwhile, is panicking about another of her announcements – thanks to a clerical error, they may not have been divorced. It's all quite silly, and it comes, of course, with an unfeasibly happy ending. Tony discovers that he and Myrtle were not married in the first place; Dorothy gives birth to twins, a girl and a boy, the latter arriving just after the deadline has passed; Myrtle decides to share her legacy, thus solving Tony and Dorothy's money worries once and for all. Hooray. Let the titles roll.

To Dorothy is, however, more than the sum of its parts. It might feel tired now, but to those who saw it on its release – Friday night, local flea pit, quarter of sherbet lemons to share – it would have seemed much livelier, something dark at play beneath the surface fluff. In 1954 the divorce rate was six times what it had been before the war. Add to this figure the countless number of women who were involved in phoney second 'marriages', their surnames changed by deed poll the better to make them appear respectable, and you will understand why many people believed that marriage was in crisis. *To Dorothy a Son* longs to please, but it also reflects this anxiety. It's all here: the untimely reappearance of a first wife/husband; the dread exposure of a bigamous/sham marriage and its shameful consequence, illegitimacy; and, most noticeably of all, the painful post-war recalibration of the respective roles of men and women. Even as Dorothy makes demands on Tony she fears his resentment. 'I don't want the baby,' she tells him at one point. 'I hate babies.' But what she really hates, you suspect, is her own powerlessness – and, perhaps, the sight of her husband running around in an apron.

'Men were made to wear the pants, and the pants were made to carry the dough,' says Myrtle sarcastically, amused by the change in her ex (at a preview screening of the film, the men in

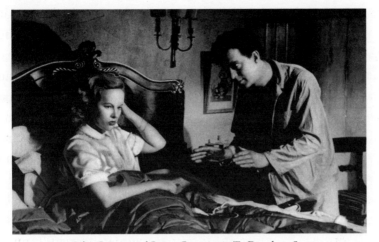

John Gregson and Peggy Cummins in To Dorothy a Son

the audience endorsed this sentiment with hearty laughter, much to its director's disappointment). But she only half means it. Myrtle is a ballsy woman, independent and forceful, and it is clear that after years as a struggling singer she is thrilled to have her own money to spend: if Dorothy has two babies, she will have two mink coats. Hunkered in my screening room for one at the BFI, it was with some amazement that I realised the two women would end as friends, not rivals – a weirdly feminist twist in a film whose female characters are, at first glance, mere archetypes. Myrtle splits her inheritance not in half but three ways, and in doing so silently asks the question of the hour: why should only Tony escape the tyranny of the feather duster?

Every year, during the film awards season, the cry goes up: where are all the women? But in Britain, in 1954 they were everywhere. It's hardly surprising that *To Dorothy a Son* came with a subliminal feminist message, for its director was Muriel Box, a passionate feminist. Amazingly, this was Muriel's second picture of the year. Even as she was shooting it – Shelley Winters driving her halfway round the bend with her refusal ever to learn her lines until she arrived on set – she was editing *The Beachcomber*, a comedy drama starring Donald Sinden and Glynis Johns that she had filmed on location in Ceylon. And no sooner had she wrapped it than she was thinking about her next picture, *Simon and Laura*, on which she would start work in May 1955.

Alas neither *The Beachcomber* nor *To Dorothy* was a hit for Box: 'Spent nearly £8 on a pair of evening shoes ... shocking!!!' she wrote in her diary, having spent a consolatory day shopping after the 'lousy' reviews for the latter. Many of her colleagues, however, were having better luck. Wendy Toye, a recent winner of the prize for best short film at Cannes, had directed a respectable if rather baggy thriller, *The Teckman Mystery*, starring Margaret Leighton. A former debutante called Joan Henry* had adapted her best-selling prison memoir *Who Lie in Gaol* for the director J. Lee Thompson, and the result – *The Weak and the Wicked*, starring Glynis Johns as a gambling addict – had grossed two hundred thousand pounds at the box office. *The Belles of St Trinian's*, the third most popular film of the year, had been edited by the brilliant Thelma Connell.†

Most stunning of all, though, was the success of Betty Box, the sister of Muriel's husband Sydney. Betty had produced *Doctor in the House*, the film that had made a star of Dirk Bogarde, whom she

---

* The cousin of an Earl, Henry was a reckless gambler. In 1951 she was jailed for fraud, having borrowed money from a 'friend' to pay her racing debts (the cheques of this friend were forged). *Who Lie in Gaol* was based on her time in Holloway and Askham Grange prisons, and attracted controversy for the allegations it made (some women, she said, were forced to give birth in their cells). Her next book, *Yield to the Night*, was a novel set in the cell of a young woman shortly to be hanged for murder. J. Lee Thompson, who was by now her lover, turned it into a 1956 film starring Diana Dors. At the time many people believed it was based on the case of Ruth Ellis, hanged in July 1955 for the murder of David Blakely, but this was not so: the novel was published in 1954. Spookily, Henry appeared to have seen the future. For more on Ellis and Dors, see the Introduction.
† Connell began her career as editor on *In Which We Serve* (1942), Noël Coward's patriotic war film. She went on to edit *Alfie* (1966), starring Michael Caine, for which she received a BAFTA nomination.

had cast as the duffle-coated student medic Simon Starling in the face of stiff opposition from her bosses at Rank. It was the biggest film of the year by a mile and there was already talk of a sequel. 'An uproarious, devil-may-care, almost wholly ruthless picture of the goings-on in medical training at a London hospital,' the critic Dilys Powell had written of it, a view with which Muriel, who did not always adore the work of her more commercially minded relative, wholly concurred. Oh, yes. That was the other thing: women film critics were ten a penny. The most famous were Powell at the *Sunday Times* and C. A. Lejeune at the *Observer*, but there were others too: E. Arnot Robertson at the *Daily Mail*, Isabel Quigly at the *Spectator*, Elspeth Grant on the *Daily Sketch*. In 1956 a woman, Penelope Houston, was even appointed editor of *Sight and Sound*, the highbrow journal of the British Film Institute, a job that would be hers for more than three decades.

Muriel was a curious mixture: easily disheartened yet doggedly ambitious. When she heard that the distributors of *To Dorothy a Son*, her fifth film as director, would not be giving it a West End run she fell into a depression; in the days before it opened the headaches that plagued her became worse. But she also knew the territory. You had to keep going. Even as the critics sneered at it she was working on a script – it was called *The Truth about Women* – that she believed would change her fortunes. The one thing that she and Wendy Toye, Joan Henry, Thelma Connell and her sister-in-law Betty had in common, apart from their sex, was that they were as tough as boots. They ate setbacks for breakfast. Muriel was perfectly aware that directing, in particular, was difficult for a woman. It wasn't only the men who were against you (Michael Balcon, who ran Ealing Studios, would tell anyone who would listen that women lacked the qualities necessary to control a large film unit). Some women were too. Kay Kendall, soon to appear in *Simon and Laura*, would later say that it had felt 'strange and uncomfortable' to be directed by Box; Muriel Pavlow, her co-star, acknowledged Box's capabilities but insisted 'I think I respond better to a male director.'

The other thing Muriel had by the bucketload was experience. She was forty-nine years old by the time she made *To Dorothy*; her hair, about which she tended to fret, would have been threaded with grey were it not for her fortnightly trips to the hairdresser, and her doctor was always telling her – somewhat unhelpfully – that the tiredness she sometimes experienced was down to her impending menopause. She had been working in the film industry since 1929, when she quit her typing job at a corset factory in Welwyn Garden City and joined British Instructional Pictures. There was a sense in which she had seen it all before. On her sideboard at home stood the Oscar she and her husband had won in 1946 for the screenplay of *The Seventh Veil*, a film starring James Mason that was one of the first pictures to take psychiatry seriously. But thrilled though she'd been to receive it, the distinct sense of anti-climax she felt when the statuette arrived from Hollywood in a straw-filled packing case had turned out to be something of a portent. Three years later she directed her first feature, *The Lost People*, and the reviews were 'foul, on the whole'. Beginning a new diary in 1950, she wrote that she was glad to see the back of the old year, 'the worst yet for us [her and Sydney] as far as reputation goes'. It was probably best, she thought, not to take anything too seriously. If the doldrums could follow hard on the heels of an Academy Award, then a flop could be succeeded just as swiftly by a smash hit.

Violette Muriel Baker was born in 1905, in New Malden, Surrey. Her father was a railway clerk, her mother an assistant in her uncle's magic lantern shop. The family, as she put it in her autobiography *Odd Woman Out*, belonged to the 'respectable poor'. Her parents often rowed about money and sometimes physically fought over it; her mother, who would weep and sing hymns to herself after these altercations, occasionally had to pawn her wedding ring in order to buy food. Caroline Baker was slightly snobbish, the kind of woman who hearthstoned her doorstep every week the better to keep it bright white, but surreptitiously, so as to avoid detection (her neighbours all had maids or daily help). Thanks in large part to her, the household was gloomy yet tinged with hysteria. By the time Muriel was thirteen her parents no longer shared a bedroom, her mother having discovered that her father was having an affair with a woman who lived close by.

Prone to self-dramatisation, Muriel had one of those indelible childhoods, bulging with incident. She claimed, for instance, to have lost her virginity at the age of six to a twelve-year-old boy who had come to stay one summer, and who liked to 'snuggle' in her bed while they played noughts and crosses. Not that she found this traumatic. 'As the weeks went by, his play in the mornings became more intimate,' she writes in *Odd Woman Out*. 'But since he was a jolly boy and I liked him, I found nothing objectionable in what he did. The reverse in fact ... Not until many years later when I happened to be discussing the subject of sex with a male friend who inquired whether I had found defloration painful and unpleasant, did I realise that I had never experienced it in the usual way.' Certainly, it made much less of an impression than the accident that befell her older brother around the same time. Badly burned by boiling oil in the kitchen, Vivian required grafts, the skin for which Muriel provided in an operation that took place at the same time as a tonsillectomy. It was performed by the family doctor in an upstairs bedroom at home; the same man operated on Vivian too. (The tonsillectomy was successful, but the grafts failed and Vivian was transferred to St Thomas's in London for further treatment.)

The children – Muriel also had a sister, Vera – spent their holidays with their maternal grandmother, who owned a genteel boarding house at Southsea in Hampshire, an establishment crammed with Victoriana: music boxes, ostrich eggs, fans, a lizard in a glass box. Even more fascinating, on the first floor lived a retired actress, Mademoiselle le Thière, a creature who was reputed to have been in the original cast of one of Oscar Wilde's plays. Thanks to this long-term tenant, her grandmother had once seen such greats as Henry Irving and Herbert Beerbohm Tree perform, and now, when funds allowed, she took Muriel to see the stage heart-throbs of her own day: Gerald du Maurier, Matheson Lang, Owen Nares.

In 1914, war broke out. At first, this was exciting: two Tommies, cheerful cockneys, were billeted with the family and the mood indoors lifted. But after they were drafted to France the house was more of a mausoleum than ever. Everyone was preoccupied with food, or rather the lack of it. Muriel began to live for her visits to the Kinema in Kingston upon Thames. She and her siblings had to walk the two miles there and back, and they had to watch the picture from low wooden benches just under the screen, necks aching. But it was worth it: 'It was the heyday of the cliffhanging serials, the one and two-reel slapstick comedies, and the flickering newsreels. King Edward the Seventh's funeral was the most impressive spectacle we had ever seen.' When an old friend of her mother's – an immigrant she'd befriended some years before – turned up offering the family free seats for any show they cared to see in the cinema he now ran (also in Kingston), Muriel took him at his word, presenting herself twice weekly at its door. For a while, this was tolerated. One day, however, she was shown a high wooden chair on the deserted stage behind the screen and told that from now on this was where she would watch the film.

This wasn't ideal. She missed the theatre's plump upholstered seats and the whirring of the projector almost drowned out the music from the orchestra pit (this was still the era of silent films). It was difficult to read the subtitles, which now appeared in reverse; she deciphered them with the help of a mirror that hung on the theatre wall. But there were advantages: when the show was over she was sometimes allowed to rewind the spools, and if the film had broken the projectionist would let her help him stick it together again, which made her feel important. Even better, she was allowed to take home the frames that were 'lost' in the course of this operation: 'I had a fine collection of tiny clips in a secret store for many years, examined and gloated over with the passions of a connoisseur.' Her interest in film was becoming a passion. At school she took to reading *Picture Show,* a weekly cinema magazine, in the most tedious lessons.

By the time she hit puberty her older siblings had left home, which meant that the full force of her mother's 'didactic, despotic personality' was directed only at her. Mostly, her inclination was to give as good as she got, with the result that the two of them would spend hours at a time verbally tearing each other apart. But on other occasions she would take the silent approach, wondering how long her mother could carry on without getting any response. All she could think about was the day when she could start earning her own living and begin her escape. Her father was content for her to be a shorthand typist or a railway clerk like him. Her mother, though, had other, grander ideas and knowing this Muriel, ever the opportunist, took her chance. 'I want to go on the films,' she said. To her amazement, this was not dismissed out of hand, perhaps because it seemed such a remote possibility.

But in the summer of 1920 the films came to her. On a train to Southsea she fell into conversation with a stranger. He asked her if she liked the movies – she had her nose deep in *Picture Show,* as usual – and when she told him that yes, she did, very much, he plied her with questions. In the end they talked about D. W. Griffith, the pioneering American director of the civil war epic *The Birth of a Nation,* all the way to the coast. As the train pulled into Southsea he handed Muriel his card; if ever she wanted to see a film being made, he said, she should give him a ring.

'JOSEPH GROSSMAN', she read, as her new pal disappeared into the seaside crowd. And then the miraculous words: 'STOLL PICTURE PRODUCTIONS'. This was amazing. Muriel knew all about Stoll, where Grossman was studio manager. Its latest film, *The Glorious Adventure*, a melodrama about the Great Fire of London, was being shot in a new colour process called Prizma and starred Lady Diana Manners, the famous society beauty; the word was that she looked utterly marvellous in her close-ups. And so it was that six months later she made the first of what would be several visits to Cricklewood, the home of Stoll. Muriel was too shy to broach the subject of a job, and in any case her meagre wardrobe, which consisted only of her school gym tunic, the bridesmaid's dress she had worn at her sister's wedding and one old skirt, would barely have seen her through the week. But watching the actors and technicians was heaven even if she wasn't being paid for it, and eventually Grossman gave her, unprompted, a few days' crowd work in *The Old Man in the Corner*, a silent movie based on Baroness Orczy's detective story of the same name.

It was at this point, half fainting beneath the heat of the Klieg lights, that it dawned on Muriel that she was about as likely to be 'discovered' by a director in a crowd scene as she was to fly to the moon. She needed another way in. Back at home, she set to thinking. What about the theatre? Soon afterwards she persuaded her parents to pay for her to enrol on a course at the Margaret Barnes School of Dancing in Surbiton. She understood that she had left it a little late to learn to dance; she was now seventeen, after all. But she was determined, and she worked hard at her *entrechats* and her *pliés,* and at the end of the year she was able to scrape through a preliminary examination adjudicated by the celebrated ballerina Adeline Genée. Meanwhile, she tried to pick up other skills. She sang with a local choral society; she signed up for a course taught by Sir Ben Greet, the Shakespearian actor-manager ('anything I know about acting I owe to Ben Greet,' she said later); she joined an amateur dramatics society.

But there was trouble ahead. Muriel had somehow contrived to fall in love with an associate of her father's, Stanley, an Aneurin Bevan lookalike and a keen amateur pianist. Unfortunately, he was fourteen years her senior and her mother thought him wildly unsuitable. The atmosphere between mother and daughter now shifted from tetchy to poisonous and continued that way until, one summer morning, Muriel simply walked out. In one pocket of her mackintosh were three shillings, a toothbrush, some soap and a sponge; in the other a couple of apples, some raisins and a copy of E. V. Lucas's *The Open Road* ('A Little Book for Wayfarers'). She took a train to Dorking and for three days she lived rough on the downs. Meanwhile, her father went round to see Stanley and threatened to give him a good horsewhipping. This was wildly unfair: poor Stanley had known nothing of her plan.

When she returned – it was humiliating, but her money had run out and she was hungry – things were even worse. Her mother began censoring her post, and cross-examined her after her every outing. Muriel felt like she could kill her, sometimes. 'To avoid striking her, my fists clenched with such force the nails dug into the palms and drew blood. I would catch myself staring at her as she ranted on about some misdemeanour of mine, amazed at my own sinister thoughts: "Now I know what it feels like to commit murder!" and wondering how long it would be before I lost control and throttled her.' In the end, she did not wait to find out. A couple of days before her twentieth birthday, Muriel put everything she owned into a bag and left home once again. This time, it was for good.

She went to Welwyn Garden City, where her sister's mother-in-law had offered her a room on the condition that she helped out with the housework. Of course she would also need a job, and there seemed nothing for it now but to admit that her father had been right: she would just have to become a secretary after all. Stanley lent her fifty pounds. It wasn't much, but if she was careful it would see her through a course at Pitman's College. For the next six months she spent nothing at all save for the cost of her daily train ticket to London and lunch at the ABC restaurant in Southampton Row, an establishment whose three menus she would remember for the rest of her life: (1) a roll, butter, St Ivel cheese and a cup of tea; (2) a sausage roll, biscuits, butter and a cup of coffee; (3) macaroni cheese, a roll and a cup of tea. The soles of her shoes she patched with cardboard; when the winter arrived she had to bulk out her summer coat with newspaper.

The course completed, she found a position as a secretary at Barclays Corsets in Welwyn. It was dull work and she was lonely too, the long-suffering Stanley having finally ended their seven-year affair. The only way to survive was by filling up the evenings. Luckily Welwyn, a suburban utopia popular with Fabians and Quakers, fairly throbbed with societies. She joined the Welwyn Folk Players and soon landed herself the lead in *Hindle Wakes*, Stanley Haughton's 1912 play about a Lancashire mill girl who, despite pressure from her family, refuses to marry the man with whom she has spent the weekend. She perfected her accent by listening to the girls in the canteen at the corset factory, most of whom had been recruited from Lancashire.

Two years passed. In 1929 Muriel landed a new job. The work was the same, and she would still be stuck in Welwyn, but her employer was British Instructional Films, where she worked in the Scenario Department. 'Life suddenly became very interesting and unpredictable,' she said later. 'Everything was in a state of flux, the company turning over from silent pictures to "talkies", an operation fraught with anxiety and many pitfalls.' Loopy as it sounds now, it was a while before producers realised they would need to hire dramatists to craft proper dialogue – at first they stuck with the scenarists who had written the clipped

subtitles that accompanied the silent movies – and this gave
Muriel a small opportunity. Directors would sometimes accept
her suggestions for improvements to the scripts she typed up,
and though her efforts were doubtless just as 'execrable' as those
of the scenarists, slowly she was able to pick up the rudiments
of screenwriting. Sometimes she was also required as a last-
minute extra, which meant she got to see the new films being
made.

She got another small break when the continuity girl on Puffin
Asquith's* first talkie, a drama about Gallipoli called *Tell England*,
fell ill with appendicitis. Asked to step in until a substitute could
be found, Muriel worked on the film for the next three weeks. It
wasn't easy: as she later admitted, she had only the vaguest
notions of how much the director, editor, camera-operator and
even the costumier relied on her notes. She watched the scruffy-
looking Puffin – Asquith was famous for his dishevelled
appearance – direct his stars Fay Compton, Ann Casson and Carl
Harbord in blissful ignorance of the effect her shortcomings
might be having on the film's progress, not to mention its budget.
But she hardly needed to worry. No sooner had it wrapped than
she found herself back at her desk, and soon after this a third of
BIF's staff were laid off, Muriel among them: the silent films the
company had on its stocks could not now find distributors, and
its debts had piled up. Her only consolation was that Asquith
wrote her a reference.

Joe Grossman would now make another serendipitous appearance in her life. Having applied to British International Pictures
at Elstree for continuity work, Muriel discovered that he was the
studio's latest boss. And he remembered her. Hired by Joe in spite

* Anthony Asquith was the son of the Liberal prime minister Herbert Asquith and his second
wife, Margot Tennant. Puffin was his childhood nickname. He would go on to film Shaw's
Pygmalion with Leslie Howard, and Terence Rattigan's plays *The Browning Version* and *The Winslow
Boy*.

of her inexperience, she could only muddle through at first. On day one the function of the clapper board had to be explained to her (this bit of kit had not been a feature of her brief stint on *Tell England*), but somehow she survived. By the time she lost her job several movies later – continuity girls were hired by the film, so it was always a precarious living – she was competent enough to be able to pick up work as a freelance.

In 1932 she joined Michael Powell's company in Wardour Street. Powell was then directing four-reel pictures, or 'quota quickies': B movies, shot on a shoestring, often in a matter of days.* Tired of train journeys, Muriel decided to move to London and found herself an attic in a house overlooking Regent's Park. The room was not luxurious. Water had to be hauled up a flight of stairs in a bucket, and her underwear washed in a pan on top of the stove. But she could have coped perfectly well with these things if she hadn't felt so lonely. 'The utter blankness which confronts one on trying to be self-sufficient and philosophical,' she confided to her diary one day after a walk in the park. 'The condition became so acute I was even forced into tears when eating my supper. It's strange crying alone ... At these moments, I almost wish some accident would finish me off completely.' In an effort to lift herself out of this depression she auditioned for RADA: she would be perfectly happy to forfeit her so-called career in the movies for the chance to act again. But when the big day arrived and she launched into Mirabelle's speech from Congreve's *The Way of the World*, her courage ebbed, replaced with 'a suffocating, creeping despair which, three quarters of the way through, literally choked

---

* Michael Powell, the director celebrated for his partnership with Emeric Pressburger. In the Forties they made such celebrated movies as *The Red Shoes* and *The Life and Death of Colonel Blimp*. The quota quickies were the result of the 1927 Cinematograph Film Act, which required exhibitors to screen a greater percentage of British movies. The idea was to give the industry a boost, but this huge new market only encouraged film companies to supply the demand for as little cash as possible. Cinema charladies, so the story goes, used to hoover while they were on; they were so bad no one wanted to see them.

me'. Back in her room, she cried for several hours: 'My last
chance! And I had muffed it!'

Sydney Box was a journalist and aspiring playwright whose roots
were even humbler than Muriel's. Aged seven, he had helped to
supplement the income of his seamstress mother with two paper
rounds while his father, a sometime florist, fought in the trenches;
he and his four siblings might have starved otherwise, especially
after his pa came home wounded. 'I still shudder at the memory
of one period of two weeks when our diet consisted solely of por-
ridge, boiled swedes and cocoa,' he would recall later. 'I have
never been able to eat swedes since.' Having begun his working life
as a cub reporter on the *Kentish Times*, he was by the early Thirties
a Fleet Street freelance; among many other things, he put in shifts
as a weekend sub-editor at the *Christian Herald*. But he still lived in
Beckenham, his home town, where he wrote and produced plays
for the local dramatic society. He was shy, balding, generous, easy-
going, flirtatious, a wheeler-dealer, energetic, full of ideas, lame
in one leg, and married.*

He had been involved in a desultory correspondence with
Muriel since the summer of 1932, when his one-act play *Murder Trial*
had won a prize at the Welwyn's annual drama festival (hearing
of its brilliance from her friends there, Muriel wrote to him asking
if she might have a copy). But in 1933 things changed between
them. Sydney was invited to dinner at the attic, ostensibly so they
might discuss their respective work (Muriel was now in continuity at Gaumont-British at Shepherd's Bush; she'd also had a
stab at writing a play of her own, a comedy called *Better Halves*).

* A 1946 newspaper portrait of Sydney described him like this: 'He bites off large lumps of life.
But there's a baby face, a soft voice, refinement, sensitivity and the odd paradox of urbane
naivety.' But he never forgot his roots. Even when he was rich and famous and never out of
the papers, he would still keep two hundred pounds in his pocket for reassurance. I've always
got this, he would think to himself.

However, they seem to have spent most of the evening exchanging confidences. Muriel told Sydney all about Stanley, and he told her about his four-year marriage. Perhaps not everything, though, for the next day she received a long letter from her dinner guest in which he attempted to tie up what he called the 'loose ends' of their conversation. His marriage, he said, had been a mistake; he and his wife had not slept together for years; he was pleased to be able to say that she had now found, as he put it, some other box – ha ha – on which to 'strike her match'. He was, he insisted, 'released from all obligations' save for the financial.

The tone of his note, jokey and a touch unctuous, suggests that he worried he was being premature. But for Muriel his missive came as a relief: *he was free*. In the course of a single evening, it seems, she had fallen in love. Within a month she and Sydney were sleeping together. By the autumn, they had found three small rooms to rent in a house opposite a fried-fish shop off Russell Square in Bloomsbury. They were, she quickly discovered, well suited, the one an incurable optimist (him), the other an incurable pessimist (her). But she also had to admit that she liked the idea of living in sin. She felt adventurous, bold, sophisticated. And what a dynamo this man was! 'Since meeting Sydney I realise what I've been missing all my life and each day I offer up a blessing for the magical good fortune that brought us together,' she wrote in her diary in August 1933. 'I have a feeling our relationship will prove fruitful. Already he is working with zest and mapping out his future with a thoroughness I admire.'

She was not wrong about this. Sydney's big problem in life was that he tended to do too much, not too little. One day, soon after they'd shacked up, he arrived home with an even bigger grin than usual on his face. It had occurred to him that while the majority of Britain's amateur actors were women, most of the plays that were written with drama societies in mind had more parts for men, and on a sudden impulse he had walked into Harraps, the publishers, to tell them so (there were then some twenty thousand amateur dramatic societies in Britain, with approximately a million members; this was a lucrative market). He had walked out again with a contract to produce a book of six one-act plays with all-women casts. *In just three months' time.*

And so it was that he and Muriel first began working together – a collaboration that would last, one way or another, for the next three decades. Every evening she would settle down to work on the first draft of a play they had already roughed out over supper, or even in bed. She would then pass it to Sydney to polish. And on and on, until the work was done. The result, *Ladies Only*, and its follow-up, *Petticoat Plays*, were an instant success, and over the course of the following six years they would publish upwards of fifty further such dramas. No West End producer would have known either one of their names, but Muriel and Sydney Box were soon the most performed playwrights in Britain.

It was thanks to one of these plays that they married. A newspaper had described *Not This Man*, which won the top award at the National Drama Festival at the Old Vic in 1935, as blasphemous. When Sydney decided to sue his lawyer advised him that his domestic arrangements, were they to be revealed in court, might prejudice his case. So he and Muriel decided to get hitched (she would otherwise have been perfectly content for them to go on as they were). The wedding took place at Holborn Register Office on 23 May 1935, with two office cleaners hastily enlisted as witnesses. Afterwards they had a cup of coffee at a nearby Lyons Corner House and then they each went straight to their offices; there was no honeymoon. Somewhat predictably, Sydney lost his court case. But he didn't regret having brought it: the publicity was worth a hundred times what he had spent on legal fees. And now that they were married they could have a baby without worrying about anyone's disapproval. Their daughter Leonora arrived the following year.

For a while, life was good. But with the outbreak of war in 1939 the lights went out at Britain's amateur dramatic societies – a situation that presented Muriel and Sydney with something of a problem. Muriel had left her continuity job when she fell pregnant; Sydney had been fired by a documentary company for whom he had lately been writing scripts. Their plays were their only source of income, and who was going to want those now? Again, it was Sydney who had the bright idea. The blackout, it was clear, was going to drive people half crazy, so what about a compendium of puzzles, games, jokes, poems and prayers to get families through the long, dark nights? *The Black-Out Book* was published in November 1939 under the pseudonym Evelyn August. It was so successful that on the back of its royalties Sydney was able to establish his own documentary company. Within two years Verity Films would be the biggest producer of government-sponsored propaganda in the country. (Thanks to his disability, Sydney was not called upon to fight.)

For the first months of the war Muriel stayed in London. But once the bombing began – a house in the Highgate street where they were now living received a direct hit – it was decided that she and Leonora would have to be evacuated. She dreaded this. She didn't want to leave Sydney; their goodbye in the sepulchral gloom of King's Cross, to the sound of heavy ack-ack fire, filled her with foreboding. But you sense, too, that she feared missing out. 'It was obvious,' she said later, 'that attitudes to everything were changing, mine included.' When she arrived in Dumfries after a fourteen-hour train journey she felt she had landed in another world. The Scots were suspicious, unwelcoming – something she found odd, given that they were fighting the same enemy as the English. It was impossible to make telephone calls or to send telegrams – the lines between London and Scotland were permanently jammed – and the post arrived too late to be reassuring (by the time a letter arrived its sender could very easily

be lying underneath a pile of rubble). The only consolation was
that she had her sister-in-law for company (she and Betty, along
with Sydney's mother, occupied two rooms in the home of a shoe
salesman and his family): 'A petite, very pretty blonde, with an
engaging manner which effectively disguised a remarkably keen
brain. In a great many ways, she resembled Sydney, being possessed of artistic flair and considerable organising ability.' They
became friends, though rivalry would always simmer beneath the
surface of their relationship. Nevertheless, Muriel's evacuation did
not last long. When Sydney suggested that she might come to
London to help him with a ninety-minute documentary, *The
Soldier's Food* – Ralph Richardson was to be seconded from the Fleet
Air Arm to star in it – she did not hesitate. Leaving Leonora with
her mother-in-law, she hot-footed it back to London.

Making this little film about messing committees, hay-box
cooking and the importance of fresh greens took longer than
expected: location work at Richmond Park was hampered by
Messerschmitts dive-bombing the parade ground, and studio
shots were held up by the screeching of sirens and the sound of
shrapnel on the roof. Yet the experience only increased Muriel's
determination to work for what remained of the war. She packed
Leonora off to a boarding school in Buckinghamshire, a liberal
establishment recommended to Muriel by Jill Craigie* (the children learned carpentry, and grew all their own food), and then
it was back to London again. Betty, a trained commercial artist
with an accountancy qualification, followed swiftly on her heels;
Sydney had persuaded her to join Verity Films as a production
assistant.

In 1941 Sydney made his wife the director of a documentary

---

* Britain's very first woman film director, Craigie made left-leaning documentaries and wrote
screenplays. She met her future husband Michael Foot, the Labour politician, while she was
making *The Way We Live* (1946), a film about family life in Portsmouth, the most bombed town
in England.

for the British Council, *The English Inn*. Thanks to the war, directors were thin on the ground and no doubt she had been
begging him to let her have a go. But these weren't his only reasons. Sydney believed in her, something he would prove over
and over in the future. Muriel may have lacked his enterprise
and cunning, but she was a fast learner – 'I took to [directing]
like a duck to water' – and after this epic of horse brasses and
foaming ale he enthusiastically assigned her to several Ministry
of Information films. Only when the Ministry decreed that *Road
Safety for Children* was not a suitable project for a woman did this
run end; Sydney's business was not so successful that he was
willing to risk falling out with his biggest client. But in any case,
he needed Muriel elsewhere, for he was branching into features,
leaving Verity in the capable hands of Betty. In swift succession
he now produced *On Approval*, a comedy with Googie Withers,
for English Pictures, and *The Flemish Farm* (a war movie), *French
Without Tears* (by Terence Rattigan) and *Don't Take It To Heart!*
(another comedy) for Two Cities Films. Muriel advised on continuity and editing. In 1943, considering his apprenticeship as a
producer complete, Sydney acquired a lease on Riverside
Studios and he and Muriel began working on the screenplay of
what they hoped would be their first independent production,
an adaptation of the stage comedy *29 Acacia Avenue*.

All this went on, of course, against the backdrop of the continuing war. It must have been odd, even surreal, to be making
movies – and quite a silly one, in the case of *29 Acacia Avenue** – at
a time of national crisis, for all that cinema audiences continued
to be remarkably buoyant, for all that the pictures were so important for morale. (Cinema audiences reached their peak during the
war. In 1945 there were 1,585,000,000 admissions; by 1956 this would

---

* It's about a spoony boy who indulges his feelings for two girls at the same time, while his
parents are away on holiday.

fall to 1,101,000,000. Picture houses had notices advising audiences that the programme would continue during air raids – which was lucky, since most people remained in their seats when the sirens sounded). But it was amazing how work could cause even the most dramatic and terrible events to fade to grey. In 1944, for instance, London was constantly under attack from the V1s, the devastating bombs known as doodlebugs. In her diary, Muriel pasted a Giles cartoon featuring civilians with giant ears, which had a caption that read: 'It's ridiculous to say these flying bombs have affected people in any way!' Beneath it, she wrote, 'When-ever we are out now, we begin to feel like those in the cartoon above.' (People would strain to hear the dull rattle of the V1s, knowing that when they fell silent an explosion was imminent.) She was exhausted; it was impossible to sleep. On fire-watch duty she had counted thirty flying bombs in a single evening. The Warner Brothers studio at Teddington had received a direct hit. In Norwood, two of Sydney's relatives had been killed when a V2 – the doodlebug's successor – landed on their house. And yet, as she also noted, the greater part of her was preoccupied with the fate of 29 Acacia Avenue, which J. Arthur Rank was refusing to distrib-ute (audience laughter at a screening had convinced him, a strict Methodist, that it was 'immoral').*

The bombs continued, right up until Easter 1945. So did the crushing shortages: it had now been several years since she had been able to get her hands on a bottle of cooking oil. Ditto lip-stick, shampoo and stockings. She told her diary that she longed for fruit, for liver, even for suet. But she couldn't feel too glum. She and Sydney had written a melodrama about a suicidal pianist called The Seventh Veil, and it had now gone into production, starring Janet Todd, Herbert Lom and James Mason. This was thrilling; the screenplay was entirely original, and they had

---

* It was eventually released in July 1945. Audiences loved it.

Janet Todd in The Seventh Veil

always dreamed it would be a vehicle for Todd.* On balance, she would probably take the movie over a pair of nylons. A few weeks later, the news came that Germans had begun to disintegrate. Muriel was overjoyed, of course,† but she couldn't help noticing that VE day would also bring with it forty-eight hours' holiday, time she and Sydney could usefully devote to finishing their next screenplay, *The Years Between*, an adaptation of the play by Daphne du Maurier.

The Seventh Veil opened on 22 October 1945 at the Leicester Square Theatre; its title and the names of its stars could be written in lights, thanks to the end of the black out. Muriel, ever the pessimist, did not have high hopes for the film. She doesn't explain the source of this gloom in her memoir, or in any subsequent

---

* The war did affect the filming of *The Seventh Veil*. Thanks to clothes rationing, it was difficult-verging-on-impossible to get the right costumes for Todd, and the V2s that succeeded the doodlebugs often exploded near the studio; shrapnel made a chequerboard of the roof and the rain dripped on to the set. Staff and artists alike were delayed in the mornings, their cars and taxis having disappeared into bomb craters overnight, and the sirens interrupted the recording of dialogue.
† Overjoyed but also, like many people, sceptical. The news about Hitler – that he was dead – was so good it was almost 'fishy'.

interview, but perhaps it was its ending that made her nervous: after receiving psychiatric treatment, the film's heroine, Francesca (Todd), realises that the love of her life is her crippled and Svengali-like guardian Nicholas (James Mason), a romantic revelation mottled with incestuous and masochistic undertones. Even with Mason in the role – he had been Britain's most popular box-office star in 1944 – this was risky. But whatever the cause of her anxiety, she was quite wrong to doubt it. The film, which won the Oscar for best original screenplay in 1946, was loved by the critics and public alike; as Muriel would put it in *Odd Woman Out*, 'with almost monotonous yet very comforting regularity, it broke every known record'.*

It had cost only £92,000 to make.

No wonder Arthur Rank now asked Sydney to take charge of production at Gainsborough Studios.

It was Noël Coward who – following their takeover at Gainsborough – described the Boxes as 'the Brontës of Shepherd's Bush'. But while this was both delightful and very neat, it was not entirely accurate. Betty Box, the member of the family for whom the Gainsborough years would prove to be most successful, worked not in Shepherd's Bush but at the studio's Islington outpost, where Sydney had appointed her the studio head.

This was a shrewd move. Rank had contracted him to make ten to twelve pictures a year, with budgets of between £150,000 and £200,000 apiece; Islington's output would need to comprise roughly a quarter of this total if he was to meet these obligations. He needed to be sure its stages were productive, and what better way of doing so than by putting his own sister in charge? At Verity, Betty had made over two hundred short films (her

* Queen Mary asked to have a private screening of *The Seventh Veil* – and she, for one, 'heartily approved' of Francesca's choice.

favourite of these, she liked to joke, was called: *How to Use Dried Egg Powder for a Tasty Meal*), and she had proved that she was hard working, tough, pragmatic and good with budgets. She was, it was generally agreed, the absolute mistress of the cheap special effect. Night-time shots being much improved by damp slates, which reflected the light, she had been known to call out the fire brigade to spray the roofs of buildings on her locations. The only member of the Gainsborough board to object to her appointment was Michael Balcon, who insisted that it smacked of nepotism. Betty, of course, didn't buy this for a minute. 'I believe that had I not been a woman, there would have been no objection at all,' she wrote in her memoir *Lifting the Lid*.

Overnight, then, Betty Box became Britain's leading female film producer – its *only* female producer – and at the age of just thirty-one. It was a giant leap, and the transition would have crushed a lesser woman. 'I quickly learnt what a very different world I was entering,' she wrote in *Lifting the Lid*. 'At Verity, I could say to the army, "I'll need three hundred private soldiers with their officers, a dozen tanks, a column of vehicles," and they were all delivered without any charge (providing, of course, they weren't otherwise occupied dealing with Mssrs Hitler and Mussolini). But now came big deals with stars, top technicians, composers, designers for huge sets and for film stars' clothes – a very much tougher proposition. All of them had high-powered agents whose livelihood depended on doing bigger and tougher deals for the people whose careers they guided.'

But while the personnel were more glamorous, the studio was straight out of the dark ages: 'It was a filthy place. Next door to a glue factory, which stank. Very dirty and grubby, and so antiquated it was unbelievable.' There were two stages, but they were built one on top of the other, with only a tiny lift to connect them. This arrangement necessitated careful planning. Only interiors could be shot upstairs; anything of any size had to be filmed

Betty at work

on the ground floor. Speed was also of the essence. Pictures had to be made in ten weeks at the outside; most were completed in just six. A set used for one film on a Friday often had to be revamped over the weekend so it could be used for a new movie on Monday morning.

Gainsborough's reputation was, famously, for melodrama. But Betty, who had an instinctive feeling for popular taste, now turned the studio's sights to comedy; of the dozen films she was to produce between 1947 and 1949, more than half were funnies. Post-war audiences needed cheering up, and she would be the person to do it. There was *Miranda*, the story of a man who captures a beautiful mermaid and takes her to see London disguised as an invalid in a wheelchair; there was *Marry Me*, about a newspaper reporter who goes undercover at a matchmaking service; most successful of all, there were the Huggets films – *Here Come the Huggets*, *Vote for Huggett*, and *The Huggetts Abroad* – which depict the quotidian adventures of a working-class family, and thus anticipate the television soap operas of the future.

What did Muriel make of Betty's new job? Mostly, she was

relieved that Sydney had someone reliable to share the workload. It was now becoming apparent to her that her husband was a workaholic. His weight was out of control – he had recently finished the first of what would be many stints in a weight-loss clinic – and his days were impossibly long; it was usual for him to rise at 5 a.m. to 'diddy up' a script before heading into the studio. But Betty's rise must have been galling nevertheless. Her sister-in-law now had her dream job, while Muriel remained a frustrated director. Sydney had put her in charge of script development at Shepherd's Bush, and while this was highly demanding – good screen writers were perilously thin on the ground, and yet the studio's wheels simply had to be kept turning – there was a sense that she was treading water. It's striking that while Muriel and Sydney collaborated on between thirty and forty pictures over this period, including writing several screenplays together, she mentions only half a dozen by name in her memoirs, and then only in passing.* Yes, Sydney was still determined to do the right thing by his wife, and in 1949 put her forward to direct *So Long at the Fair*, a thriller that he and Betty were co-producing, but its star, Jean Simmons, soon put a stop to that idea. 'Heigh ho,' wrote Muriel in her diary. 'I see a storming future ahead of this young lady . . .'

The Boxes were by now well on their way to being extremely wealthy. Betty and her husband Peter Rogers† were able to indulge their taste for fast cars with white leather seats and, in Betty's case, for couture clothes and fur coats. Muriel and Sydney owned a Rolls-Royce and a large property with extensive grounds

---

* She was excited to meet Somerset Maugham, whose stories Sydney turned into three successful films, but was disillusioned by the reality of the man, who resembled an 'inscrutable tortoise' and whose caustic wit on set provoked 'uneasy laughter'. Maugham, she noted, was so enamoured of himself in make-up – he 'introduced' the stories on screen – that he jokingly announced his intention of wearing it permanently.

† Rogers was Betty's second husband. She divorced her first, a mechanic, when he returned from the war a stranger. She then reverted to using her maiden name, as she would do for the rest of her days.

in Mill Hill, north London, called Mote End. They had several live-in staff, among them a housekeeper, a gardener and a chauffeur. Both couples ate at London's most fashionable restaurants – the White Tower, Les Ambassadeurs, Kettners, Mirabelle – and enjoyed holidays abroad. They were able to buy homes and businesses for their siblings. But what was the use of money, Muriel sometimes wondered, if they were too exhausted to be able to enjoy spending it?

In 1949 Arthur Rank announced that he was closing the outmoded studios at Shepherd's Bush and moving production to Pinewood in Buckinghamshire, a shift that would help stem the Rank Organisation's mounting losses. For Betty, who would work at Pinewood for the next two decades, this was 'total luxury'. But for Muriel and Sydney, the move brought mostly frustration. Michael Balcon refused to countenance the idea of Muriel directing a film she had written, based on *Romeo and Juliet*, and in the spring of 1950 every script written or promoted by the Boxes was turned down. One project, though, did get the green light from the board. *Cockpit*, a film Sydney produced at Gainsborough, had come with them to Pinewood, having not been thought fit for release. Rather than leave it on the shelf, however, Sydney decided to rewrite certain sections of the script – it was set in Germany after the war, and starred Dennis Price and Richard Attenborough – and have them reshot in the hope of recouping some of the cash that had already been invested in it. In effect, what he was talking about was a cut-and-paste job. This gave Muriel her chance: it was an impossible gig; no other director would want it. She was also familiar with the material and – perhaps it was this that swung things her way in the end – would not ask to be paid. Reluctantly, Balcon and his colleagues gave their consent.

Muriel reshot almost 60 per cent of *Cockpit*, which was renamed *The Lost People* on its release. She had to use all her ingenuity to make the new sequences and the old work together. On set, she kept a Moviola – a miniature projection machine usually used in the cutting room by an editor – with her at all times, the better that she could check the original footage for lighting, quality and continuity against the scenes she was about to shoot. The experience was, she said, akin to 'solving an intricate film jigsaw', and she knew 'it would never add up to much'. But she didn't care. 'Its importance to me was that it demonstrated to those who mattered that I had the ability to handle artists and dialogue as well as move my camera around.' For all that it had terrible reviews, and only just managed to recoup its costs, the film gave her confidence. Nothing could keep her from the director's chair now.

In 1950 Sydney left Rank and set up his own company, London Independent Producers; his intention was to make four or five pictures a year. The first of these was to be a low-budget adaptation of *The Happy Family*, a stage play about a grocery store that stands on the proposed site of the Festival of Britain – it is, like the more famous *Passport to Pimlico*, a comedy about a community under siege – and he handed it, quietly but very deliberately, to Muriel. At the casting stage, to avoid ruffling feathers, he told agents that he and his wife would be co-directing the film (the large cast included Stanley Holloway, George Cole and Dandy Nichols), but the moment shooting started he left her quite alone. Muriel was so nervous that when Maud Millar, a film gossip journalist, approached her on set in the first week and asked her what job she was doing on the picture, she could not bring herself to give an honest answer. In her diary she wrote warmly of her unit and her cast: they were, she said, 'full of fun'. But she also added: 'I only hope that Sydney sticks by me to the end. I couldn't do it without him being around – at least not this first one.'

For Muriel, *The Happy Family* changed everything. She finished it on time and on budget, and at the wrap party in the studio canteen Stanley Holloway led the cast in a chorus of 'For She's a Jolly

Muriel on the set of The Happy Family

Good Fellow'. It made a substantial profit and picked up good reviews both in Britain and America on its release in 1952. In future, British producers could have no objections to the idea of her as a director, or at least none they were willing to articulate to her face (though her agent would never be able to persuade an American studio to back her). She now moved swiftly on to her next project: *Street Corner*, a drama-documentary about women in the police force for which she and Sydney had also written the script (it was conceived as a female version of the 1950 Ealing Studios movie *The Blue Lamp*, which starred Jack Warner as Police Constable George Dixon and was the film that gave birth to the television series *Dixon of Dock Green*). This was a less happy experience than *The Happy Family*: the extras were 'terrible', location work was frequently interrupted by the digging up of roads and

Scotland Yard, which did not care for the film, kept trying to interfere. But she enjoyed the research: 'While examining the cell [at Marylebone police station] where Emmeline Pankhurst was imprisoned, I could not help wondering what that eminent suffragette would have said if she could have glimpsed the future and seen me, a woman-director, in the company of a female in the higher ranks of the police force, nattering away on the spot where she was forcibly fed. A sobering thought.'

The movies now came thick and fast. *Street Corner*, released in 1953, was followed by the short *A Prince for Cynthia*; 1954 brought the release of *The Beachcomber* and *To Dorothy a Son*; and they were followed by *Simon and Laura* (1955), *Eyewitness* (1956), *The Passionate Stranger* and *The Truth about Women* (both 1957), *This Other Eden* and *Subway in the Sky* (both 1959). Muriel did not have an entirely free hand when it came to the work that she did. Her budgets were small and schedules tight. She was lucky to have Sydney's backing, but even he needed to be sure a film would find favour with nervous distributors (and, ultimately, he produced only half of the films she made). Nor was she the most creative of directors. Her shots are prosaic, and her films want for pace and, sometimes, for emotional truth. *The Beachcomber* and *The Passionate Stranger* are second rate and predictable: the former, a plodding drama adapted from a story by Somerset Maugham starring Glynis Johns as a resourceful missionary; the latter, a silly confection about a romantic novelist whose chauffeur finds her latest story and assumes she is in love with him. *This Other Eden* is a feeble Irish comedy – hilarity does not ensue – and *Subway in the Sky* is a bog-standard thriller about a soldier who goes on the run when faced with a false murder charge.

But *Street Corner* was a ground-breaking film, with its mostly female cast, its clearly feminist point of view (the women officers are good at and absorbed by their work – an asset to their male colleagues, not an impediment) and its thoughtful examination of the pressures that might lead a young woman to commit a crime.* So, too, is *Simon and Laura* in which Kay Kendall and Peter Finch play married actors whose smug portrayal of a happy couple in a television soap opera is in stark contrast to the reality at home. At the box office, this was Muriel's biggest success, and it's easy to see why. The film is witty, charming and contains delightful performances. But it's also surprisingly modern, satirising television, the coming medium, quite deftly. Ian Carmichael is expertly twittish as the BBC wunderkind struggling to build an audience for his clever new idea – and to keep his stars under control. The suggestion that 'authenticity' boosts ratings (a technical disaster causes a punch-up in the studio to go out live, and the show's audience doubles) is strangely prescient. When the film was released in 1955 all the critics noted its 'feminine angle': Laura (Kendall) and the screenwriter of her show, Janet (Muriel Pavlow), are cool, confident and keen on their careers; Laura, it is clear, has been earning much more than Simon of late. Carmen Dillon was *Simon and Laura*'s production designer, and Julie Harris designed its costumes – Muriel liked to employ other women when she could† – and thanks to them it still looks fresh, especially compared to other movies of the era. (Dillon had already won an Oscar, in 1948, for her work on Olivier's *Hamlet*; Harris would win one in 1966, for designing the costumes for *Darling*, starring Julie Christie.)

And, just occasionally, she was able to pursue a personal project. *The Truth about Women*, her favourite of her films, owed its existence more or less entirely to her. A comedy 'with serious undertones' whose screenplay she had written herself (a man writes his romantic history that he might helpfully reveal some

---

* Women first joined the Metropolitan Police in 1919. In 1949 there were 235 women police officers in uniform and just twenty-one in CID. The separate women's police unit at the Met was not disbanded until the mid-Seventies.

† *Eyewitness*, for instance, was scripted by Janet Green, later the screenwriter of *Victim*.

universal 'truths' about the opposite sex), she saw it as an explicitly feminist film: 'Virginia Woolf's *A Room of One's Own* made
such an impact on me in my twenties that I had been possessed
ever since with a strong urge to support equality between the
sexes. Thus my approach to this subject was perhaps more
enthusiastic and dedicated than to any other theme previously
attempted. Unable to chain myself to the railings, at least I
could rattle the film chains.' The movie's conclusion – cynical,
and rather brave – is that men know nothing at all about
women. When it comes to 'truths', its Don Juan of a hero can
amass only blank pages.

The Truth about Women had a big budget (£183,000), an all-star cast
(Diane Cilento, Julie Harris, Laurence Harvey) and costumes
designed by Cecil Beaton. But British Lion, for whom it had been
made, disliked it once it was complete – their line was that it just
wasn't funny enough – and refused it both a West End run and a
press show. In public, Muriel continued to fight for it: she wrote
a furious letter to the company's managing director, urging him
to show a little faith in his own investment. But in private, this

experience left her feeling extremely low: 'I've lost heart about my future – no confidence in anything – no subject S suggests has the slightest interest for me,' she wrote in her diary. Even when the critics eventually lined up to praise it – they had paid for their seats themselves – her mood did not lift. She felt she had been badly treated, even lied to. Would a male director have been treated like this?

Muriel was addicted to her work; even as she was battling with British Lion, deflated and depressed, she had started on new projects (she was about to begin casting *Too Young to Love*, a mildly controversial film about a delinquent teenager that would be released in 1960). On those rare days when she wasn't working, she wondered what she was *for*.* But life as a director could not be said to have made her happy. In the course of shooting a picture she would lose at least a stone, and her diaries record in miserable detail the many ailments, psychosomatic or otherwise, that followed her from set to set: headaches, low moods, painful joints, exhaustion, various infections and fevers (though her libido, you notice, was quite unaffected: she and Sydney did not share a bedroom, but they had a busy sex life). In spite of all that she had achieved, a part of her still felt only tenuously connected to the movies. One summer evening in 1959, she thought about Sydney,† who still worked late most nights, and found herself wondering if he would die at his desk. She wrote in her diary: 'Me, I want different things from life, and always have done. I wouldn't

---

* She did work very hard. In addition to her directing, she was still writing: plays, novels, screenplays; her work rate is astounding. She was also required to do publicity for her films: unglamorous tours to provincial hotels with coin-operated gas fires in their bedrooms; appearances on local television and radio; interviews for the newspapers. On top of all of this, she was a keen Labour Party activist – Jennie Lee and Nye Bevan were friends – and a passionate gardener.
† Sydney's business affairs were increasingly vast. In addition to his movie production business and his writing, he had interests in television and a three-hundred-acre dairy farm. He was a mainstay of the newspapers, his latest moves always reported in the gossip columns.

care if I never directed another [film] if it was a choice between making the sort Betty and Ralph [Thomas, the director] produce, or Peter Rogers. Highly commercial and successful financially. I can't look back on one [of theirs] I would have cared a jot about directing. If S had offered them to me, I should have refused. I am a queer fish, and no doubt will remain so.'

Ah, yes. Betty. What had she been up to all the while?

Soon after she arrived at Pinewood in 1949, she met the director Ralph Thomas. The son of a commercial traveller from Hull, Thomas had begun his career in the movies as a clapperboy at the Sound City studios in Shepperton. After the war – he'd served with the 9th Lancers and won the Military Cross – he'd worked as the supervisor of Rank's trailer department, in which capacity he produced Betty's mermaid film *Miranda*. Sydney had been so impressed with this he'd promptly invited him to direct at Gainsborough. Thomas had duly made three comedies for the studio, winning a reputation for efficiency. It was thanks to this that he'd survived the move to Pinewood.

He and Betty first worked together on the film with which he made his name, *The Clouded Yellow*, a taut thriller by Janet Green. Betty took to him straight away; she recognised a kindred spirit. When the film got into financial trouble halfway through shooting and Rank refused to bail her out, she borrowed heavily against her own home, determined not to lose the stars she'd signed. But she didn't tell Ralph this was what she had done until the picture was finished, something for which he was profoundly grateful – and this sealed the deal. They were now a team. Their partnership would last for thirty years and thirty films. They suited one another: their pictures always ran on schedule and to budget; they were eager to please, sensible, flexible, unassuming in the sense that neither of them longed to make great art, and they had a feeling for what the public wanted. Their sets were famously happy. 'You looked forward to going in each morning,' Donald Sinden recalled. 'We were always encouraged to enjoy ourselves – I mean to find enjoyment in our work.'

Betty, Ralph, Joy and Peter

But their relationship wasn't only professional: Betty and Ralph were also lovers. No one knew this officially – and yet, everyone knew.* When they were away – Betty loved to shoot films in exotic locations, which meant that they were often abroad for weeks at a time – they were a couple; they took rooms next door to one another in hotels. When they were at home, however, they went back to their real lives. Ralph had a wife, Joy, and two children. Betty had Peter. (They were childless by choice. Norman Hudis, the *Carry On* screenwriter, once asked Betty what

* I have no proof of this relationship: no letter, no photograph. But every single one of my interviewees for this chapter mentioned it to me, unprompted.

she thought about having children. 'Oh, I can't be bothered,' she said.) It was all unspoken, polite, arranged, according to the custom of the day. The two families could socialise perfectly happily, splashing about in their Buckinghamshire swimming pools as if all was right with the world. And perhaps it was. Marriages, in a funny sort of way, were more pliable, more accommodating, then – and histrionics to be avoided. No one seemed unhappy. Joy was devoted to her home, which was beautiful and luxurious, and to her young family. Peter had his own films to produce – the *Carry On* series, which were directed by Ralph's brother Gerald – and his dogs, which plenty of people believed he loved better than any human being. (The actor Leslie Philips says that when his dog had puppies, Peter Rogers sent him a bouquet: 'I thought the flowers were for me, but they were for the dog. I don't know how Betty took that sort of thing.') Glasses clinked and the sunshine kissed the women's immaculate blonde up-dos and their sunglasses shaped like cats' eyes, and everyone smiled. Between them, these two couples made about a hundred movies, films that now read like an index of the varying fortunes of the British film industry from Churchill to Wilson, from Kenneth More to Roger Moore.*

Betty was undoubtedly a hit maker, but she really owed her nickname in the industry – Betty Box Office – to one movie. In 1952, at Cardiff station (she was in the city for a screening of her thriller, *Venetian Bird*), she picked up a comic novel by Richard Gordon about the misadventures of a group of medical students at a fictional hospital called St Swithin's. Reading it on the train to London, she laughed so hard her carriage emptied – or so she would later claim. At Paddington she promptly bought another six copies. This book, she had already decided, would make an excellent film. 'It wasn't an easy one to script,' she writes in *Lifting*

---

* Kenneth More, star of *Genevieve, Reach for the Sky* and Wendy Toye's hit *Raising a Riot*.

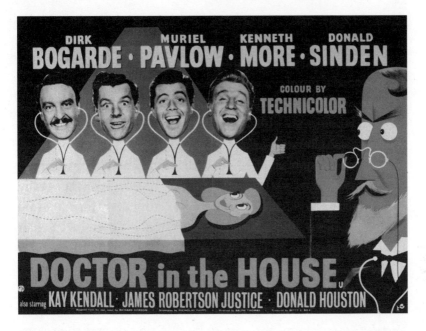

the Lid. 'It had no real storyline. It was mainly a string of anecdotes. Ralph and I worked with three writers before we licked it into shape.' The final screenplay was largely the work of an urbane old Etonian called Nicholas Phipps.

Betty fought for *Doctor in the House* all the way. The studio wasn't keen on the idea of a medical comedy – *jokes? About doctors?* – and it told her, over and over, to keep costs down. There was also strong opposition to her casting of Dirk Bogarde as Simon Starling; hitherto known mostly for playing spivs, according to her bosses Bogarde was not funny. When the film was complete, Rank's sales force wanted to call it 'Campus Capers', on the grounds that no previous film about hospitals had ever been successful. Betty thought this a dire idea: 'They produced a poster with four or five young, American-type students sitting on the grass under a blossoming tree, eating apples and studying anonymous-looking books. I seem to remember the girls even had ribbons in their hair. I almost vomited then and there.'

Previews usually had her throwing up with nerves, but not the one for *Doctor in the House*: 'From the first scene to the last, the audience was with us, and the laughter nonstop.' The reviews were fantastic. The film was profitable within six weeks; it was a hit in New York and in Australia. Kenneth More won a BAFTA for his performance as Richard Grimsdyke, perpetual student. '*What's good for them is good for you,*' ran a Guinness campaign of the day, featuring the film's stars (Bogarde, Kenneth More, Donald Sinden and Donald Houston) drinking pints. '*Guinness is as good as a Doctor in the House.*' Bogarde, a star at last, was thrilled: 'I honestly have never been so happy,' he wrote to Betty. 'Or felt more confident in my director and producer. My admiration for you both is colossal!' The following year, 1955, she and Ralph made a sequel, *Doctor at Sea* (escaping boredom as a GP, Dr Starling becomes the medical officer on a cargo ship, the SS *Lotus*). It was the third most popular movie of the year, after *The Dam Busters* and *White Christmas*.

Betty would grow increasingly reluctant to produce *Doctor* movies (there would be a further five, though Bogarde eventually bowed out, to be replaced by Leslie Philips); she didn't want to push her luck. But their astonishing success – even the later sequels made money – did give her and Ralph some room for manoeuvre. Among all the light comedies, the melodramas and the thrillers, you do find riskier Box/Thomas films: *Conspiracy of Hearts* (1960), a film about Italian nuns who rescue Jewish children, deals fairly explicitly with anti-Semitism; *No Love for Johnnie* (also 1960), about a Labour MP seduced by power, helped its star, Peter Finch to two awards for best actor, a BAFTA and a Silver Bear at the Berlin Film Festival.

Did Betty's instincts ever fail her? Only rarely. She chose to make *A Tale of Two Cities* (1958) in black and white rather than Technicolor, thinking that this would give it some arthouse

*Betty with Katharine Hepburn and Ralph Thomas during
filming of The Iron Petticoat*

cachet – a mistake, she felt afterwards.* The story goes that she
turned down the script of the first James Bond film, but she
always denied this: 'I didn't turn them down. I didn't want to
make them. I could have made two or three films of my own
choice while the Bond people were spending a year setting up and
a year shooting and finishing.' What really happened was this. In
1956 she was co-producing the Cold War comedy *The Iron Petticoat*
with Harry Saltzman. The film, which had a screenplay by Ben
Hecht, starred Katharine Hepburn and Bob Hope. Hepburn had
stipulated that she would do no interviews during shooting, but
the journalist Nancy Spain was a friend of Betty's, and as a favour
she arranged an interview for her alone. 'As a token of her appre-
ciation, Nancy sent me a proof copy of Ian Fleming's *Dr. No*. The
book lay on my desk when Harry Saltzman came to see me.

---

* Though not as bad a mistake as the fact that in the guillotine scene a man in a beret can
be seen riding a bicycle. Seeing this on the rushes, Betty made the decision that it would be
too expensive to reshoot the scene. 'I decided to take a chance. Dirk [Bogarde] and Marie
[Versini] were so good in the sequence – if anyone in the audience had eyes dry enough to
focus on the far right background, we had failed anyway, I figured.'

When he'd gone, the book had gone, too. He eventually made the film and started the series. I didn't want to do it.'

At Pinewood's restaurant every head would turn when Betty walked in. And in a room full of movie stars! She was immaculate in Dior and Courrèges and Balenciaga. Her jewellery jangled. Her honey blonde hair shone. There she would sit, surrounded by her coterie: Bogarde, More (until they fell out*), Phipps. She had, by all accounts, a tough exterior. Somebody in publicity once made the mistake of writing in a press release that Petula Clark would sing a 'little' song (this must have been in the film *Don't Ever Leave Me*, a 1949 Gainsborough comedy in which Clark played the teenage daughter of a Shakespearian actor who is kidnapped by an elderly crook). 'I never produce anything little,' said Betty, putting a line through it. Unlike Muriel, she was offered two multi-movie contracts by major American studios. But she was perfectly happy at Pinewood, playing Queen Bee.†

This is not to say she was grand. On set she made a point of mucking in. Shooting *Campbell's Kingdom* (1957) in Italy, she spent her evenings helping the crew to make poppies from orange and yellow crêpe paper so they could replicate a Canadian spring. (David O. Selznick, working on *A Farewell to Arms* in the next valley got to hear about these poppies and asked her if she would consider selling them to him for his picture.) On the same film, she would drive every morning through the deep snow to pick up the British newspapers for her crew, who couldn't live without them (a desperate race against Selznick's emissaries, sent out in search of the same booty, for the same reason). In India to shoot *The Wind*

---

* When More left his wife in 1968 for the actress Angela Douglas, who was twenty-six years his junior, he became estranged from his family and he was also ostracised by some in the industry – including, it seems, Betty. According to one source, this was because she had once made a pass at him, and he had turned her down.

† Though she loved her first trip to Hollywood. She stayed with David Niven, met Ida Lupino, then Hollywood's only woman director, and watched Cecil B. DeMille at work on *The Ten Commandments*.

Betty with Dirk Bogarde

Cannot Read (1958), she got the wardrobe department to build half
a dozen pockets into her poncho, the better that she could hide
small bottles of gin and whisky in them on India's dry days
(another way to keep the crew happy). When she was awarded the
OBE in 1958 her first instinct was to turn it down: 'I was paid hand-
somely for doing work I loved. Why should I be rewarded further?'
(In the end, she accepted it for her mother's sake.)

Like her brother, Betty never forgot her hardscrabble childhood; she liked being rich and felt no need to apologise for it:
'Goodies I'd never in my wildest dreams hoped to have were now
mine for the taking, and I seized them with both hands . . . I
already owned five fur coats, so I ordered a white mink, floor
length, and wore it with pleasure, even if it did make me look like
I was rolling along on casters – all five foot three inches of me.'

She never bought one of anything, even cars: she and Peter owned a Rolls-Royce and an Aston Martin – *each*. By the end of the Fifties, she and Peter were living at Drummers Yard, a grand house near Beaconsfield which they had bought from Dirk Bogarde. It stood in extensive grounds, and because part of it was a tower some of their furniture had to be specially made so it would stand against the curved walls. But as someone who truly adored her work she insisted that she would have been happy to work for less.

Though not, of course, for less than the men. When she discovered that in spite of all she had done for the company, her fees were still lower than those of Rank's male producers, she went to see its director, John Davis, a man as unpopular as he was parsimonious, and demanded that the figures be 'adjusted'. Davis blustered. 'What do you need the money for? Another mink coat? You have a rich husband – you don't need a rise.' But, somehow, she faced him down. By the time she removed herself from his office her request had been 'amicably granted'.

In 1959, Muriel's fears about her husband's health came true when Sydney suffered a cerebral haemorrhage. His doctors told him that he must give up work completely for a least a year and while he rested in Spain and the South of France – he handed the reins of his business to Peter Rogers – Muriel made only one picture: *The Piper's Tune*, for the Children's Film Foundation. She also wrote a novel, *The Big Switch*, a satire about what would happen if women ruled the world. It was eventually published in 1964.

Sydney made a surprise return to the industry in 1963 when he launched an unsuccessful bid to acquire British Lion films. He made his last movie – and Muriel's – in 1964: *Rattle of a Simple Man*, a second-rate comedy about a naive young man (played by Harry H. Corbett) who travels to London from Manchester for the FA Cup, where he unwittingly falls in love with a prostitute. Betty's film career continued a little longer but it too came to a halt in the end. Her last movie, directed by the stalwart Ralph, was the lamentable *Percy's Progress* in 1974. A sequel to *Percy*, it was a comedy — I use the word loosely — about the recipient of the world's first penis transplant.

The Boxes' time had passed. They were middle-aged people at a moment when middle-aged people suddenly seemed very old indeed — a trend that the movies, as ever, ruthlessly exaggerated. First there had come the films of the New Wave, muscular and bitter: *Room at the Top*, *The Loneliness of the Long Distance Runner*, *Look Back in Anger*. Then London had begun to swing, and the pictures with it: *Georgy Girl*, *Darling*, *Here We Go Round the Mulberry Bush*. In this context, even the best of the Boxes' films felt tattered. Their gentle comedies, their plucky, proud-to-be-British affairs about love and war, were relics to be put away, like antimacassars and the novels of Neville Shute.

Betty took this in her stride. She said she was retired, and she meant it. She wafted around in her kaftans and natty trouser suits, she embroidered exquisite cushions and she thought about all the good times. 'I cherished them,' she said. 'The opportunity I was given to show that a woman could do the job as well as any man.'

For Muriel, things were more difficult, at least at first.

On 30 October 1964 the telephone rang at Mote End, and though she somehow managed to stand at the hall table long enough to politely take a message she felt as though she was falling, that her head would hit the floor at moment. Sydney, she grasped in as long as it took to find a pencil, was having an affair. The flat in town he had been keeping as a writing den was in fact a love nest, shared with a woman called Sylvia Knowles.

Unable to sleep or to eat she left for a hotel, where she put herself under the care of her doctor. Half mad with grief, she began to think. This man she had loved so devotedly for so long: hadn't he always been disappearing to Brighton to hole up in a hotel while he rewrote his latest script? It was as if she had been blind, and now she could see.

For a time she rallied. She remembered his spoony notes, the frequent and lavish bouquets. (Sydney, perhaps because he had a guilty conscience, had the outward appearance of an exceptionally uxorious husband.) More soberingly, she considered the way her destiny seemed always to have been tied to his. But over dinner at Maxim's in Paris, where she and Sydney were seeing in 1965, it only took one cool question on her part and several martinis on his for it all to seep out, noxious as gas. As if he was merely talking her through a film budget or a casting list, her solid, loving, reliable Sydney now told her that he had never been faithful; that he had slept with any woman who had offered herself to him over the years; that he enjoyed and participated in 'every known kind of sexual perversion'. His sex life, he went on, was compensation for his 'gammy leg'. Living half the time with Sylvia had calmed things for the present. But if he felt the need he would, rest assured, soon 'indulge' again.

Reading Muriel's diary for this period is painful. Her terrible suffering (she was undone). His cruelty (he would not leave, but nor would he give Sylvia up). For Muriel, the humiliation of it all. The walking-dead separations. The eager, pathetic reunions. Her dignity in pieces, just like the collection of movie clips she'd had as a child.

Eventually they made an arrangement. Sydney would live with Sylvia and Muriel would be his new lover — and for a while, though she knew she had debased herself by agreeing to this, she had hope. At least she had something to look forward to, and perhaps an hour on a Saturday afternoon would eventually lead to a holiday.

But it could not last. In 1966 Sydney suffered a heart attack. Muriel was now reduced to hounding her husband and Sylvia from afar: with letters, phone calls and, on one occasion, a clandestine visit to their flat, made when she saw its front door standing ajar. In 1967, they escaped her by moving to Perth in Australia, and in 1969 Muriel and Sydney were finally divorced.

In 1992 Betty Box received the first UK Women in Film lifetime achievement award. She died of cancer at her home in Gerrard's Cross on 15 January 1999. Peter Rogers died on 19 April 2009.

After her divorce, Muriel Box, fully recovered and utterly sane once again, co-founded Femina, Britain's first feminist publishing house. She edited its first book, *The Trial of Marie Stopes*, herself. She now became an active campaigner for women's rights, working with her friend, Edith Summerskill, the Labour politician, to reform Britain's divorce laws. In 1970 she married Gerald Gardiner, the Lord Chancellor.

Sydney Box died in Australia on 25 May 1983.

Muriel Box died on 18 May 1991. In 2012 *To Dorothy a Son* was, unaccountably, released on DVD.

Digging for Victory

Jacquetta Hawkes, archaeologist

'Let me ... behave badly'

It was painfully obvious what the Blitz had done to urban Britain: rubble was all around; hundreds of thousands of people had been made homeless; houses needed to be built, and in vast numbers. But in time the destruction had other, more curious effects. The most badly affected cities seemed almost to have been turned inside out by the bombs (not for nothing did the French describe their own destroyed towns as *éventré*, or 'disembowelled'), with the result that their inhabitants could hardly help but consider the churned earth and what might lie beneath – and when archaeologists began digging at sites newly revealed by bomb damage or reconstruction work the response could be swift and hungry. In September 1954 W. F. Grimes, the director of the Museum of London, started excavating the site of the Roman Temple of Mithras in the City of London; it was a race against time, for the temple stones would soon have to make way for the new offices of Legal & General.*

* This site, in Walbrook Street, was initially thought to be a relatively unimportant villa. Shortly towards the end of a two-month period of excavation, however, exquisite carvings were found, including one of the head of a faintly smiling Mithras. Walbrook Street was close to Fleet Street, with the result that a photograph of the young god appeared in the *Sunday Times*, and the following day the row over its fate was heated enough for Churchill to order his minister of works, Sir David Eccles, to go straight to the City for a look-see. Grimes won an extension for the dig, and more finds followed. The remains were then rebuilt in a more convenient location close by. In January 2012, however, it was announced that the temple would shortly be returning to its original home, the better to make way for a new HQ for Bloomberg. W. G. Grimes, incidentally, was one of the team who excavated the ship burial at Sutton Hoo in 1939 – a race against time of a quite different order (see John Preston's marvellous 2007 novel, *The Dig*).

The excavation of the Temple of Mithras

During the two hours the site was open to the public every evening some eighty thousand people came for a look. There were moments when the crowd was so swollen the police had to be called in to control it.

This wasn't the first time the British had fallen in love with archaeology. In 1922 newspaper readers had feverishly followed the story of Howard Carter's discovery of the tomb of Tutankhamun, as told by H. V. Morton in the *Daily Express*. Now, though, their passion was to be more enduring. Exciting things would keep happening. In 1949 the process of radiocarbon dating was discovered. In 1953 it was revealed that the bone fragments long known as Piltdown Man, and supposedly of an early human, were in fact a hoax. In 1959 excavation began at Henry VIII's magnificent Nonsuch Palace in Surrey. And then there was the media. The BBC television game show *Animal, Vegetable, Mineral?*, in which distinguished academics competed to guess the origin and purpose of an artefact on loan from a British museum had made stars of Glyn Daniel, its presenter (later Disney Professor of Archaeology at Cambridge University), and Mortimer Wheeler,* a regular panellist (Wheeler was a professor at the Institute of Archaeology at the University of London, whose major excavations included Roman Verulamium and the Iron Age hill fort at Maiden Castle, Dorset). In 1954, Wheeler was named Television Personality of the Year; twelve months later, Daniel succeeded him. Also popular were the series *Buried Treasure* and a Home Service documentary programme, *The Archaeologist*. According to David Attenborough, who began his career as an assistant producer on *Animal, Vegetable, Mineral?*, the BBC's output caused a sudden rush to the dusty and hitherto ignored archaeology sections of Britain's libraries. 'It was a sensation,' he recalled in a speech to the Personal Histories Project at Cambridge University in 2009. 'Librarians around the country wrote to us at the BBC, and said the shelves on which archaeological books had sat for decades untouched, were suddenly empty. Archaeology became a huge success. Archaeology became a matter of interest to anybody with any intellectual curiosity at all.'

But it was a woman who led the pack. In 1951 the poet and archaeologist Jacquetta Hawkes published *A Land*, a slim volume

* Mortimer Wheeler – Rik to his friends – was one of the great popularisers of archaeology. His excavations in 1926 at Caerleon in Wales were, for instance, sponsored by the *Daily Mail* in exchange for the exclusive right to cover the dig. His 1955 memoir *Still Digging*, which had for its cover a drawing of Wheeler in which he looks remarkably like the actor Terry Thomas, was a surprise best seller. An unstoppable womaniser, he also had a crazy private life. Wheeler was married three times: first to the archaeologist Tessa Verney, then to Mavis de Vere Cole and, finally, to Margaret Norfolk. Mavis de Vere Cole, a mistress of Wheeler's friend Augustus John, was the second wife of the notorious prankster Horace de Vere Cole who was, for a time, in the frame for the Piltdown hoax. In the Fifties, having long since divorced Wheeler, Mavis achieved a strange kind of fame of her own when, in a jealous rage, she shot her lover Anthony Vivian in the abdomen – a *crime passionnel* for which she served a six-month prison sentence. Mortimer Wheeler died in 1976 at the age of eighty-five. His biography, written by Jacquetta Hawkes, was published in 1982.

with illustrations by Henry Moore. On the surface of it, the book's prospects should have been dim. Ardent and strange, *A Land* is a literary peculiarity. Part archaeology, part geology, part memoir, it tells the story of Britain from the moment the 'white-hot young Earth' dropped into its place 'like a fly into an unseen four-dimensional cobweb' to the present day, with daring recourse to both science and culture. It is patriotic and romantic and crammed with arcane information. Why did Queen Victoria favour granite? Where will you find Dudley locusts? What is the connection between ammonites and fifteenth-century knights?* But it also hums with something akin to what we would call New Age-ism. Hawkes's affinity with the ancient past is so intensely felt you would not be surprised to turn the page and find her taking part in some half-baked Druidical rite.

---

* Answers: 1. 'The Queen loved granite because she hated change; at her express wish nineteen varieties representing the principal Aberdeen granites were used to ornament the pulpit at Balmoral.' 2. Wenlock Edge, in Shropshire: 'So common and so conspicuous are the fossil trilobites in some parts of the Wenlock limestone that they have won the local name of Dudley locusts.' 3. Both were protected from extinction by a kind of shell – for a time.

Nevertheless, it struck a chord. The critics, almost without exception, adored it. 'Mrs Hawkes is that rare and necessary combination,' wrote Cyril Connolly in the *Sunday Times*. 'A reverent scientific aesthete.' In the *Observer*, Harold Nicolson described the book as 'an enchantment'. Hawkes, he wrote, was trying to arouse in her readers 'the child-like wonder that we experience when we see our own house from a long way off . . . there is a weird beauty in this prophetic book . . . [it was] written in a passion of love and hate'. It was a *Daily Mail* Book of the Month and the recipient of a special prize from the *Sunday Times*. Readers loved it, too. It sold madly well, quickly running into several editions, and in 1959 its popularity was acknowledged with its appearance as a Pelican paperback: yours for only 3/6 pence. Its author, meanwhile, rapidly became an intellectual celebrity. She, too, began appearing on *Animal, Vegetable, Mineral?*

What few people realised at the time was that *A Land* was forged *in extremis*. Its author was out of love with her husband and passionately in love with one of Britain's most famous and beloved (not to mention married) writers. Her book, meanwhile, was dedicated to the memory of a third man, a lover who had died suddenly in 1946, leaving Hawkes with 'an all-consuming sense of loss'. *A Land* can be read as precisely what it purports to be: a book about Britain and the influence its land forms had on its civilisation. But it may be understood, too, as an expression of longing. Jacquetta Hawkes, outwardly at least, was a rather starchy figure: thin-lipped, stern-eyed, with a voice that even by the standards of the day sounded strained and formal. (One afternoon in the British Library Sound Archive I listened to several recordings of Hawkes; she made Celia Johnson sound like Olive from *On the Buses*.) Yet she begins *A Land* with a wild, almost sexual description of herself lying, late at night, on a meagre patch of grass in the garden of her Primrose Hill home. 'Exposed'

in this 'open box or tray', she likes to feel the hard ground press-
ing against her bones; it makes her 'agreeably conscious' of her
body. 'In bed I can sleep,' she writes. 'Here I can rest awake.' The
image that is evoked, though this seems to have passed by her
reviewers (they were, needless to say, all men) is of a woman on
the run from a certain kind of domesticity. Like the cats that
rustle in the creeper on the garden wall, she is temperamentally
unsuited to the myopic quiet of the carpeted hall, the lino-
floored kitchen. No wonder, then, that at the sounds of the
night – a barge on the Regent's Park Canal, a train pulling out of
Euston Station – her ears prick. She pictures the huge city
around her, and all the people in it. Some of them are asleep,
'stretched horizontally a few feet above the ground'; others,
more excitingly, are in transit, 'moved about the map by
unknown forces'. As metaphors go, this is hardly subtle. Hawkes
had written a book about the past, but it was the future that was
pulling at her heart.

Jacquetta Hawkes was born in 1910, in Cambridge, the youngest
of three children. Her mother, Jessie, had trained as a nurse; her
father, Frederick Gowland Hopkins, was a biochemist who in
1929 was awarded a Nobel Prize for the discovery of vitamins,
along with Christian Eijkman. It was a formal, self-disciplined,
undemonstrative but mostly happy household. The family villa,
commissioned by her father in easy walking distance of his lab-
oratory, was distinctly grand (it was approached via a gravel
drive that curved round a semi-circular lawn), and the family
income sufficient that her mother could employ a cook, parlour
maid and nanny. Jacquetta's childhood was 'steeped in sweet-
ness and light with no awareness of harsher ways'. Her parents
were liberal agnostics who believed in the education of women,
and in women's rights in general. When Jacquetta was four her
nanny took her to see the smouldering beams of a house that

Jacquetta the tomboy

had been set alight by suffragettes. Tiny as she was, she assumed, not unnaturally, that such women must be monsters. Why else would they commit such a horrifying crime? But when a suffragette march was held in Cambridge her mother – surely she would go to prison for this! – pinned a large rosette to her lapel and headed out to join it. The Gowland household is missing from the 1911 census, of which the suffragettes famously organised a boycott: 'If women don't count, neither shall they be counted.'

Jacquetta was a tree-climbing tomboy who detested dolls – on one occasion she deliberately smashed a large blue-eyed china doll on her mother's rockery – and preferred to play with her bow and arrow. It was a point of pride, too, that she never appeared to be a wimp in front of her brother, who was eight years her senior; aged about five or six, she would make herself endure mild pain, and set about conquering her fears of mice, bats, earwigs, spiders and the dark (the last she mastered by walking a little further down the garden every night). Later on, at the Perse School for Girls, she would periodically refuse to wear uniform or take part in organised games. She also founded a Trespasser's Society: members were awarded points for daring to enter illegally 'gardens, college properties, farms with ferocious farmers and estates with outstandingly fierce gamekeepers'.

She knew she wanted to be an archaeologist from an 'absurdly tender age'. In the garden, a large hydrangea stood proxy for a prehistoric cave, and she would draw bison and mammoth on the walls beside it. The family home had been built where a Roman road lay beneath an Anglo-Saxon cemetery, and at the Cambridge Museum of Archaeology and Anthropology she saw an amber necklace that had been unearthed near one of its gateposts. She longed to find some similar artefact herself – perhaps something as extraordinary as the Grunty Fen armilla, which dated from 1000 BC and the golden curls of which had sprung up as though by magic through the covering peat – but having been denied permission to embark on her very own dig, resolved to slip out into the garden at night, in secret. 'I took a torch and my garden trowel and laboured greatly in the middle of the lawn to remove about one square foot of turf in many fragments,' she recalled. It would, she imagined, be easier the deeper she went. But, to her chagrin, she was wrong about this: 'I drove the trowel downwards again; it came up with only a dessert-spoonful of dull earth. Every time a bicycle went by, usually with a bobbing and wobbling front light, I put out my torch and squatted over the hole. My right palm was beginning to blister, and I seemed to have been at work for hours. I stood up to survey my excavation by torchlight. The sides sloped inward, meeting at a point about eighteen inches below the surface. It was no good.'

In 1929 Jacquetta began studying for an archaeological degree at

Cambridge.* She was a diligent student – she had her father's powers of concentration – but also, by her own account, an extremely innocent one. Her first two 'proposals' came from men who shared her interest in ornithology: 'My "bird-watching" became something of a joke among my Newnham friends.' This inexperience led her into 'serious involvement long before I was ready for it'. During her second year, needing some practical knowledge of excavation, she was dispatched to Camulodunum, the Celtic site at present-day Colchester, where the work was being directed by a young man called Christopher Hawkes. At just twenty-seven he was the leading authority on Celtic Britain. He was also, in spite of his diminutive stature and horn-rimmed spectacles, in possession of a dashing and slightly intimidating rep-utation as an 'ardent and successful charmer of women'.

Jacquetta expected to be invisible to him. His girlfriends up in London – she had heard the gossip – sounded so sophisticated and glamorous. How could she compete, especially in her work-ing clothes? But before the digging season was out he had declared his love for her. 'Of their very nature archaeological digs produce a fine tilth for love affairs,' she wrote years later. 'And Camulodunum was no exception. I soon found that I could have a choice of suitors, but Christopher Hawkes could not fail to eclipse the rest.' Did she love him? She thought she did (though it worried her that she found their physical relationship – so far unconsummated – unexciting). Her lover seemed so worldly, with his flat in London and his friends who moved, like his family, just on the edges of what was known as 'society'. He was so . . .

* In 1929 women could study for the tripos but would not receive a degree after taking it; they did not become full members of the university until 1948. Jacquetta was a member of Newnham College, whose principal was Pernel Strachey, aka the Streak. Strachey was the older sister of Lytton, and surprisingly conservative for someone associated with the Bloomsbury Group. For instance, women students who attended the theatre were allowed to do so only in the company of a fellow student, and were required to sit in the dress circle. She did, however, permit members of the boat club to wear shorts on the river.

impressive. It isn't clear at what point Hawkes proposed to Jacquetta, but in 1932, when she set off on a travel scholarship to join a dig on Mount Carmel in what was then Palestine she took a framed photograph of him with her, the better to try and work out whether she should marry him on her return.*

By the spring of 1933 they were engaged, Jacquetta having accepted Christopher's proposal during a visit to Grime's Graves, a Neolithic flint mine in Norfolk. This should have been a happy time, but she began to have doubts almost immediately. First, there was the discovery that, in spite of his reputation, Christopher was a virgin ('absurdly immature though I was, I remember a feeling of betrayal'). Then there was Christopher's mother, who had taken against her, disliking her for her cleverness, her shyness and her lack of sophistication. The class-obsessed Mrs Hawkes was horrified to learn that Jacquetta had not 'come out'. 'She will be no use to you,' she is supposed to have said to Christopher. 'She doesn't wear gloves.' In a note she urged her son to tell Jacquetta to use make-up.

Finally, there was the wedding itself, over which Jacquetta

---

* The director of this dig was the great Dorothy Garrod, who in 1939 would be elected Disney Professor of Archaeology at Cambridge, thus becoming the first woman to hold a Chair at Cambridge or Oxford. She made a huge impression on Jacquetta, who remembered her like this: 'Small (5ft 2in), composed and neat beside her fellahin workers – girls in bright ballooning skirts and a few lusty pick-men – her command of them was absolute. When a builder tried to cheat her, she overwhelmed him, thumping the table, her normally calm eyes glaring. In the cool peace of the evening after a good dinner there were a few classical records to be played or she might take up her flute. Her talk (low-pitched) was sometimes witty, always congenial.' Garrod spent seven tough seasons at Mount Carmel (1929–34), the most important of her career. Her finds enabled her to establish a sequence of some six hundred thousand years of human activity in the region. Hawkes's experiences in the 1932 season were also formative. A Neanderthal skeleton was unearthed – the first to be discovered outside Europe. 'I was conscious of this vanished being and myself as part of an unbroken stream of consciousness, as two atoms in the inexorable process to which we all belonged,' she said. It was on Mount Carmel, too, that she 'took full possession of a love and confidence that have not yet forsaken me'. Watching a camel train in the moonlight, she was filled with a sudden comprehension of the beauty of the physical world. This was an intensely spiritual experience, but it was also deeply erotic – 'I had the heightened sensibility of one in love' – and, as such, the beginning of a restlessness that would endure for the next two decades.

Jacquetta and Dorothy Garrod on donkeys in Palestine

seemed to have no control whatsoever. Christopher, a high
Anglican, was determined they would marry in church, but she
felt, having not even been baptised, that this would be wrong and
for a time had tried to resist. In the end, though, she surrendered. 'There was a day at Winchester College [his alma mater]
when he marched me, weeping, round and round the cloisters
until I surrendered and agreed to be wed in my father's college
chapel.'* After this her future mother-in-law, perhaps realising
that Jacquetta's parents weren't at all up to organising a *proper*
wedding, 'assumed a masterful command'. Her satin gown
would be made by Elspeth Fox-Pitt, who had designed the costumes for H. K. Aycliff's controversial jazz-age production of the
The Taming of the Shrew in 1928, and her bridesmaids' dresses – all six

---

* Frederick Gowland Hopkins was a fellow of Trinity College.

of them – by Motley.* There would be champagne, and a great number of guests. Meanwhile, Jacquetta and Christopher made, rather more quietly, their own preparations for what would come after the ceremony. She was fitted with a 'birth control device' and had her hymen stretched. He turned gratefully to a booklet given to him by a kind but obviously rather beady female friend – a guide to what would be expected of him in bed. Through all of this, Jacquetta hung on to her self-respect by working on her first scholarly article.† But only just. Work had to be squeezed in between writing letters to people she barely knew, thanking them for their mostly unwelcome wedding presents. At home her unease must have been obvious; her mother asked several times if she really wanted to marry Christopher. Jacquetta, though, was reluctant to speak her mind. Christopher had made two previous proposals. The first was turned down; the second was accepted, only for the girl in question to tell him soon afterwards that he must place a notice in *The Times* announcing that the engagement was off. Jacquetta was unwilling to inflict on him a third humiliation.

'I recall a sense of bewildered incredulity as I went up the chapel on my father's arm,' Jacquetta wrote afterwards. 'I saw through my veil that Christopher was wearing spats.' The reception was crowded – A. E. Housman was supposed to have been among the guests, though if he was, she never saw him – and she 'floated through it all, lost in unreality'. In the wedding photographs she looks doubtful, animated by duty rather than excitement. Thanks to her heels she stood a touch taller than her

---

* Motley were John Gielgud's designers during the Thirties. One of their number, Sarah Harris, was the first wife of George Devine, who would go on to run the Royal Court Theatre, where he staged one of the most important cultural events of the Fifties: the first production of John Osborne's *Look Back In Anger*.
† 'Aspects of the Neolithic and Chalcolithic periods in Western Europe'. It was published in the journal *Antiquity* six months later, in March 1934.

husband that day, a fact that would make his body language seem all the more poignant in years to come. It is quite painful to see. He looks at her, fond and obviously proud;* she looks slightly shifty, as if already contemplating her escape. After the wedding breakfast, they changed – in separate rooms – before leaving for their honeymoon in Majorca from Cambridge station. When Jacquetta leant out of the train window, and said to her husband's best man, a Count Orloff, that she wished he were coming with them, it wasn't the champagne speaking. She meant it.

According to Jacquetta, the honeymoon was not a disaster. But neither was it a roaring success. Christopher's request that the hotel replace their twin beds with a double – 'the small hotel was shaken by the tramping and banging of the removal and installation' – turned out to be a hostage to fortune, and they did not, it seems, make the most expressive use of its cool expanses. As she put it in her 1980 memoir-cum-novel, *A Quest of Love*: 'While I came nowhere near to passion, it would not be just to say that I proved frigid or altogether indifferent. I wanted to please my husband and even gained some little pleasure in the attempt. Of course this was not enough, and had I truly loved and desired him, he might well have discovered himself as a better and more joyous lover. As it was we enjoyed the sun, the bathing and visiting antiquities – and were not unhappy.' One day, needing to be alone, Jacquetta disappeared for several hours. It was an absence neither one of them referred to again following her return.

The couple made their home in a flat near Paddington Station. Christopher was working at the British Museum and Jacquetta planned to continue her own work: she was writing a book about the archaeology of Jersey, which would be published in 1937, the

---

* Christopher sang 'lustily' throughout the wedding service. Afterwards his stiff wing collar was signed by all those close to him. 'He really needed a trophy [bride],' his son Nicolas told me. 'Before that word was invented. There had to be some fine woman who would be a suitable partner for Christopher Hawkes.'

The wedding: Trinity College, Cambridge

same year that she was elected a Fellow of the Society of Antiquaries by some extremely distinguished peers. She was expected to entertain – and be entertained – but it wasn't difficult to find time in which to write; her new husband was a workaholic. When he wasn't at the museum he was closeted in his study. Often he would work through the night. In 1934 he had a breakdown – the result, his doctor said, of overwork rather than 'any inherent nervous disability' – and a month of enforced rest followed. For Jacquetta, this must have been alarming. She had only just married him, and now he was crumpling in front of her very eyes.

In 1937 Jacquetta gave birth to a son, Nicolas, and soon after the family moved to Fitzroy Road in Primrose Hill. Relations with her mother-in-law were no better – things were so bad, in fact, that Christopher wrote an angry letter to the other Mrs Hawkes, warning her that if she failed to moderate her language she would cause 'serious and irreparable harm' and might never come to know her grandson – but the move north marked the start of a new chapter. It was in this house that Jacquetta's social life would begin to spark, and it was here, too, that she would write *A Land*. Though her marriage was moribund – every year it became 'more lifeless and stultifying'; she and Christopher were, she thought, now growing 'positively unhappy' – her confidence was growing. In 1939, for instance, she travelled alone to County Waterford, Ireland, for the excavation of a Megalithic tomb of which she was in sole charge (Nicolas was left with his Irish nanny, Kathleen O'Toole). It was a tough summer. The hotel was awful and crammed with priests, who disapproved of the study of pre-history almost as much as they disapproved of a married woman being so far from home. She was, she told her friend Diana Collins, rather lonely. But was she tempted to give it all up? No. As it had been during her engagement, work was a distraction and a balm.

She and Christopher were quite clear about the fact that war

Jacquetta in Ireland

was coming – he had been involved in the operation to move items from the collections of the British Museum to the safety of Aldwych station – and in September, just a few days after her return to London, it was duly declared. On Primrose Hill trees were felled and a gun emplacement erected. In 1940, driven by the threat of a German invasion, Jacquetta and Nicolas left London for the relative safety of rural Dorset, where they stayed with family friends, the Pinneys, at their manor house. The thought was that Nicolas would enjoy playing with the Pinney children, and that life away from the city would be a good deal less hairy. In fact, their new situation proved to be tumultuous: even Nicolas, then just three years old, sensed something was amiss. In Dorset Jacquetta, experiencing 'a sudden undamming of feelings of an intensity I did not know I possessed', fell violently in love with Betty Pinney.

What did this relationship involve? It depends who you believe. According to Jacquetta, her emotions, though fierce, were platonic, 'romantic and ideal' (she would later describe herself as an 'adolescent longing to be able to rescue my lady from some dragon or other'); it was the lean and aristocratic-looking Betty – I'm told that she resembled Maudie Littlehampton, the cartoon character created by Osbert Lancaster – who wanted a physical relationship, and on the one occasion she tried to persuade Jacquetta to sleep with her, Jacquetta at once 'retreated'. Other reports have it the opposite way round. But whatever the truth of the matter, at some point in the summer of 1940 Jacquetta was in such a state over the relationship that she threw herself from a first-floor window. The ambulance that was called took many hours to arrive: thanks to the threat of invasion all the local signposts had been dismantled, the better to foil any German visitors. Lucky, then, that she was not badly hurt.*

The strange thing was that even in the throes of this passion Jacquetta felt 'a curious apartness, being always conscious of the absurdity of my condition', and it was, she believed, this sense of her own ridiculousness that eventually sent her back to London and to Christopher, with whom she would remain throughout the Blitz, the only time in her life she 'had to experience and resist extreme physical fear' (Christopher had been seconded to the Ministry of Aircraft Production; Nicolas and his nanny were sent to his maternal grandparents in Cambridge). Primrose Hill was bombed regularly, the planes aiming at the gun emplacement at one side, and the railway line out of Euston Station at the other.

---

* Nicolas Hawkes believes his mother's jump was attention-seeking rather than a serious attempt to commit suicide. Over the years Jacquetta was to brood on the matter of her sexuality. In *A Quest of Love*, she wrote: 'I do not think it was timidity that confined it to emotion. My body was only mildly interested, if at all. From that time, I have loved men, but still, on meeting other women, I can feel that instinctive message, the tremor of a nerve just penetrating consciousness, that triggers a true Sapphic presence.'

It also fell victim to some of the earliest doodlebugs; one landed close to the Hawkes's home, breaking windows in many of the houses in their street. But while all this was frightening, such adrenalin-fuelled privations also had a useful side-effect: although she and Betty continued to write to each other for many years, the Blitz put paid to any true backward glances.

In the city again, Jacquetta became a civil servant, first in the Ministry for Post-War Reconstruction and later in the Ministry of Education, where she was editor-in-chief of the film unit. She also embarked on a couple of 'experiments' – her word for minor affairs ('I remember that I first became an adulteress to the sound of Mozart'). Then, in 1942, her college friend Peggy Lamert, who was working at the publisher Chatto, introduced her to Walter J. Turner, an Australian poet and one-time friend of Ottoline Morrell (their friendship ended after he caricatured her in his 1927 book, *The Aesthetes*). Turner, two decades her senior, was a notorious (and married) womaniser, hugely intelligent, passionate, unconventional and uninterested in any of the usual proprieties – and Jacquetta swiftly became 'wholly infatuated' with him. It was a devotion that came on like sudden illness. Meeting him unexpectedly at an exhibition one day, she promptly fainted.

Their affair lasted for four desperately exciting years. But in 1946 Turner died suddenly of a brain haemorrhage. He was just sixty-three. Jacquetta was distraught – unable, once again, to hide her emotions behind her usually gelid exterior. Both her son and her husband found themselves in the uncomfortable position of having to console her for her loss. 'Poor mummy,' said Nicolas, touching her arm.* Christopher, who had recently been appointed Professor of European Archaeology at Oxford, even wrote her a letter of condolence (he knew about the affair, clearly). 'My darling,' it reads. 'I

---

* Jacquetta was a conscientious mother, but not a warmly affectionate one. She once said she had no instinct for motherhood.

do feel your grief for Walter's death inexpressibly much and do assure you of my very deepest sympathy. It is a dreadful shock and sorrow and loss to you which I know is irreparable. Loneliness I feel sure is what you feel worst, and a sense of being cut off from vitality and happiness.'

Just as before, it was work that pulled Jacquetta through. Throughout her relationship with Turner she had written reams of poetry, and she now prepared the best of this for publication: *Symbols and Speculations* would be published in 1949. Meanwhile, there was also her day job. In 1943 she had been made principal and secretary of the UK National Commission for UNESCO, and preparations for the first meeting of this new organisation, which would take place in 1947 in Mexico City, were now under way.

It had fallen to Sir John Maud, the most senior civil servant at the Ministry of Education, to assemble the British delegation. He had selected J. B. Priestley, the novelist, playwright and broadcaster, to represent the world of the arts: a sensible, if somewhat unexciting, decision. Priestley was hugely famous, his greatest plays already written and widely revered: at the start of the war, he had broadcast to a rapt nation every Sunday night (until, that is, Churchill – or someone – stopped him).* But Jacquetta disagreed. Still under the influence of Turner and his circle, who fancied themselves rather more avant-garde than Priestley, she thought him too lightweight, too popularist, too downmarket.

Maud, though, would not be moved and Jacquetta slunk back to her office to begin a correspondence with Priestley. Soon after this the delegation gathered for a reception at an office in

---

* These broadcasts, *Postscripts*, which ran from June to October 1940, were sometimes funny and sometimes serious. The more serious of them reminded the public what had happened to soldiers after the first war, when they returned to unemployment and poverty. As a result a critical minority, led by the MP Brendan Bracken, demanded that they be stopped on political grounds. The BBC did drop him, though letters from the public were running 300:1 in his favour – possibly on the orders of Churchill.

Belgrave Square. It was here that the two of them met for the first time, Jacquetta handing the playwright some kind of comedy pink pudding (you imagine her raising her eyebrows ironically as it wobbled on a plate). This first encounter was swiftly followed by another, at a UNESCO meeting in Paris for which Priestley was allocated two assistants, Jacquetta, and her friend Helen de Mouilpied, who also worked at the Ministry of Information. On this trip Priestley operated a divide and rule policy. First there was dinner with Helen, during which he quizzed her about Jacquetta, with whom he was clearly taken. (As her answers came back, he is said to have to exclaimed: 'What a woman! Ice without and fire within.') Then there was dinner with Jacquetta, in whom he confided his worries about his daughter Mary (she would shortly be hospitalised having suffered a complete nervous breakdown). Did he also tell Jacquetta that his marriage was as unhappy as her own?* Perhaps. But more likely he simply took stock. A long voyage to Mexico loomed – and according to his biographer Vincent Brome, whenever Priestley travelled by sea it was his habit to select a woman to sleep with en route. A little bit of advance planning would not have gone amiss.

The *Queen Mary* left Southampton for New York in November 1947. Priestley's plans, however, were immediately thwarted: Jacquetta, a terrible sailor, spent the entire voyage confined to her cabin. Installed in the Hotel Maria Cristina in Mexico City, moreover, she fell ill again, this time with gastroenteritis (the entire delegation had gone down with it, thanks to the hotel's dire plumbing). This time, Priestley was not to be put off. He went up to her room bearing a medicinal bottle of brandy, a visit which left her feeling grateful and cared for; and when she recovered he

---

* Priestley was at this time married to Jane Wyndham-Lewis, his second wife and the mother of three of his five children. His first wife, Pat Tempest, had died of cancer in 1925, leaving him with two daughters to bring up. Priestley also had a stepdaughter from Jane's first marriage, to D. B. Wyndham-Lewis. He had been unfaithful to Jane on many occasions.

took her out for dinner over the course of which – the high alti-
tude and martinis having gone straight to her head – Jacquetta
told him she didn't think much of his work. Priestley was hurt,
particularly when it became clear how little of his writing she'd
actually read. But perhaps her words came as a challenge too, for
it was as they walked back to the hotel that their affair began.

The conference lasted six weeks. Their clandestine relationship
seems to have thrilled them both – 'Now, in my late thirties, I was
to discover the pleasures and spiritual transformations of total
love,' wrote Jacquetta, 'I seemed to be created anew' – but they
also told themselves it could go no further. Priestley had to leave
for New York before the conference closed, and they agreed that
once he had gone there would be no communication between
them. They would quietly return to their own lives.

How easily promises fall from the lips! Priestley's archive is kept
in an inhospitable windowless basement at the University of
Bradford, his home town, and there you can read the first of the
many love letters he wrote to Jacquetta. This one was written on
a train, on hotel writing paper, his wobbly script even less deci-
pherable than usual, and it begins: 'My darling, I know I shouldn't
be doing this – it's against everything I meant or even said – but
I can't help it. I must write one letter to you . . . to try and relieve
myself of this terrible weight of sadness and loss . . . Missing and
missing and missing you. I'll get over the worst of it soon, I suppose, but just now I feel older and emptier and sadder than I ever
remember feeling before.' He had, he told her, 'feasted on beauty
and strangeness and comradeship and fun', and now it was time
to pay the bill. Would she write to him care of his hotel in New
York? That would be wonderful. Because back in England con-
tacting him would be fraught with danger: all his post went
through his secretaries.

Jacquetta was thrilled to receive his letter – my impression is that
she had taken him at his word when he told her the relationship

would go no further – and wandered through Mexico City in a happy daze, looking for a post office that she might put him out of his misery by sending a telegram. Priestley responded to her missive swiftly with another love letter, an ecstatic note in which he attempted to pin all that he adored about Jacquetta to the page: her wiry body, her strong legs, her 'non-feminine gallantry'. He pictures the two of them as a couple of 'chaps', a Trojan and a Greek sentry meeting and finding, perhaps reluctantly, 'much value' in each other. Already he is telling her that he loves her.

But Priestley, when he turned his mind to it, could be quite the pig. In his third letter, he complains that her last reply was cool and cagey and, having been thus provoked, informs her that their relationship must pass two tests. The second of these will be the return home, with all its complications. And the first? The fact that he has so many other temptations: 'Ordeal by glamour girls – it has already passed here, for while beautiful young actresses look at me with such adoring eyes, I think of you.' This is a funny kind of a compliment. No woman could fail to notice the note of warning in it – nor the horrible inference that Jacquetta is past the bloom of youth. (At the time of their meeting, Jacquetta was thirty-seven and Priestley fifty-three.)

Back in England, however, the relationship prospered in spite of both their circumstances, and Priestley's boorish moods. Over the course of the next six years they would meet whenever and wherever they could – Priestley's marital home was a grand house on the Isle of Wight, but he also kept a flat at Albany, Piccadilly – enjoying sex 'indoors and out, by day and by night, in borrowed offices and flats, in the box of a provincial theatre or the garden of the Institute of Archaeology' (these are Jacquetta's words, not Priestley's). It's difficult to picture, this snatched love-making: you think of the times, of Priestley's fame, of their relative ages and of their respective personalities, and you wonder that they dared. But for Jacquetta, at least, this new relationship had a strong element of compulsion and she surrendered to it completely, with a certain amount of flamboyance and not a little pride.

And Priestley? He was more conflicted. His letters to his wife, for a while at least, grew suddenly fonder – a guilty conscience, one assumes. 'Unlike you,' he told Jacquetta early on, 'I don't want to be in love.' He convinced himself that he'd been ambushed in Mexico, though how consciously Jacquetta had done this, he could not tell.

They were, you see, so completely different. Priestley, the son of a Bradford schoolmaster, had left school at sixteen to become a clerk in a local wool firm; he did not attend Cambridge until after the First World War, which he had spent in the trenches watching other men of his background die. His first instinct, always, was to put any criticism Jacquetta made of him down to her social class; she was, he feared, an intellectual snob, a hide-bound elitist for whom the things most people liked (detective novels, say*) were infra dig. She was blunt and he was thin-skinned, with the result that some of his early letters to her are appallingly snitty. Even their strong physical connection seemed to have been wrought from difference. As he put it in a note of 1948, 'It is odd how everything is reversed for us. I, the easy sensualist regard you most unsensually, except when immediately excited by you; whereas you find love for me in your body, but little or none, alas, in your mind.' Look at a photograph of them together – Jacquetta, queenly and elegant, the possessor of a singular 'folded-in handsomeness'; Priestley, stout and balding and froggy, the very image of a well-to-do northern alderman – and you understand that Priestley used the word 'odd' for a reason.

We know a lot about what Priestley thought of his lover. He is always describing her 'mannish walk', her 'exquisite long eyes',

* Jacquetta had apparently ticked off Priestley for reading too many detective stories.

her 'donnishness', her 'witchcraft', her 'astringent talk', the way their connection seems to take place 'below the conscious level'. He refers to her, more than once, as looking like a 'high priestess from some strange race'. We know, too, that for the first years of their affair he was careful to manage her expectations; he is always telling her not to expect a letter, or warning her that he will be too busy to see her. He was also apt to moan, seemingly unworried that he might bore her with the details of his domestic arrangements. He mithered about his weight ('my contours'), and in a letter of 1952 he notes that his Teasmade is broken. But what did Jacquetta feel? This is more difficult. Only one of her letters to him survives, Priestley having been determined to conceal the relationship, the better that he might lead a double life. It's clear that she was eager to see him; also, that the sexual side of things was fulfilling. On the other hand, having given Priestley the impression in Mexico that she was inclined to take what he called 'a rather tough detached masculine line' with regard to their affair it was painful to find him taking her so much at her word, treating her almost as if she were 'another man'.

There were rifts – at least one of them serious. Some time in 1948 Jacquetta's attention was caught by a young woman across a crowded restaurant. According to Priestley, her physical attraction to the girl in question was plain to see and it sent him into a tailspin, for he was nothing if not priggish. (Jacquetta had clearly told him all about Betty Pinney; my sense is that his resentment was born of disapproval as much as jealousy.) In a letter he wrote: 'I felt you had moved clean away from me, unconsciously resented the surrender of the few days before, and so were swinging over to that attitude you had known some years before.' Witnessing 'this queer little scene' had, he insisted, left him exhausted and depressed, and he needed to be left alone for 'some weeks' to brood. In a later letter – written after they had finally met – he blames his continuing inability to work on this encounter and wonders whether it wouldn't be better for both of them if they stopped seeing one another.

Their relationship was spiky, prone to ebb and flow. But if these 'mysterious surges of antagonism' got Jacquetta down, she rarely showed it. By 1950 Priestley's home life was painful and difficult. Jane now knew he had another woman, and the thought of his continuing infidelity often drove her to her bed; Priestley, in turn, had trouble controlling his temper. Jacquetta's home life, by contrast, was smooth and replete with interest. Christopher was away in Oxford much of the time; in London, where she was determined to remain, Jacquetta was free to work and to entertain (Nicolas was sent to boarding school in 1951). Work was as important to her as ever. Her son remembers being told by his mother, at around this time, that her income after tax was only just enough to cover the cost of domestic help: 'She was clearly telling me that she went to work because she wanted to.'

In 1949 she was appointed adviser to the Festival of Britain – she masterminded the display *Origins of the People*, for which she helped to create painstakingly accurate dioramas of Iron Age settlements – and in 1950 she became a governor of the British Film Institute.* As a result, her circle widened. Among her new friends were Laurie Lee, Henry Moore, Cecil Day-Lewis and Jack Pritchard (the furniture manufacturer whose company Isokon produced the Penguin Donkey, a dinky modern bookshelf designed for his friend Allen Lane, the Penguin publisher). Mortimer Wheeler was also on the scene, trying desperately to chase her into bed. The parties she threw could be boisterous; poor Christopher, assuming he was in town, was usually to be found hiding in the kitchen.

The following year was a turning point. In June 1951 Laurie Lee, who had written the captions for Jacquetta's dioramas of early

---

* It was also the year she visited Robert Graves at his home in Deià, Majorca, where they discussed Goddess Theory.

Jacquetta, smoking a cheroot, on the beach at Deià with Robert Graves

man, wrote to say that her new book had 'pride of place' in the Lion and the Unicorn, the Festival of Britain pavilion celebrating Englishness, and that it was 'well-thumbed already'. Lee called *A Land* 'a book to hold and to have', and he wasn't the only one to feel its unlikely power. The letters poured in from a public who seemingly couldn't get enough of it. By August the first edition had sold out; in libraries the wait to borrow a copy was six months. 'We thought at first we couldn't afford a guinea,' wrote a Mrs Cecily Hadley of Swanage. 'But after reading another chapter or two, my husband said: it ought to be two guineas.' Freya Stark wrote, comparing Jacquetta to Proust. Vita Sackville West sent a letter begging her to come to stay at Sissinghurst.*

The usual line when it comes to Priestley's decision to separate from Jane – their divorce was granted in July 1952 – is that it was

---

* Jacquetta did indeed visit Sissinghurst, on at least two occasions. Nigel Nicolson, Vita's son, always insisted that there was nothing between his mother and Jacquetta but writerly admiration. Maybe so. Nevertheless, I believe that there was an attraction. A note from Vita to Jacquetta of 1959 includes the following: 'I well remember our brief encounter in the Rope Walk [at Albany, where Vita's husband Harold kept a set]. You were running both physically and mentally, and you were wearing a most becoming Russian-looking fur hat. So you see.' The clue is in the last three words.

mostly her doing: she had finally had enough; their children were grown up; she had met the man who was to become her third husband. And this is certainly the impression Priestley liked to give. He worried about his reputation, about attacks from the 'cheaper' Tory press. If he and Jane had to part, he favoured a legal separation. 'I do not particularly want a divorce myself,' he told one confidant. 'And in some ways would find it more convenient (and safer) to be officially married.' But it seems to me that he had another, more vital reason for letting Jane go: Jacquetta's success. His lover was now a star in her own right, and with a legion of male admirers.* She might, if he was not careful, drift away. Adding to his anxiety was the sense that his own powers were beginning to wane. As a first step he asked Jacquetta to collaborate on a play, *Dragon's Mouth*; this would allow them to spend legitimate time together. Its reception having been somewhat chillier† than that of *A Land*, however, he then contrived to make himself wholly available to her.

How did Jacquetta respond? With verve. In 1952 matrimonial law was silly and archaic. There were four main grounds for divorce: adultery, cruelty, desertion and incurable insanity. Where the first of these was the reputed cause, it was usual for the man to assume the official role of adulterer, and for him to hire a 'professional co-respondent', book a hotel room and ensure that a private detective was there to see the couple enter and leave it.

---

* At least one man was passionately in love with her: the writer Edward Hyams, whose history of farming, *Soil and Civilisation*, was published in 1952. In the Jacquetta Hawkes archive at the University of Bradford there is a long letter from Hyams, written when he finally realised the relationship was hopeless. In it, he tells her that he is prepared to suffer a great deal of pain on her account – anything than be cut off from her completely. 'To be with you, see you, hear you is exquisite pleasure . . . The choice is between being very much alive and in pain, and half dead.'

† *Dragon's Mouth* was a dramatic quartet – each of them wrote two voices – inspired by Jung, about whom Priestley was quite dotty. The four characters represent Jung's four functions of sensation, intellect, intuition and emotion. It is rarely, if at all, performed today – and with good reason.

Jacquetta, ever proud, thought this dishonest and hypocritical. She would, she told Priestley, go with him herself to Paris. Why they chose Paris rather than, say, Bournemouth is not entirely clear. Yes, Priestley would be less likely to be recognised there. But in Paris the mood was altogether less conducive to procuring the necessary legal evidence. The hotel's manager refused to provide Priestley's detective with any information he could use in court on the grounds that the 'English monsieur' should be allowed to take his pleasure where and with whomsoever he pleased. In the end, 'a sort of retired police inspector' was found in Exeter, where the divorce proceedings were to be heard, and it was his statement that was read to the court.

The farce did not end here. Priestley had been invited to Japan to give a series of lectures, and Jacquetta now decided to accompany him. She had so far said nothing to Christopher about a divorce, but perhaps she didn't need to: the trip would last from September until shortly before Christmas. It is impossible to see this as anything other than a declaration of intent. Christopher turned to his father, a lawyer. Divorce, Fifties-style, was complicated by the fact that the law said that if a husband or wife was found to have condoned or colluded with the behaviour of a partner to obtain a divorce it would be refused. What effect, Christopher wanted to know, would Jacquetta's trip have in the event of their separating? His father advised him to ask Priestley to set out in a letter his motives for taking Jacquetta with him as a precaution against Christopher ever being accused of collusion. Priestley duly did so, citing their theatrical collaboration and work for UNESCO.

Three months later Jacquetta returned home bearing extravagant gifts for her long-suffering husband. But it was no good. If she had intended to go on as before – I suspect she rather liked what she called her 'half-and-half arrangement' – the reality of a family Christmas soon put paid to that idea. On Boxing Day she asked Christopher for a divorce. He took this more calmly than she had expected, perhaps because he had done his grieving while she was away. But she wept, and so did Nicolas: 'She called me into their bedroom. There were twin beds: Grandma Hawkes's idea, I think. The curtains were drawn. It was the middle of January. I can't remember the preamble. She said: "Your father and I are going to separate and I will marry Jack Priestley." I wept buckets. "I'll always love daddy as a father," I said.' To Nicolas, Priestley was just someone who'd come to the house a couple of times; he was remembered for playing the piano. Looking back, though, he had known something was amiss with his father. On Boxing Day evening the family had gone to party, where his father danced 'dashingly' with a good-looking young woman in a beautiful brown dress. 'He didn't look very happy about it, but he was very determined.' Jacquetta had looked on, silently.

Was Priestley delighted to have bagged his prize? Not exactly. In letters from this period he is cruelly equivocal, banging on about his latest health kick – a regime of cold baths, which were supposed miraculously to shrink him – and worrying about the consequences of this second separation: 'I certainly don't want people to get the impression that I was responsible for breaking up a happy home.' His advice is rather chilling in the circumstances: divorce, he tells her, would be the best path, even if he were not around. It is as if he cannot bear to take responsibility for his part in the proceedings. Then again, he was also telling his stepdaughter Angela that he would soon be free to marry Jacquetta. (Not that Angela, or any of his children, had met his lover.) He wanted Jacquetta, it seems, but feared, metaphorically speaking, the sight of her baggage cluttering up his hall.

And that letter of Priestley's to Christopher was now to spring up and bite the playwright on his not inconsiderable backside.

Jacquetta's divorce came to court on 5 June, a date which, being so soon after the Coronation, Priestley fervently hoped would pass unnoticed by the newspapers. But, alas, the headlines were all his. The divorce was to be petitioned on the grounds of Jacquetta's 'misconduct' with Priestley while in Japan; on the advice once again of his father Christopher made full and unexpected use of the letter he had extracted from Priestley the previous autumn. Its contents were duly revealed, but minus the reason for its existence. As a result the judge read it as evidence only of its author's duplicity: Priestley, a writer of fiction, had indulged in a 'deliberate and cunning attempt to deceive Professor Hawkes', and his conduct was 'mean and contemptible'.

Priestley was horrified. So was Jacquetta, who despised the judge for his attempt to 'stir up beastliness in a case where all those concerned were entirely free from it' (there is no record of what she thought of Christopher's ignoble role in this affair, though he came to regret it deeply). And the heat of it – a prickly blend of embarrassment and indignation – must surely still have been upon them when, a month later, they married at Caxton Hall, Westminster.* It certainly was in the eyes of the press; as they emerged from the registrar's office they were greeted by the flashbulbs of some thirty photographers. But perhaps this episode drew them together, too, for thereafter you sense something closing down – in Jacquetta, at least. She was happy. She loved her new husband. But there was now a placatory spirit abroad. The 'sudden antagonisms' of old would be replaced with a careful public smoothness. 'Let me have the guts to behave badly,' she had written to a friend shortly before she

---

* An appropriate place for Jacquetta to marry. The Women's Social and Political Union used to hold a 'women's parliament' at Caxton Hall at the beginning of each parliamentary session before marching to the real thing, where they would attempt to hand a petition to the prime minister.

Jacquetta and J. B. Priestley marry. Thirty photographers awaited them outside

asked Christopher for a divorce. She would not need such guts again for almost three decades.

After their marriage Jacquetta went to live at Brooke Hill, Priestley's house on the Isle of Wight. It was fabulously grand, the entrance hall alone large enough to accommodate the small orchestras Priestley liked occasionally to hire, and she took to life there – cossetted, formal, lavish – with gracious ease. The day was oiled by Priestley's loyal staff Gertrude and Miss Puddock, and one always dressed for dinner; guests were sent off for hot baths and told to return at the cocktail hour, which Priestley would host in a velvet jacket (he mixed an 'exhilarating' martini). Her new husband's income was such that she was now free to indulge her passion for clothes. She adored his collection of art, which included work by Sickert, Derain, William Nicholson and Utrillo, and added to it with buys of her own; in her bedroom at Albany there was a Turner and a Gwen John nude (she and Priestley kept separate bedrooms, believing that this was better for 'sleeping and sex'). Was part of Priestley's attraction that he was rich? Perhaps. She certainly enjoyed his money. 'She wasn't vulgar about it,' says Nicolas Hawkes. 'But they were in agreement that people who were creative who did well were perfectly entitled to live well. What they believed in [politically] was that the rewards of life should be spread to all people. Denying themselves wouldn't have helped anyone else.'

She continued to work, of course. In 1954 she published *Man on Earth*, a follow-up to *A Land*, and in 1955 she and Priestley co-authored *Journey Down a Rainbow*, an account of their travels in the south-western states of America. She also scripted a film, *Figures in a Landscape*, a celebration of Barbara Hepworth* that had its premiere at the 1954 Venice Film Festival. Thereafter, her output continued to be prodigious. There were two novels, a biography of Mortimer Wheeler, several more archaeology books and a collection of fables; she was also the archaeological correspondent of the *Observer*; co-editor of the prehistory volume of a vast UNESCO project, *The History of Mankind*; and author of *The Shell Guide to Archaeology* (this her last publication, in 1986). But she never repeated the success of *A Land*. Jacquetta had, for the time being, lost her taste for risk, in her work as in her life. The feelings she had poured into *A Land* were in abeyance and it was important to keep them that way. What had been instinctive now seemed daring – perilously so. As she later noted, 'at no earlier time [in

---

* Jacquetta's script, a hypnotic prose poem, was narrated by Cecil Day-Lewis, and the effect is mesmeric. The making of the film, however, was not a happy experience, not least because it coincided with the death of Hepworth's eldest son, Paul, in an aeroplane crash. Hepworth and Jacquetta, cut from the same cloth, should have been friends, or at least allies, but this was not to be. Jacquetta found the artist needy and difficult, while Hepworth worried that the film would be 'overcrowded' with words. For more on Hepworth and the Fifties, see the Introduction.

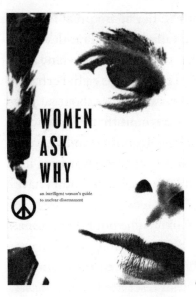

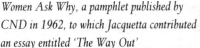

Women Ask Why, a pamphlet published by CND in 1962, to which Jacquetta contributed an essay entitled 'The Way Out'

history] would it have been thinkable for a middle-class English woman to have lived this story without social ostracism and submergence'. She and Priestley rarely mentioned the past, and after their marriage lost touch with many of their old friends.* Most people continued to think of her as cool, daunting, a touch haughty: a man's woman, who did not suffer fools. The 'fire within' was no more visible than before.

Much of her energy she now put into political causes. In 1958 she and Priestley played an active part in founding the Campaign for Nuclear Disarmament. She was a regular Aldermaston marcher, helpfully visible to newspaper photographers by dint of her height and large red hat. Later, she organised CND's Women's

---

* It's possible to put a different spin on this, as Tom Priestley does: 'After the divorce they got rid of a lot of the old friends. I remember Ralph Richardson saying, "Why don't I see your father any more?" This is a slightly delicate thing, but I think that Jacquetta felt that she owned my father, that he was hers and hers only, and it was difficult for her to accept that he'd had a whole other life ... I can also tell you that [my sister] Rachel felt that Jacquetta interfered with the relationship with her father.' The children, according to Tom, were 'put on a rota' in terms of visiting.

Committee (other members included Iris Murdoch, Peggy Ashcroft and Dorothy Hodgkin). At rallies she was a highly effective speaker; women were known to immediately hand over watches and jewellery to be sold to raise money for the cause. In the same year, she and Priestley also became founding trustees of the Albany Trust, a charity established to complement the campaigning work of the Homosexual Law Reform Society.*

In 1959, she and Priestley left the Isle of Wight for Alveston, near Stratford-upon-Avon. Gertrude and Miss Puddock, and even the gardener, Hales, came with them. Their new home, Kissing Tree House, was just as splendid as Brooke Hill: there was a tennis court, and glasshouses to keep the house supplied with fruit and fresh flowers; the lawn was so big the local cricket team were known to use it. It was a good deal more convenient for London. They settled into a routine, writing in the mornings and afternoons, with a break for a proper lunch and a walk for Priestley; dinner followed by the evening news. At weekends there were house parties. Priestley was now the proud owner of a study with a secret door behind which was stowed a sink, a refrigerator and a variety of bottles.

And so life went on.

Then, in 1980, when she was seventy and Priestley was eighty-six, Jacquetta did something extraordinary. She published *A Quest of Love*. She called this book a novel, but it isn't really. Yes, it has a heroine of sorts: a reincarnated Everywoman figure who looks back on her sexual awakening in her various lives, from the court of the Minoans at Knossos to the England of Queen

---

* In 1954 there were 1069 men in prison for homosexuality. In the same year the Conservative government set up a Departmental Committee to investigate British sex laws. The result of their work was published three years later as the Wolfenden Report. John Wolfenden's fifteen-strong committee included three women. It says quite a lot about Fifties mores that, for their sake, he suggested everyone use the terms 'Huntleys' and 'Palmers' (after the biscuit manufacturers): Huntleys for homosexuals and Palmers for prostitutes. Sadly for everyone involved, the law was not changed until 1967.

Victoria. In this respect, it is rather *Orlando*-like. Except that this lusty heroine seems also to be – or at least to sound like – the book's author and her story, which has come to her in a series of dreams and which she refers to as the memories of her 'Long Body', is bookended by two slices of confessional autobiography in which Jacquetta reveals the failure of her sex life with Christopher, the affair with Betty and the details of her early encounters with the nation's most famous living playwright. (She also tells us, a propos nothing, that she did not masturbate as a teenager.) The result is bizarre and quite terrible, as though Mary Renault had suddenly come over all Anaïs Nin.

From start to finish, no one knew what to make of it. D. J. Enright, Jacquetta's editor at Chatto, begged her to make the book less explicit (someone told me that he asked her not to use the word 'cunt' so often, though I have not been able to verify this). She refused. When it came out – as part of the publicity campaign, Snowdon photographed the Priestleys for *Vogue* – readers were baffled and horrified in almost equal measure. Even her most devoted friend, Diana Collins, was somewhat nonplussed. 'I think that her keyword is imagination,' she wrote in her own memoir, trying to make the best of an embarrassing job. As for her family, only Priestley was (albeit tacitly) supportive. Nicolas never really forgave her for writing the book; Christopher Hawkes, though happily remarried, was still alive and it caused him some pain.* 'The general feeling was: why did she feel it necessary to say all that?' Tom Priestley told me. 'For someone who seemed very controlled, it was an aberration. She had to get it out ... but she didn't have to publish it.'

So why did she? I'm not sure. It's easy to see *A Quest of Love* as a form of attention-seeking by a woman who fears her power is

---

* He did not find out about the book for several years. 'When he did, it was quite tricky,' says his son.

Jacquetta and Priestley at Kissing Tree House

diminishing and is determined not be forgotten, or not completely ('I am an old woman now,' it begins. 'I had better admit
that both to myself and to all those other women who I hope will
listen to me.') But something else is going on too. Read it closely,
and *A Quest of Love* – so feverish and insistent, so embarrassingly
sincere – suggests what might have been had its author dared to
remain outside the establishment, had she not tamped down her
emotions so definitively. Look, she is saying, this is what I'm capable of when I let myself go. I don't dispute that Jacquetta loved
Priestley deeply, that they were perfectly contented most of the
time. But he was a place of safety too, and the home they built
together a kind of gilded cage. There is regret among this book's
pages, as well as late-life ardour. 'One must forgive oneself,' she
writes, carefully omitting to say for what.*

J. B. Priestley died in 1984, a month before his ninetieth birthday.
Jacquetta was holding his hand. Outside his bedroom, owls were
hooting. A memorial service was held at Westminster Abbey.

Jacquetta, who had grown into a somewhat difficult old woman,
died in a Cheltenham hospital in 1996, at the age of eighty-six. The
obituaries remembered her as 'compulsively honest', 'demanding'
and 'imperious', though for many of those reading them she was
already forgotten, her once glittering career always superseded by
that of her more famous husband. There are those, such as Michael

---

* In *A Quest of Love*, Jacquetta writes of two states of being: 'absence from oneself', which is akin
to being invisible, and its opposite, *'participation mystique'*, in which 'the other flows into oneself and becomes extraordinarily concentrated'. The latter enables one to empathise not only
with strangers, but with animals and birds too. It was something she experienced often as a
child and young woman, but hardly at all in the years thereafter. Whatever its cause, this was
a blunting of the senses and clearly the source of some regret. It's interesting, too, to read her
contradictory responses to feminism. She derides Women's Liberation for its extremism in
one breath, and in the next makes the case for a woman's right to have a career now that
'childbearing is largely voluntary and the social and religious tyrannies devised and imposed
by men have been exposed for what they were'. Like many women of her age and class, she
worried that feminism was unfeminine.

Shanks of Stanford University, who believe that the archaeological establishment moved explicitly against her, scandalised by her private life and disapproving of her sensuous, discipline-muddling engagement with the past (archaeology went through a severe period of scientism in the Sixties and Seventies). But though I'm not entirely convinced by this argument – I believe it was her marriage that marginalised her, not the academy – it's certainly the case that *A Land* was out of print, and had been for years.

Happily, though, you can't keep a good book down. People talk of the New Nature Writing, by which they mean (best-selling, award-winning) authors such as Richard Mabey, Roger Deakin and Mark Cocker, whose responses to landscape are singular, personal, lyrical, unsentimental and, sometimes, indignant. But it's only 'new' because memories are so short – and I'm not the only one to think so. In 2012 *A Land* was reprinted in a handsome new edition with a foreword by Robert Macfarlane, the poster boy for the literary outdoors. Macfarlane describes Jacquetta as 'a missing link in the literature of nature and landscape', and *A Land* variously as a 'geological prose-poem', 'a Cretaceous cosmi-comedy' and a 'lusty pagan lullaby'. It is, he adds, 'flamboyant enough that I can imagine it re-performed as a rock opera'. He's wrong about the rock opera; *A Land* is more Benjamin Britten than Ray Davies. But he's right about everything else.

She is a missing link, too, in the world of what we have learned to call 'heritage' – a connection, perhaps, between the neo-Romanticism of the Thirties,* which insisted that the 'modern' need not be at war with the past, and the mob-cap-and-tearoom culture of the National Trust today (though she would, I think, have despised the latter; as she once said, 'every generation gets the

---

* Among its leading lights were Paul Nash, Graham Sutherland and the garden designer Christopher Tunnard. For more, see Alexandra Harris's excellent book, *Romantic Moderns*. Jacquetta admired Nash and Sutherland, and owned works by both.

Stonehenge it deserves – and desires'). Her 1943 film, *The Beginning of History*, made while she was at the Ministry of Education and starring a specially commissioned reconstruction of an Iron Age site at Pinewood Studios, is one of the earliest instances, if not the earliest, of a historian using the medium to illustrate to the public how people used to live – to explain us to ourselves. Such things, of course, have since become commonplace.

And once you know about her, you see her everywhere.

In 2012 the Blagdon Estate, home of Viscount Ridley, and the Banks Group, a land development company, unveiled a huge piece of land art they had commissioned in Cramlington, Northumberland. Designed by Charles Jencks, it is called *Northumberlandia* and was built using the by-products of open-cast mining. At 112 feet high and 1300 feet long, it is the largest representation of the female body anywhere in the world.

When this unlikely public park first opened – a hillside nude on whose breast any visitor may idly stand – I gazed at the newspaper photographs and felt amazed. The work of twenty-first-century bulldozers, the sculpture's vast curves speak of Picasso and Matisse. But she looks over her shoulder, too, embracing in her form, in her swirling paths and her generous mounds, our brooding hill forts and our hunkered long barrows, our exquisite chalk drawings and our bounteous ancient goddesses. My mind was full of Jacquetta then, and I wondered, What would she have made of this?

Sometimes I think she would have adored it. I imagine her marching right to the top of *Northumberlandia*'s nose, the better to contemplate her majestic proportions. But then the doubts creep in and I know that she would have loathed it, this ersatz monument-cum-camouflage job.

I see her at the breakfast table, crossly folding her copy of *The Times*. Her lips are a narrow line, pressed tight with distaste. The air is heavy with her husband's pipe-smoke and, just possibly, with thoughts of a wild new book.

All Rise

Rose Heilbron, QC

'I am serious about my career. But that does not mean I shall give up dancing . . .'

On the night of 16 May 1956 there were eight people on board the *Windmill*, a forty-foot wooden houseboat moored at East Creek in South Benfleet, Canvey Island. In one room, sleeping on a pair of bunks pushed tight together, was forty-seven-year-old Grace Richardson, her daughter Ann, seventeen, her two-year-old granddaughter Beryl and Colin and Reggie, the two-year-old twin sons of her neighbour Violet 'Vicky' Clark. In a second were Grace's own sons: thirteen-year-old John and sixteen-year-old Charlie. Finally, crammed into the boat's kitchen-cum-living room, was thirty-five-year-old Vicky.

Vicky had been living with Grace since 17 April, when Reg Wright, the man she called her husband, had died suddenly. She had told Grace that she could not face remaining on her own houseboat, the *Buchra*, until she had redecorated, and Grace had invited her to stay. It was only one more soul, after all. But then, overnight, the situation changed. On 14 May the *Buchra* had gone up in flames and Vicky had found herself homeless.

Two nights later, Grace and her children woke up to find their own houseboat on fire, the flames coming at them 'like a wall' from the direction of the kitchen. There was no time to think. Ann acted first, pushing Beryl through the bedroom window – this was the only way out – and on to the mud outside. Then she looked around. Chaos, and in the middle of it was Vicky, a basket of clothes over her arm. On top of the basket was her handbag. She swayed a little, but she didn't move. By now, Charles and John had climbed out of the window too, and Ann quickly followed them. Grace shouted at her, 'I'll throw the babies after you.' Her mother duly tried to pick up one of the twins, but it was no good. According to Ann, Vicky had a foot on the boy, making him impossible to move. When she came to life a moment later, Vicky didn't attempt to help Grace. Rather, she began to push her basket through the window and then clambered after it.

Grace was the last person to leave the boat alive. On the towpath she saw Vicky on her knees; she was looking for her handbag. Her friend seemed preternaturally calm. Only when the police arrived did she become hysterical and attempt to return to the burning vessel; PC Ronald Wall and three others had to restrain her. A Mr Reeves, who lived on another houseboat, heard her saying, 'My babies, my babies. Save my babies.' But no one could. The fire had taken over. By dawn the boat, coal-black and half collapsed, resembled nothing so much as a vast crow's nest, fallen from a mammoth tree. The charred bodies of the twins were discovered soon afterwards by a fireman. It was said that when they were found they were holding hands.

Though barely thirty miles from London, Canvey Island is a strangely remote place. It has the feeling of being cut off, and all the more so in 1956. Everyone knew everyone else, and after the fire on the *Windmill* the briny Essex air was soon thick with rumour. Each week brought fresh developments, reported in full in the *Canvey News & Benfleet Recorder*, which had never known a story like it. By the time of the twins' funeral on 24 May, the police had already interviewed more than a hundred people. By early June they had decided to exhume the body of Reginald Wright, Vicky's common-law husband. In mid-June, a voluminous report was ready for the Director of Public Prosecutions. It was, the paper informed its readers, eight inches thick and a hundred thousand words long: 'HOUSEBOAT POSER NEAR END', promised the front-page splash. Up in London the nationals got in on the act, one of them even managing to secure an interview with Vicky Clark herself. She denied any involvement in either one of the house-boat fires.

On 26 June the police made two arrests. It isn't known how Grace Richardson responded to the arrival of officers outside the hostel where she was staying, but Vicky Clark remained 'perfectly composed' as the constables led her out of the building where she was billeted, even taking the time to wave to someone inside. At Southend police station, both women were charged with murder, a move that did nothing whatsoever to calm the mood on Canvey Island over the next few days. When the women were brought back from Holloway Prison for a hearing at the beginning of July, people queued from six o'clock in the morning for a seat in the courtroom. Outside, the crowd was so febrile – the *Recorder* reported that it was one thousand strong – the police had to appeal for calm via a loudspeaker. Meanwhile the local spivs

Vicky Clark

were out in force, selling houseboat 'remains' for half a crown a piece.

The trial began at the Old Bailey on 29 October and lasted for two weeks. The prosecution alleged that the two women had been in cahoots, Clark having persuaded Richardson to order a gallon of paraffin and help her burn down the *Windmill*; with the twins gone her lover, Bill Smith, would agree to take her with him when he emigrated to Australia. Grace's prize was to be rather more prosaic: with the *Windmill* destroyed, she would be free to move to a better houseboat, the *Intruder*. But since the prosecution's star witnesses were Grace Richardson's son Charlie and her daughter Ann, it was perhaps predictable that the case against her soon collapsed, and on 7 November she was sensationally freed by the judge. After this there seemed to be little hope for Vicky Clark, as she seemed to realise; in the dock she often had to be passed a bottle of smelling salts. The evidence of Ann Richardson, dressed in an emerald green coat, lasted for more than five hours and pointed strongly to Clark's guilt. First of all there was her account of events on the night of 16 May. 'She could have saved her babies if she'd let the clothes go,' Ann told the court. Then there were the conversations she claimed to have overheard, during one of which Vicky told Grace, 'Bill won't take me [to Australia] with the boys, but he will take me without them.' Clark, Ann insisted, was desperate to be with Smith: when he had travelled to Australia on a previous occasion, leaving Vicky behind, she had tried to commit suicide.

Shortly before the fire, the court heard, Vicky had moved various of her possessions to yet another houseboat, the *Beta Glen*. She had also had the foresight to put fifty pounds in the basket she'd pushed through the window of the *Windmill*, whereas the Richardsons claimed to have lost £180 in the blaze. Vicky insisted Bill Smith was only a father figure to her, but the prosecution had got its hands on a letter she had written to him when he visited

Australia: 'You have done the very thing you promised never to do,' it said. '[But] no matter how you have deceived me, I will always love you and if you ever come back, I will be waiting because deep in my heart I still cannot believe you could do such a despicable thing to me. Are you really no better than the rest?' Another houseboat resident was called: Winifred Bowling. Mrs Bowling reported that Bill Smith had suggested that the twins, being such 'beautiful kiddies', could be sold 'for a hundred pounds apiece' at a nearby American airbase.

Gerald Howard, QC and his team had been diligent; the prosecution case was damning and Vicky's cross-examination relentless. Again and again she was asked why she hadn't tried to save her children herself. Again and again she failed to come up with a convincing answer. But there were other things – helpful things, in the circumstances – that the prosecution didn't need to spell out. Clark's lifestyle spoke for itself.* Her five children had two different fathers, only one of whom she had bothered to marry. Three of them lived apart from her, and the other two she had allegedly considered giving up for adoption. She had been seen openly kissing Bill Smith, a married man. To the public, and perhaps to members of the jury too, she was, as people used to have it, no better than she ought to be. While no one would ever know for certain whether, on the fateful night of 16 May, Vicky Clark really had struck a match and set fire to a gallon of paraffin, her private life left no room for doubt: her reputation was deserved.

And so the trial entered its final stage: the defence began its summing-up. Clark's counsel pointed out that in the days before the first fire she had been busy repainting the *Buchra*. Why would someone destroy something on which they'd worked so hard? And what about the Richardsons? The family was behind on a number of hire-purchase agreements and in arrears on its rent. If

---

* It also gives the lie to those who believe that the Fifties wanted for disordered families.

they had really been in possession of £180, why hadn't they used it to pay off these debts? It was, the defence argued, all very well to lay all the blame on Mrs Clark for the deaths of Colin and Reggie, but there was no denying the fact that two able-bodied young men had escaped the burning boat ahead of her. At this point the subject of Vicky Clark's morals was at last tackled head on. Yes, she was an 'immoral' woman, but immorality was not a crime – and even if it was, she was not charged with it.

As closing arguments go, these were straightforward enough. However, in the next day's newspapers it would be the defence's final and most unexpected flourish that would grab the column inches. Would Violet Clark, her barrister asked the court, really have gone to bed in her curlers on the night of 16 May if she had planned the fire? If she had known that just a short while later she would come face to face with firemen, police officers and her staring neighbours? Surely not.

On the face of it, drawing attention to what the *Daily Herald* referred to as 'this foible' of the female sex should have had little impact on the jury. ('It is just one of those things with women,' said the paper. 'They won't be seen with their hair in curlers, or not if they can help it.') In 1956 it wasn't vanity that stopped women wandering about in their rollers so much as their sense of what was respectable, and in the minds of most Vicky Clark had been a stranger to the idea of respectability for most of her adult life.* But for those listening in court such thoughts were suddenly fugitive. It was, you see, Clark's great good fortune

* I can't help but think of my grandmothers, born only a few years before Vicky Clark, who as young women had hairstyles very similar to hers (which is to say, they wore veritable helmets of curls fixed with setting lotion). My maternal grandmother, the more middle class of the two, would rather have died than be seen in her rollers; she wouldn't so much as step outside the front door without having first applied lipstick and swapped her 'flatties' for heels. My paternal grandmother, more working class, would have been less flustered by the idea of a strange man seeing her rollers. But only a little less. They weren't vain, either of them. It was a matter of what was 'nice'.

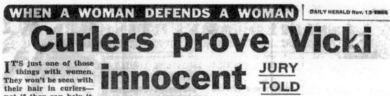

Curlers prove Vicki

innocent JURY TOLD

DAILY HERALD Nov. 13 1955

WHEN A WOMAN DEFENDS A WOMAN

IT'S just one of those things with women. They won't be seen with their hair in curlers— not if they can help it.

A woman, Miss Rose Heilbron, Q C, reminded an Old Bailey jury of this foible of her sex yesterday.

It shows, she said, that Mrs. Violet Clark is innocent of murder.

WOULD SHE?

For 35-year-old Mrs. Clark (known as Vicki Wright) put her hair in curlers on the night the houseboat Windmill caught fire at Benfleet Creek, Essex.

Would she have done this if she planned to start the fire? Miss Heilbron asked.

Would any woman be prepared to face firemen, neighbours and police with her hair up if she could avoid it?

The prosecution says Mrs. Clark did start the fire, killing her two-year-old twins, Colin and Reginald, who were burned to death.

ROSE HEILBRON, Q C
She was eloquent

to have for a barrister an elegant, highly intelligent, much-photographed woman whose own hair, always immaculate, the jury would often have seen in the press, and whose own distaste at the thought of such a nocturnal encounter – it was there in her manner if not in her words – worked on her audience like a spell. Her mildly outraged tone suggested that this aversion was something she and her client had in common, for all that they could not be more different outwardly, and for a few fleeting moments Clark, the hard-faced goodtime girl, was made to seem just a little vulnerable.

What happened next astonished everyone. On 13 November the jury returned its verdict. Vicky Clark was found guilty not of murder but of manslaughter, for criminal neglect in the duty to her children, a crime for which she was sentenced to just three years in prison.*

Hearing the news in Fleet Street, the headline-writers rubbed

* She served only eighteen months.

their hands with glee. Rose Heilbron, the housewife lawyer – the
most famous lawyer in the land – had won yet again, and in a case
that had seemed, right until the end, to be cut and dried.

It would be difficult to overstate how well known and admired –
loved, even – Rose Heilbron was in her day. Partly, this was the
nature of her business. Thanks to the death penalty, murder trials
were followed far more avidly than now; a life was at stake, which
gave even the most straightforward of cases a queasy import. A
decade after the end of the war, moreover, there was still wide-
spread unease about what the violence people had experienced
meant for civil society. Were its long-term effects on display in the
criminal courts? But even among the famous lawyers whose
names filled the newspaper columns, Rose was in a class of her
own. In 1956 there were only two women Queen's Counsels in
England: Heilbron, and Helena Normanton.* They had taken silk
together in 1948, the first barristers of their sex to do so.
Normanton, however, was some three decades Rose's senior and,
owing to poor health, had not practised for several years. To all
intents and purposes, the beautiful, determined and highly successful Rose was in a class of one.

The papers reported everything she said and everything she
did – including, on one occasion, the news that she had dared to
wear a calf-length evening gown. In the eyes of the press, she was
a 'housewife Portia', her brilliance in the courtroom and her

---

* Helena Normanton (1882–1957), who was called to the Bar in 1922, was the first woman in
England to lead the prosecution in a murder trial. She was also the first married British
woman to be issued a passport in her maiden name (in 1924), though she used Mrs for work
because it was better for business. A former suffragette, she was a committed campaigner for
the rights of women in general, and for women lawyers in particular – and thus an avid
writer of articles and letters to the newspapers. Responding to a piece in *Strand* magazine in
1932, in which Margot Asquith had claimed that 'a judicial mind is not the strongest part of
a woman's intellectual equipment ... few of us would like to be tried by a female judge',
Normanton told the editor, '[Your magazine] will rapidly disappear if you publish inaccurate
articles of a frumpish and out-of-date point of view.' She probably deserves a book of her own.

Helena Normanton and Rose Heilbron take silk

hefty earnings – facts that might otherwise have irked them – softened and made more acceptable by the knowledge that she was also married with a small daughter, and kept a delightful house. As the *Daily Mirror* put it, '[At home in Liverpool] Rose Heilbron leaves behind her wig and gown, and the majesty of the law becomes the quiet attractive housewife in a fawn coat who, as the tradesmen say, "wouldn't dream of trying to use her position to jump the queue".' The same article noted approvingly that her family's favourite foods included liver sausage, olives, gherkins and salad, and that she owned a 'magnificent' collection of classical records and drove a Triumph. Others wrote of the Bechstein piano that stood in a bay window of her house, and of the pink geraniums blooming cheerily in its porch. In the weekly magazine *Tit-Bits*, a musical actress called Joanne Heal, who'd met Heilbron at a reception, reported happily that, for all her cleverness, what she was most anxious to talk about was 'the

'I washed it this morning and I can't do a thing with it'

thrill of owning a new dish-washing machine'. Even the cartoonists treated her with affection. A good example dates from
shortly after the case of the Burning Houseboat, when she was
appointed Recorder of Burnley, and thus became England's first
female judge: a Rose-like figure, wearing a judge's long wig, leans
over the bench and whispers to the barrister below, 'I washed it
this morning, and I can't do a thing with it.'

On the part of the press, this love affair represented quite some
U-turn. Until the advent of Rose, the newspapers had been firmly
on the side of those who still regarded the admittance of women
to the English Bar* as an unhappy experiment, and who lived in
fear of the arrival of women QCs or – God forbid – judges. Barely
a week went by without yet another columnist taking up his pen
to complain that it was thoroughly unnatural for a woman to
appear in court. Of course, women made 'splendid solicitors'.
Being very conscientious, they excelled at correspondence, at
dealing with wills and conveyancing, at running around getting
things filed and stamped and served. But barristers? *No.* As Hervey
Middleton (a pseudonym, presumably for a male lawyer) put it
in the *Daily Mail* on 29 June 1938, not only were women unable to
see that there were two sides to every question, their 'righteous
indignation' meant they would never be able to remain sufficiently cool to open a case. And then, of course, there were their
physical handicaps: their stature, their hair. 'How is a woman to
wear a wig?' asked Middleton. 'If she waves her hair and puts her
wig on top of it, she looks as if she were carrying a beehive.
Alternatively, if she wears a close-fitting wig over short, straight
hair she looks like a female convict when she takes it off.' As for
the female voice – this was the thing that 'concerned' these men
almost to the point of obsession – it was 'designed by nature' to

* Women were admitted to the Bar in 1919, following an Act of Parliament for which Helena
Normanton and others vigorously campaigned.

carry about ten feet and no further: 'A man can pitch his voice so that it fills the courtroom without losing any of its resonance or character. A woman, attempting the same feat, only produces a noise like the hooting of an owl; a noise which is unendurable in the course of a long speech, and grotesque in cross-examination.' Contrast this with the courtroom hacks' admiring descriptions of Rose's voice – low, mellifluous, and with a warm touch of the Mersey at its edges – and you wonder, what was her secret? Extraordinary enough that she had made silk. But to have won the press over too? How on earth did she do it?

Rose Heilbron was born on 19 August 1914, in St James Road, Liverpool, the younger daughter of Max and Nellie. The family was Jewish. At the time of her birth Max, who had begun his working life as a watchmaker, was in business with his father and one of his seven older brothers. The Heilbrons had various inter-ests: they were cigar merchants, and they owned several boarding houses; Max also invented a beauty aid known as 'Max's Panstick'. But the bulk of their living came from Heilbron's Cunard Hotel in Great George's Square, where emigrants en route from Europe to a new life in America stayed while they awaited passage. In the early part of the last century there were several establishments like this in Liverpool, the bulk of whose clients were Jewish refugees fleeing the pogroms of eastern Europe. For their home-sick guests, they weren't happy places; at night, passers-by could sometimes hear the mournful sound of violins and Russian folk songs coming from the windows. But for their owners they were extremely lucrative, and in 1931 Max and his family were able to leave the city centre and move to a five-bedroomed house in the prosperous suburb of Allerton.

Nellie Heilbron wanted her daughters to get on, and to this end Rose was sent to the Belvedere School, then a direct-grant gram-mar school. She also arranged for her to have elocution lessons.

Heilbron's Cunard Hotel

Rose was good at elocution, winning several prizes. In 1930, in a strange foreshadowing of her future career, she gave a recitation at St George's Hall, which housed Liverpool's assize courts; the following year she became the youngest person in England to pass the Licentiateship of the Guildhall School of Music in elocution.* Her carefully trained voice undoubtedly gave her the confidence her parents longed for her to have, but they must have been more alarmed than pleased when, at seventeen, she left Liverpool for London, where she hoped to make it on the stage (an enthusiastic schoolgirl actress, the *Liverpool Post* had already praised her 'finely swaggering Petruchio'). Their daughter was very bright; they had hoped for something better. Did she and her father fall out over this decision? No one seems to know. But if they did, it must have been difficult when, six months later, she admitted defeat and returned home – and perhaps this is also why she kept her brief theatrical career a secret thereafter. It became public only in 2012 when a biography by her daughter Hilary revealed

---

* According to her daughter Hilary Heilbron, Rose noted in an exercise book from this period that elocution lessons were important because they helped one 'to speak well in one's intercourse with men'. Hilary Heilbron is also a QC; her mother encouraged her to change her surname by deed poll (from Burstein, her father's name) when she left school.

that her mother had adopted the stage name Rose Bron, found herself digs and joined the cast of a play called *Hokuspokus* (a version of the Curt Goetz play, later a movie, in which a woman is put on trial for the murder of her husband only for him to turn up again alive).

Luckily, Rose had a plan B. In October 1932 she took up a place at Liverpool University to study for a law degree. Why law? Again, no one seems to know. It may have been that a career as a barrister (for this was her ambition) was the next best thing to a career on the stage. Or it may have been connected to the wider culture of the hour; this was, after all, the golden age of detective fiction and, in the real world, the heyday of Sir Bernard Spilsbury, the famous forensic pathologist. But whatever the attraction, she worked extremely hard. Her diaries record the long hours she put in, and by some accounts she was rarely to be seen at social gatherings. 'She was a pretty girl,' a contemporary said years later, 'but she was always working in the library. I don't remember seeing her at any dances, and I know that although I continually asked her out, she only came out to tea twice.' Happily, though, her efforts paid off. Three years later she was awarded a first-class degree, the first woman at Liverpool University to achieve such a distinction, and only the second in the country. In November 1935 she joined Gray's Inn, having been awarded the Lord Justice Holker Scholarship,* and in 1937 received her LLM (Master of Laws), after which she began to read for the Bar. As a result, even before she had begun to practise she found herself a minor local celebrity, the *News Chronicle* reporting her degree in the headline 'HER AMBITION – YOUNGEST BARRISTER'.

It all sounds straightforward, even easy – if perhaps a little lonely. But this was not the case at all. At home, where Rose was still living, circumstances had changed dramatically. The

---

* She was the first woman to receive it.

Depression had had a serious effect on Max Heilbron's business and, if the family was to stay afloat, an alternative source of income needed to be found. In 1935 the Heilbrons opened a small hotel, the Dorchester, in a Georgian terrace in Rodney Street, and here it was all hands on deck. Luckily for Rose, her sister Annie took on the greater burden. 'Let Rose get on with her studying,' Nellie said to her older daughter. 'Our Rose was always Mummy's pet,' Annie would later tell the newspapers.

Much worse, a few weeks after Rose received her LLM her mother was diagnosed with breast cancer. According to Annie, while their mother was ill Rose appeared at her bedside in a hired wig and gown, knowing that she would not live to see her called to the Bar: 'Mother's face lit up,' she said. But once Nellie was gone – she died in May 1938, at the age of just forty-nine – her younger daughter had to put her ambition on hold; by one account, she considered abandoning her career altogether. Her father needed her. When she did return to her studies six months later her resolve was rooted in the practical. The family business was still in a parlous state and she needed to earn a living (once the war came, moreover, the hotel would be requisitioned). And so it happened that in May 1939, a year almost to the day after her mother's death, Rose did indeed become Britain's youngest woman barrister.

Her call to the Bar attracted the attention of the national press, something that seems to have unsettled her not at all. One interview in particular stands out, for its clear-sightedness, but also for its guile. Rose knew exactly how to position herself: plucky but not threatening, serious but with her girlishness winningly intact. 'I am no bluestocking,' she told the Daily Express. 'The general impression of a woman lawyer seems to be a sober old maid. I have not adopted the law as a hobby. I am serious about my career, but that does not mean I shall give up dancing, swimming, golf or tennis. Legal problems will not keep me from the other jobs I love – housework and gardening. When I marry I intend to continue as a barrister. I have many men friends. Some have possibly fallen in love with me, but I have no plans for marriage. I am not in love. This does not mean I am sacrificing my life for my career. I am a home-lover. I have kept house for my father since my mother died, so the job of running my own home when I am married will not be a strange one.' Talking about a career, however, was not the same as having one, and it soon became apparent that securing a pupillage – a twelve-month apprenticeship to a barrister five years her senior – was going to be more difficult than she had assumed. At least one set of chambers turned her down specifically on the grounds of her sex; she had to understand that while its members didn't object to women barristers in principle, some of the men would feel 'constraint and diffidence' if she was working alongside them.

Nevertheless, by September 1939 she had been taken on by chambers in Castle Street, Liverpool. Her timing, though she would not have grasped this in the moment, was fortuitous. In the same month Britain declared war on Germany. Across the city her male colleagues would soon be leaving to fight, or to take on other forms of war work.* For all that it was unnerving to see sandbags appear outside the city's buildings – she gathered together her most precious possessions so they were easy to grab if there was a bombardment – a lot more work was going to come her way in these circumstances than it might have done in peacetime. In 1939 barristers were paid considerably less than now, and many of them were often woefully underemployed (even at the height of her career, Helena Normanton was compelled to let rooms in her house in Mecklenburgh Square, Bloomsbury, the better to supplement her income; there simply wasn't enough

---

* Women were not conscripted until 1942. Rose was lucky not to be called up between 1942 and 1945, and she did not volunteer for one of the Services, as some women did.

work to go round); all the same, solicitors who might otherwise have been wary of Rose would now be biting off her hand.

The next few years weren't easy. Either she was overwhelmed by work, devoting her entire weekend to preparing her cases, or things were so slow she worried about paying her bills. She had persuaded her father to take on a housekeeper – she shared the cost – which meant she no longer had to worry about what they would eat for dinner, but she was still running their home (Annie had moved out) and there was the Blitz to contend with: Liverpool was savagely bombed, and in 1941 her chambers were burned out. Slowly, though, her practice began to thrive. Divorces, motoring accidents, breaches of wartime regulations, she dealt with them all, and in October 1942 she became the first woman to lead in a murder trial, securing a manslaughter charge for her client Henry Larkin, a dock worker who'd cut the throat of his live-in lover with a razor. By April of the following year her finances were in rude enough health that she was able to buy the family home from her father.

The war ended. Rose's reputation was now such that the return of her male colleagues was unlikely to have much impact on her status: some solicitors were already talking of her making silk. 'Rose has a sense of form in court,' said one, trying to explain her success to a newspaper reporter. 'She's no mumbler and she puts over a case with lucidity, persuasion and perfect courtesy. But she's a pugilist at heart. You can't knock Rosie off her feet with an unexpected thrust of argument.' However, she was also about to meet another, more important ally. In April 1945 she was introduced to Nathaniel (Nat) Burstein, the sports-mad son of Polish émigrés and a local GP. Burstein had seen Rose at the assizes, which he had visited with a friend who was involved in the prison board, and having admired her from the public benches had engineered an invitation to a party he knew she would be attending. Their courtship was swift; an engagement followed two weeks later. They were married on 9 August in Harrogate, by a rabbi cousin of Rose's. She wore a pink dress and a black hat with a veil. The couple honeymooned in Torquay.

Nat would play a crucial role in Rose's future success (their marriage would last sixty years). The first time he'd laid eyes on her, after all, she had been dressed in her robe and wig. For him, that had been part of the attraction; he was certainly not about to try to persuade her to give up her career. Nor, having been a bachelor for so long, was he desperately in need of someone to keep home for him (a decade her senior, he was forty when they married). His own work came with manageable hours and did not involve, as Rose's soon would, trips away from home: if they had children he could be around in the evenings, even when she wasn't. He was easy-going and funny: an asset when it came to the social events that greased her professional life. And he had a steady income, something that was no doubt in the front of her mind when in 1946 she leased premises in Castle Street and became head of her own chambers.

'THAT GIRL ROSIE ... the greatest lawyer in the world'

Rose fell pregnant in the early spring of 1948 and worked throughout: the story goes that she even took her legal papers into hospital with her when she went into labour. Hilary, her only child, was born on 2 January 1949, and though the baby was delivered by emergency caesarean section – Rose nearly died during the birth – it was only six weeks before she was back in court. Eight weeks after this a letter from the Lord Chancellor's Office arrived. At the age of just thirty-four she had made silk, momentous news that was splashed across front pages throughout the Commonwealth. (As if it wasn't enough that she was the first woman to take silk, she was the third youngest KC ever appointed.) Every court reporter had his own special memories of the great Rosie – she was often called Rosie in headlines, and in Liverpool this was the name by which she was generally known – reminiscences that now came into their own. 'Miss Heilbron has impressed me on scores of occasions,' said Norman Cook of the *Daily Post*. 'She has brought a refreshing sparkle into the most wearying of assize civil actions. Her admirable air of confidence, her twinkling eyes, and – more often than not – the tilt of her wig with just that slight suggestion of rakishness, make her presentation of a case an affair of interest no matter how dull its content.'

There is a well-known photograph of Rose Heilbron and Helena Normanton, taken on the morning a fortnight later when they were sworn in as King's Counsels at the House of Lords; it, too, made all the front pages. While Normanton gazes into the crowd donnishly, a pair of wire-framed spectacles on her nose, Rose looks straight at the camera. Her eyebrows are pencilled, her lips are painted, her nose is powdered. She looks wonderfully glamorous. Her smile, though, is surprisingly cool. Oh, it was satisfying to be standing there on the steps of the Palace of Westminster with all the other new KCs. She was pleased, and proud. But however significant the moment, it was only that: a pause for breath. She certainly didn't intend to let it go to her head.

Rose's career as a KC began with the case with which, in Liverpool at least, she is still most strongly associated: the Cameo Murders. On the night of 19 March 1949 Leonard Thomas, the manager of the Cameo Cinema in Wavertree, and his assistant, John Catterall, were shot dead by a masked man demanding their takings. Rose's involvement began when she was instructed to defend Donald Johnson, supposedly an accessory to the murder (arrested for stealing thirty shillings from a labourer on his way home, Johnson claimed – apparently in exchange for bail – that he had been asked to hide the Cameo killer's gun). Having argued that Johnson's statements to the police had been obtained by inducements such as the provision of a surety, Rose won him an acquittal – and a round of triumphant headlines.

Three months later George Kelly, a small-time criminal, and Charles Connolly, a former boxer, were arrested for the murders. The Crown's case was built on the evidence of Jacqueline Dickson, a prostitute, and her pimp, James Northam, who claimed to have heard Connolly suggest a 'stick-up' at the Cameo, and to have seen Kelly produce a gun. When Kelly heard that Rose would be defending him, he was the opposite of delighted. 'Why couldn't I have a fella, like you've got?' he asked Connolly. 'Whoever heard of a judy defending anyone?' But then he met his barrister, and his attitude changed. The story goes that in the hospital wing of Walton prison, where he was on remand, he could be heard singing, Al Jolson-style, '*Rosie you are my posy. You are my heart's bouquet. Come on out into the moonlight, there's something sweet love I wanna say.*'

In the end, though, his heart's bouquet couldn't save him. The trial that followed – at thirteen days, the longest murder trial in British legal history – resulted in a hung jury, at a time when majority verdicts were not yet acceptable. The judge had no choice but to order a retrial, but this time the two men would be tried separately. Six days later, after a summing-up by Rose that lasted three hours, George Kelly was found guilty. It seemed the jury had largely believed the prosecution's star witness, Robert Graham, a criminal with a history of mental illness who claimed to have helped Kelly and Connolly communicate with each other in Walton prison. According to Graham, their messages supported the prosecution's case. His appeal dismissed, Kelly was hanged by Albert Pierrepoint on 28 March 1950. He maintained his innocence right up until the moment he died.*

For Rose, this must have been painful: over the course of the two trials she had built a relationship with Kelly. Those who knew him thought that he was telling the truth when he said he did not know Connolly before their arrest, and that he had never fired a gun in his life – and in 2003, after a long campaign by his family, the Court of Appeal quashed his conviction. Kelly, it seemed, had been fitted up by the police. According to Hilary Heilbron, Rose and Kelly travelled back to Liverpool from his appeal on the same train and at some point the guard came to ask her if she would speak to the prisoner; he was concerned about him. Rose never forgot Kelly's parting remark to her, made as she returned to her own compartment. 'Don't you worry about me, love,' he said. 'You just look after yourself.' The consoler, he could see, needed to be consoled.

Her performance in the case – meticulous and controlled – sealed her reputation as an advocate, and not only among her colleagues. The newspapers relished the way she had battled, noting that on one occasion her arguments with the judge had

---

* After the verdict at the Kelly trial, George Connolly was advised that if he pleaded guilty to robbery the murder charge would be dropped. This he did, and he was released from prison in 1956. In 1993 he wrote to Rose Heilbron, asking her if his decision to plead guilty had jeopardised George Kelly's appeal, a worry that had haunted him. This was a hugely complicated case and I have had to summarise. For more information, see *The Cameo Conspiracy* by George Skelly.

lasted so long the jury had to be sent home for the night (the judge in question was the forensically brilliant George Lynskey, who had chaired of the 1948 Lynskey tribunal, investigating corruption by government ministers and civil servants – an inquiry that had resulted in a ministerial resignation). As a result, Rose found herself in demand not only as a barrister but as a public speaker too. Look at these after-dinner speeches – seemingly indefatigable, she accepted a great many invitations – and you can almost feel her confidence growing. Her views, avowedly feminist, were straightforward and unembarrassed. Prejudice was still rampant, she told her audiences, and women must not flag in their efforts to overcome it. Nor should they ever forget those who had won for them such rights as the vote. She believed in equal pay for women and was disdainful of laws such as the Income Tax Act of 1918, which bracketed women with lunatics, idiots and insane persons. Why, she wanted to know, was it still the case that if a married woman saved money from her housekeeping, such savings still belonged in law to her husband?

In the years after the Cameo trial the cases came thick and fast, each one seemingly more sensational than the last. In 1951 she represented three Liverpool dockers who, it was claimed, had gone on strike unlawfully. She won, and when her train pulled into Lime Street Station a crowd of dock workers was waiting to cheer her walk along the platform. The newspapers reported that she received £750, plus £150 a day, to represent the dockers, then the highest brief fee ever paid to a woman. This was followed by the Bootle Bath Murder, in which she defended twenty-seven-year-old Anna Neary, accused of drowning her neighbour Emma Grace in her bath. ('Another victory in a series of triumphant cases conducted by thirty-six-year-old, petite, dark-haired Miss Heilbron ...' said the News of the World, reporting the acquittal.)

Nineteen fifty-two brought a stunning hat-trick of victories.

First of all there was the case of Louis Bloom, a Hartlepool solicitor accused of murdering Patricia Hessler, a former client with
whom he had been having an affair. Bloom had been trying to
end the relationship – Hessler was a drinker with a complicated
past – and when she had loudly objected to this one night he had
grabbed her throat. Soon afterwards, realising that he'd strangled
her, Bloom rang the police and admitted what he had done. For
Rose, it was a difficult trial. Bloom's early confession stacked the
odds against him, and the judge, Mr Justice Hallett, seemed determined to give her a hard time. Nonetheless, she was undaunted,
dragging a two-foot-high red and yellow plastic model of a
human neck into the court to illustrate the medical evidence to
the jury. 'She showed sufficient knowledge of the human larynx
to tackle a medical exam on the subject,' commented one journalist. Under cross-examination she was able to get the Crown
pathologist to concede that there were no outward signs that
Hessler had died from asphyxia, and that death from inhibition of
the vagal nerve (pressure on it causes the heart to stop) is not
always the result of violence.

But it was her closing speech – made to a court in full mourning, following the news that George VI had died – that seems to
have been most impressive; Justice Hallet warned the jury afterwards that 'common sense should not be moved by oratory,
however much you admire the oratory or the orator'. It was theatrical, even by her standards. First, she spoke of Bloom's passion,
his infatuation, the fact that he did not want to hurt a single hair
on his lover's head. Then she moved on to his account of Hessler's
death. 'How truthful Bloom's story rings!' she said. 'There is a
woman screaming . . . What more natural thing than to press on
her neck and tell her to be quiet . . . But if you make a mistake and
press a little too hard, the damage is done . . . The whole thing
happened like that. One, two, three [she rapped on the bench
with a knuckle three times to show the fatal speed with which the

tragedy occurred] and she is dead.' The jury returned a verdict of manslaughter, and Bloom was given just three years. 'No fuss please,' said Rose emerging into the crowd from the court. Afterwards a fan wrote to her: 'Dear lady,' said his note. 'You can't go around persuading juries that men are entitled to strangle their lady friends.'

Bloom was followed by Mary Standish, charged with murdering her husband with a knife. Rose argued in court that Standish had only meant to frighten her husband, who had been drinking and who had hit her earlier in the evening. It took the jury just seventeen minutes to find her not guilty. Afterwards she told the *Sunday Express* that Rose was not at all the 'stern poker-faced sort of woman' she had been expecting. 'She was so friendly and quiet, the kind of woman whom when she asks you a difficult question, you don't think twice about giving an honest answer to ... I'll never forget it. She remembered to smile at me across the court. I don't expect to meet anyone like her again.'

Finally, there was the murder of Lord and Lady Derby's butler, Walter Stallard, and their under-butler, Douglas Stuart, by Harold Winstanley, a trainee footman at Knowsley Hall. (Lady Derby, watching television in the smoke room, was also attacked, though she escaped with her life.) Boldly – a masterstroke, people said afterwards – Rose called just one witness in Winstanley's defence: a psychiatrist. But this was enough. The jury accepted that he was insane, and he was sent to Broadmoor.* The press now began to speculate that Rose would one day become Britain's first woman judge.

---

* This trial was held at the same time as that of Christopher Craig and Derek Bentley for the murder of a policeman, a case that later became a cause célèbre. (Bentley, who had learning difficulties, was hanged, having shouted the words 'Let him have it, Chris.'; sixteen-year-old Craig, who fired the gun, was too young to be hanged.) According to Hilary Heilbron, had she not been appearing for Winstanley, Rose would have been instructed to defend Craig.

For the most part, the newspapers were swoonily reverential. 'Success has not spoiled Rose Heilbron, QC,' purred the *Liverpool Post*. 'She is charming, unaffected, modest and likes nothing better in her spare time than doing her own shopping.' But this didn't mean that she welcomed interest in her life. It was uncomfortable, wondering who would be standing outside every time she opened her front door, and she resented the way the press tried to get quotes from friends and local shopkeepers. (Not that these scraps of information were particularly revelatory. 'The main thing about Miss H,' one shopkeeper said, 'is that you can't sell her any old rubbish. Just good, plain clothes.') It was also against the rules of her profession for a barrister either to give or to authorise interviews. This caught her both ways. Not only was it impossible for her to correct reporters' misapprehensions; on more than one occasion she had to reassure the Bar Council that she had not in fact supplied a newspaper with a photograph, or details of her earnings.

Perhaps, too, the press occasionally touched a nerve. She seems to have taken particular exception to an article that appeared in

the *Empire News* in August 1951 under the headline 'Two Sisters, but
They Live in Different Worlds'. The writer of the story, Arnold
Rosenfield, had tracked down Annie to the 'one and threes' – the
cheap seats – at her local cinema, where she had been watching
Walt Disney's *Cinderella*. Annie, he revealed, was a former teacher
of music who now lived with her foundry-worker husband
Arthur, their four-year-old daughter Elaine and her father Max
in a modest terrace near Penny Lane, a working-class area of
Liverpool where, according to Rosenfield, 'the only flowers that
bloom thereabouts are the ones they buy'. Rose, Annie said, visited her father dutifully every week. But the inference of the piece
was clear: while Rose soared, Annie only scraped by. 'Rose always
knew what she wanted,' Annie told the reporter.*

The year 1955 brought Rose her greatest triumphs yet. The first
took place at Manchester Assizes, where a young man, Dennis
Murtagh, stood accused of the murder of William Jackson, a
stock-car racer. It was an unusual case: the murder weapon was
alleged to be a Ford Zephyr, which Murtagh had used to crush his
victim against the wall of his house.

Rose's client had been involved in a fight with Jackson two days
earlier, after which the accused had repeatedly driven past his
house. The first time he did this Jackson's wife had, it was alleged,
thrown a brick at Murtagh's car; the second time Jackson had
thrown an iron coal scuttle, breaking its windscreen. Both inci-
dents had been reported to the police. The issue for the jury
involved a third occasion on which Murtagh had driven by, for this
was when Jackson had been killed. Had he intended to murder his
victim, or had he, as the defence contended, lost control of the car,

* This narrative seems to have had no effect on Rose's reputation, not even in the sisters'
home town. '[Liverpool] wears Rosie like a medal,' wrote Drusilla Beyfus in the *Sunday Express*
in 1953. 'She will always be bright and new and young to the ordinary people there. "I
wouldn't miss a word of Rosie," they say.'

having swerved to avoid the coal scuttle for a second time? The jury thought the former was the more likely scenario and found him guilty of murder, for which he was duly sentenced to death.

Rose lodged an appeal on the grounds that the judge had misdirected the jury on the issue of burden of proof. But the three-man Court of Criminal Appeal could not agree on a verdict, and for the first time in legal history a second appeal would be heard, this time before a five-man court. 'In this case,' she told the reconstituted court, 'the dividing line between murder and accident is so thin, so narrow and so close that it was exceptionally important for the judge to put accurately, clearly and in full the direction as to burden of proof.' It was, she added, the 'pride of these courts' that a case had to be proved beyond reasonable doubt. Why had the jury not been reminded of this? The appeal was allowed. Murtagh, who had spent the last nine weeks in the condemned cell at Strangeways Prison, was released. 'We want Rose! We want Rose!' chanted the crowd outside the court, but as usual Rose slipped off to catch her train, unseen. The case attracted a great deal of press attention. Murtagh had come perilously close to being hanged; from his cell to the gallows in the room next door, had he but known it, was a walk of just ten seconds.

And then – cue mambo on the jukebox – there was Jack Comer, aka Jack Spot, the self-styled King of Soho whose nickname he owed to the large black mole on his left cheek. Born Jacob Comacho, Comer was the son of a Jewish tailor's machinist from Lodz in Poland, and grew up in the East End where he claimed to have been involved in the Battle of Cable Street as a young man (a fat lie, sadly). In 1955 Comer was arrested following a bloody knife fight with Albert Dimes, one of the henchmen of Billy Hill, Comer's former partner and now his major rival when it came to betting rackets and all the other business of the criminal underworld. Comer, who lost so much blood after the fight he had nearly died, and Dimes, who had an injury to his head that required twenty stitches, were charged with unlawful fighting and causing affray. The issue for the jury would be which of them used their knife first, and whether it was in self-defence. Two days into the trial, however, the judge ruled that Comer and Dimes be charged separately on a charge of wounding with intent to cause grievous bodily harm. Comer – unlike Dimes – was also charged with being in possession of a knife.

At his trial, Comer insisted that he had been the victim of an unprovoked attack. As for Dimes's injuries, those were (preposterous, this) self-inflicted. Sophie Hyams, the tearful wife of the proprietor of the Continental Fruit Shop, where the two men had rolled on the ground, was called. 'Mrs Hyams,' said Rose, 'you are a frightened woman, aren't you?' The judge intervened. 'Perhaps you are frightened of Miss Heilbron,' he said, to much laughter. The defence also called a surprise witness in the Reverend Basil Andrews, an octogenarian priest who had seen the whole thing with his own eyes. Rose, who had done her homework, visiting the Soho street where the fight had supposedly taken place under police protection, made an impassioned closing address in which she referred to the *Alice in Wonderland* feeling of a trial in which her client was accused of wounding a man who had wounded him just as badly – and it worked. (Her description also stuck; the fight soon passed into gangster folklore as the 'Mirage of Soho' and 'the fight that never was'.) The jury, which retired for just sixty-five minutes, returned a verdict of not guilty and Comer punched the air delightedly. 'Don't write about me,' he told the journalists gathered outside the Old Bailey. 'Write your story about Rose, [the] greatest lawyer in history.' (This, his counsel felt, was 'something of an exaggeration' – though at least one newspaper took him at his word, beginning a serial that told the story of 'the greatest lawyer in the world' that very month.) Only later was it discovered that the doddery priest, a man who had seemed so sweet and so upright on the stand, had been paid twenty-five

DAILY MAIL: SATURDAY, SEPTEMBER 24, 1955

Miss Rose, QC, triumphs

TRIBUTE AFTER OLD BAILEY VERDICT

By Daily Mail Reporter

MISS ROSE HEILBRON—brilliant 39-year-old Queen's Counsel, surgeon's wife, and devoted mother—had a crowded day yesterday fulfilling all three rôles.

At the Old Bailey, in London, she had added to her long list of legal victories when Jack "Spot" Comer, whom she defended, was acquitted in the Soho stabbing case.

Then—with moments to spare—she doffed wig and gown to rush home to Childwall, Liverpool, to join husband Dr. Nathaniel Burstein and their seven-year-old daughter.

She was home for a well-earned restful week-end—before Mrs. Burstein must become Miss Heilbron again. The attractive daughter of a Liverpool hotel proprietor showed no signs of strain after the arguing at the Old Bailey the fine legal points of a case which has made news for weeks.

Mrs. Comer insists: "We go straight home to the family."

JACK SPOT BOWS THANKS TO JURY

pounds to perjure himself* – and since Comer could not be tried for the same offence twice, he was safe.

It was a big deal to appear in a trial like this one. The newspapers had close relationships with Comer and Hill, and were apt to write of them as if they were celebrities, with the result that the coverage was exhaustive. (The crime reporters even claimed to have discovered that the victorious Comer kept a framed photograph of Rose on his sideboard. 'A Jewish lady, she is,' said Moisha Bluebell, one of his associates. 'It's an education just to listen to her speak.') It was also fraught with danger. Soho gangsters treated their lawyers as they would any other employee: Patrick Marrinan, QC was struck off after it was revealed that he

---

* Comer's associates Moisha Bluebell, Sonny the Yank and Tall Pat, as well as his wife Rita, were later found guilty of conspiring to pervert the course of justice. The Reverend Andrews gave evidence against them.

was in the pay of Billy Hill. It seems that vague attempts were
made to nobble Rose too: in a Soho street prosecution witnesses
asked her to buy fruit, their sales pitches rather too firm in the
circumstances, and during the trial a 'sinister Italian' deliberately
bumped into her. But the *Daily Mail* reported that she showed 'no
signs of strain' afterwards; she simply rushed home to Liverpool
for a 'well-earned restful weekend'.

Whether people grasped it at the time or not, the trial of Vicky
Clark for the murder of her twin sons in 1956 — Rose's next big
case — suggested that when it came to life in Britain the stays were
beginning to give. Even as people remained conservative enough
to buy the idea that a woman would not choose to let a strange
man catch sight of her rollers, it found itself in thrall to a successful and tough working woman who, it was clear, thought of
herself as a trailblazer rather than an aberration. (Rose's speeches
at this time, with their emphasis on such things as maternity
leave and childcare, never failed to look to a future in which
'trained women' were increasingly the norm.) The Houseboat
Murders trial threw over the old order, the idea of 'good' girls
versus 'bad'. Instead of tutting about Vicky Clark's morals and
whispering that she had got away with it, attention was focused
instead on the triumph of the clever, indomitable Rose: a 'good'
girl, to be sure, but one who resembled other women of one's
acquaintance hardly at all. The public's response to Rose, like the
media's, was increasingly striking. People responded to her with —
to use one example — far less anxiety than they would to another
successful barrister, Margaret Thatcher, some years later.* Her

* Margaret Thatcher would be elected MP for Finchley in 1959. In 1952, when Thatcher was studying for the Bar, she wrote a newspaper article in which she said she hoped to see more and more
women combining marriage and a career. 'Unless Britain, in the new age to come, can produce
more Rose Heilbrons — not only in the field of law, of course — we shall have betrayed the
tremendous work of those who fought for equal rights against such misguided opposition.'

Wives Queue To See Miss Heilbron Installed

A CROWD of housewives and schoolgirls waited almost two hours today to see Miss Rose Heilbron, QC, Britain's first woman Recorder, installed with traditional ceremony at the opening of Burnley Quarter Sessions, the first since her appointment in November.

dazzling ability, combined with her looks, her earthy Liverpudlian roots and a set of professional rules which dictated that she could not accept the invitations she received to appear on popular panel shows, meant that she was, rather like the Queen, a person to be admired from afar. Such distance contrived to put her beyond the reach of envy and spite. Fondly claimed by popular culture – she was the inspiration for Mary Randall, QC, Anna Neagle's character in the 1958 film *The Man Who Wouldn't Talk*, and the subject of a flattering joke in an episode of *Hancock's Half Hour** – a woman who might otherwise have represented a threat became instead a star, a national treasure. And she wasn't done yet. On 26 November, thirteen days after Vicky Clark's surprise conviction for manslaughter, Rose was announced as the new Recorder of Burnley and thus England's first woman judge. This was news that produced not only more headlines, but also editorials, letters, cartoons, invitations, telegrams, speeches and, from the *Women's Sunday Mirror*, two dozen red roses.

On 6 January 1957 unprecedented numbers of 'housewives and schoolgirls' waited two hours to see her installed. The mood was

---

* In *The Lawyer*, James Hancock, QC is ticked off for having spent most of his afternoon in court 'trying to sit on Rose Heilbron's knee'.

celebratory, almost *en fête*. 'It was the most exciting quarter sessions Burnley has known,' wrote the *Daily Herald*'s reporter, rushing to convey the mood. 'Because the Recorder was a pretty woman; because barristers stumbled over the new address [Rose had decided she would be called Madam Recorder]; because all Burnley turned up to see what was going on. A pushing, curious crowd strained to find seats in the crowded courtroom: in the public gallery were women shoppers who had brought out their best hats for the occasion; in the Press seats were 16 men on a bench made for six. Policemen guarding the doors told the Press that there was no room left; told the jurors to push their way through. They even told one of the prisoners to go away, but he obligingly persisted in establishing his identity and they let him through. The prisoners, indeed, were nearly overlooked. They were the men with the walking-on parts in a cast that had bigger stars.' Other journalists noted the way Rose fussed over her starched neckbands, twisted her wedding ring and touched her crimson lipstick to check for smudging. That first day she sent two men to prison and another to Borstal, though there were also several conditional discharges; she presided over twelve cases in all. One can only imagine how this must have felt: the strange solemnity of it – a first for her, if not for the defendants – dissipating far too quickly in a courtroom turned party-warm by massed pride and expectation.

Rose was an unusually energetic person. But then, she needed to be. Her work as a Recorder had to run alongside her own busy practice and by the early Sixties she was also sometimes chosen to prosecute cases for the Crown. Then there were her speaking engagements, the many dinners and opening nights to which she was now invited, and the good causes to which she was asked to put her name – in 1958, she was one of several high-profile women who wrote to *The Times* arguing there should be a national monument to Christabel

Rose, Nat and Hilary on holiday in Brittany, 1953

Pankhurst.* She had a new role, too, as an honorary colonel in
the Women's Royal Army Corps. She and Nat were also building themselves a house, Parklands, in a street close to
Calderstones Park in Allerton (smart, and modern: five bedrooms, an acre of landscaped gardens, tennis court). How did
she manage? Staff, and plenty of them. In addition to her secretary and clerk she employed a cleaner, a cook and a gardener.
It was a pay roll that caused her no anxiety; she hoped only to
be able to afford it. One of the great up-sides of being the first of
a kind was that guilt, at least as it pertained to working women,
had not yet been invented. You looked at magazines for recipes

* In 1904 Christabel Pankhurst had been refused permission to become a barrister.

and dress patterns, not to be told how bad you should be feeling for the way you chose to live your life.

Her career continued to build. Rose was a good lawyer as well as a good advocate, and many of her cases made it to the Law Reports, the legal equivalent, I suppose, of a novel being published as a classic. Some continued to be reported by the press too, albeit in less detail than before: the Homicide Act of 1957, which limited capital punishment to only six categories of murder, was the beginning of the end for the death sentence in Britain, and as fewer people were hanged or at risk of hanging, interest in murder trials fell away.* One question, however, remained: would she be appointed a high court judge? Or was this as far as she would be allowed to go?

If it was going to happen it all, it was clearly going to take time. The legal world, fusty and bigoted, showed no sign at all of wanting to modernise. Women were still excluded from Bar Mess, the twice-weekly dinners held during assizes – it was said that their presence would 'spoil' the atmosphere.† She was also barred from judges' dinners and, when she was away from home, would have to eat alone. In February 1962 she was the first woman to be appointed a Commissioner of Assize by the Lord Chancellor, a role that involved assisting a high court judge with a heavy caseload, and which meant staying at the judges' lodgings: in effect, a trial run. But in 1965 it was announced that Elizabeth Lane QC‡ would be the first woman high court judge, sitting in the Family

---

* The six categories were: murders committed in the course or furtherance of theft; by shooting or causing an explosion; while resisting arrest or during an escape; the second of two murders committed on different occasions; of a police officer; of a prison officer by a prisoner. Capital punishment was finally abolished in 1965.

† Women on the Northern Circuit did not become full members of Bar Mess until 1970.

‡ Elizabeth Lane (1905–88) was a remarkable woman. She did not go to university and only studied law after she was married, joining her husband when he decided to read for the Bar. In 1950 she became the third woman to take silk. Between 1971 and 1973 she chaired the committee working on the Abortion Act.

Division. Even if Rose did not make her feelings public, this was entirely baffling; Lane was so much less well known than her. But perhaps this in itself was part of the reason she got there first. Rose's popularity may have been the source of envy and some irritation in the higher echelons of her profession – how else to explain its slowness to award her the status she deserved? It wasn't until 1968 that she was elected a bencher of Gray's Inn, and it wasn't until 1973 that she was elected leader of the Northern Circuit.* A man with the same experience would not have had to wait half as long.

In 1972, in her capacity as a Recorder, she sat at the Old Bailey as a judge: another first for a woman. The *Daily Mail* reported that 'With a trace of deep crimson lipstick, and only an occasional pat at her wig, the first woman judge – "My Lady" as they addressed her – took her seat in the Old Bailey yesterday. The seismographs registered nil.' Outside the court, however, the moment, according to the *Evening Standard*, was 'greeted with all the camera-popping ceremonial of the birth of a film star's baby'. The *Liverpool Daily Post*, sounding unexpectedly modern, bemoaned the fact that Rose was still 'imprisoned by masculine curiosity. The gossip columnists seem more interested in finding suitable adjectives for her smile at prosecuting council – it's enough to strain the quality of anyone's mercy.'

Finally, though, it happened. In 1974 the new Lord Chancellor, Lord Elwyn-Jones, appointed Rose a high court judge assigned to the Family Division. Given her criminal work, and the many personal injury cases she had taken on over the years, it wouldn't have been unreasonable for her to have expected to be assigned to the Queen's Bench Division; in the Family Division her vast experience would be wasted, there was no getting away from that. But she had waited too long for this moment to allow it to be

* Customarily, this honour went to the most senior silk on the circuit but, as a senior barrister said in 1970, 'with a certain amount of care to avoid Rose Heilbron'.

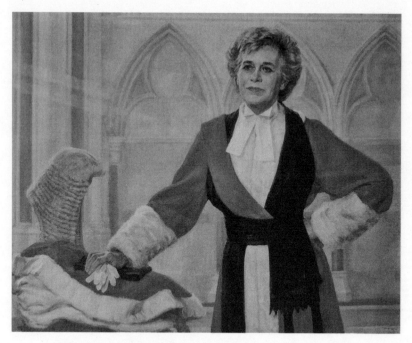

*'Only an occasional pat of her wig': a portrait of Rose in her judge's robes
by June Mendoza, which hangs in Gray's Inn*

clouded with regret. She was sworn in at 9.30 a.m. on 1 October,
queenly in a robe of scarlet.

'Heilbron rules her courtroom with a rod of silk – smooth and
elegant, but very tough.' *Daily Mail*

Rose spent fourteen years on the High Court Bench and made a
number of famous judgments. In 1976, for instance, she made an
eleven-year-old girl who suffered from a rare congenital syn-
drome a ward of court in order to prevent the sterilisation that
her mother had agreed with her paediatrician and gynaecologist.
Rose held that it was neither medically necessary nor in her interest to perform an operation that would involve 'the deprivation

of a basic human right, namely the right of a woman to repro-
duce'. More notoriously, in 1988 she held that the putative father
of an unborn child could not prevent the mother having an abortion, either on his own behalf or on behalf of the unborn child,
a judgment that was upheld by the Court of Appeal.

In 1975 she was appointed by the home secretary, Roy Jenkins,
to chair the advisory group on the law of rape, a body created to
respond to the outcry after the decision in DPP *v.* Morgan (1975)
that a man was not guilty of rape if he believed that the woman
was consenting, no matter how unreasonable that belief might
be. The report recommended, among other things, that it should
be made clear that the offence was rooted in the absence of consent, not violence; that a complainant should not have to answer
questions about her sexual history; and that complainants should
be anonymous.

Soon after she became a high court judge, Rose and Nat left
Liverpool for London, where they lived in a flat at 2 Gray's Inn
Square. And here she remained until 2000, when the vascular
dementia from which she had been suffering for some years
became too severe for Nat to care for her. She died in an Islington
nursing home on 8 December 2005, at the age of ninety-one, and
Nat five years later at the age of 104.

Rose Heilbron blazed a trail, but what difference did she make?
Not as much of a difference, one suspects, as she would have
hoped. Let's work our way up, as she did. As I write there are 1310
QCs in England, of whom just 176 are women; 1020 Recorders, of
whom 201 are women; 559 circuit judges, of whom 106 are women;
91 high court judges, of whom 17 are women. In the supreme
court, there sits only one woman. According to one recent
report, at the present rate it will be another fifty-five years before
women achieve equality in the senior judiciary. In fifty-five years,
a snail could crawl around the M25 nine times.

She would have been appalled by this, but not surprised. For all her success, for all her supreme professionalism, Rose knew what it felt like to be patronised and passed over. She kept quiet about this, mostly, but it must have rankled. How could it not? In the end, it wasn't her brilliance that was rewarded so much as her patience and tenacity, the one hidden discreetly beneath the other, an iron fist inside the finest velvet glove George Henry Lees* had to offer.

Perhaps you are wondering what happened to Vicky Clark. The story goes that, on her release from prison, she changed her name to Violet Smith and sailed to Australia, as she had always dreamed of doing, only to be turned back: the immigration authorities had discovered her criminal record.

She died in Clacton, Essex, in 2005. On Canvey Island some people, or so I have heard, still shudder at the sound of her name.

---

* The famous Liverpool department store, where Rose used to have her hair done.

Fashion in the Fifties

Audrey Hepburn models Givenchy's revolutionary 'sack' dress, 1958

Fashion in the Fifties

'It was around VE DAY that the old itch came back to me again. As the last guns rumbled and the last all-clear sounded, all the squalor and discomfort and roughness that had seemed fitting for so long began to feel old-fashioned. Instead of consenting willingly to bear them I wanted to fight them. I wanted to throw the dried eggs out of the window, burn my shabby curtains and wear a Paris hat again.'

Anne Scott-James, *In the Mink*

I don't want to get too hung up on fashion; the ethos of 'make do and mend' didn't die in 1945. In the years after the war, some people were so hard up for clothes they turned their blackout curtains into coats. But still, many of the women in this book were, thanks entirely to their own efforts, increasingly well off as the Fifties wore on. They could afford to shop, and they were interested in fashion: then, as now, clothes were an effective way of making a statement about their place in the world. And even had they been broke – as Patience Gray often was – they would still have rushed out to buy nylons and lipstick once they became available again, as women did all over Britain. Or they might have made things, as Alison Smithson liked to do (a built-in sewing machine was the sole retro reference point in the House of the Future she designed for the Ideal Home Exhibition in 1956). Sylvia Syms told me a wonderful story about how, in the early Fifties, she went to a party in a copy of a Dior dress she'd made herself – only to find Ava Gardner sitting there in the real thing. 'I told you it would look better on a blonde,' Gardner said to Frank Sinatra on catching sight of her.

In any case, last time I looked, dreams were free. *Vogue*, then as now, wasn't a catalogue; it was a repository of fantasies and yearning, a hook on which to hang one's aspiration. High fashion filtered down, just as it does today, women adopting its latest diktats when and where and how they could: a peplum here, a new bag there. A lot was going on. There was Christian Dior, whose New Look made its debut on 12 February 1947 (nipped-in waists, padded hips, sloping shoulders, skirts crammed full-to-bursting with petticoats); there was Jacques Fath (his flying saucer buttons were everywhere); and there was Cristóbal Balenciaga (women loved his balloon jackets, which enveloped the upper body in a way that lengthened one's legs and emphasised one's face). In 1954 Coco Chanel, who regarded Dior's designs as an affront to liberated women, created her first Chanel suit (collarless tweed jacket with patch pockets, and a chain sewn into the hem of the skirt the better to perfect its line). As the decade wore on tunics and chemise-style dresses became more fashionable, popularised first by Balenciaga – he was always fiddling with waistlines – and then by Hubert de Givenchy, who launched his 'sack' silhouette in 1957. Corsets were on their way out. In London Hardy Amies, who had dressed Princess Elizabeth for her tour to Canada in 1950, had installed himself in Savile Row, where he was attending to the more practical needs of a certain kind of British female. 'A woman's day clothes must look equally good at Salisbury station as the Ritz bar,' he said. Tailoring was the thing. Hemlines were getting higher and so were heels. In 1958 Roger Vivier designed a heel reinforced with steel, and thus the stiletto was revived. Trousers, which so many women had worn during the war, were also becoming more popular. Their champions were Katharine Hepburn, who was reputed not to have a single skirt or dress of her own, and Lauren Bacall.

Technical innovations made life easier all round. Before the war nylons had all been 'fully fashioned', which is to say designed and manufactured individually for legs of all shapes and sizes; stockings did not stretch. In the years following the war, however, it was discovered that stretch could be added by crimping nylon under heat, an innovation that also lead to the disappearance of the rear seam. By 1959 DuPont was ready to launch Lycra. Easy-care fabrics made life for housewives a good deal easier. Acrylic, a drip-dry substitute for wool, arrived in 1950. Polyester came on to the market in 1953. It meant, among other things, that pleats no longer had to be ironed in.

Actresses and models, as ever, were hugely influential. Women loved Audrey Hepburn's appropriation of Parisian-cum-Beatnik style in Stanley's Donen's 1957 musical *Funny Face* (skinny black pants, turtleneck, cute headscarf); it trumped even the little black dress she had worn in Billy Wilder's *Sabrina* three years before. Grace Kelly's *peau de soie* and lace wedding dress, created for her by Helen Rose, an MGM Studios costume designer, was widely admired and much copied. In Britain the most well-known models were Barbara Goalen (so famous that when she married a Lloyds underwriter at Caxton Hall in 1954 she was mobbed by crowds of fans) and Fiona Campbell-Walter, a favourite of Cecil Beaton who could earn up to two thousand pounds a day.

Younger women, however, had different ideas about what they wanted to wear: this was, after all, the dawn of the teenager. Some took their cue from music (Teddy girls wore hobble skirts, flat shoes, cameo brooches and jackets with velvet collars, and styled their hair in ponytails), and others from the movies (Marlon Brando, James Dean, Marilyn Monroe and Elizabeth Taylor all did their bit to make jeans popular). Rebellion was in the air. Another role model was Françoise Sagan, whose best-selling novel about a pleasure-seeking seventeen-year-old called Cécile, *Bonjour Tristesse*, came out in 1954, when she was still a teenager (it was made into a film in 1958). Sagan – 'a charming little monster', as the novelist François Mauriac put it – had pixie hair and was photographed for the press in gingham shirts, Breton stripes and a polka-dot bathing suit.

Françoise Sagan: 'A charming little monster'

Which brings me, finally, to the bikini. It was Louis Reard, a French automobile engineer, who invented the bikini in 1946 (he was running his mother's shoe shop at the time). He had the idea when he saw women rolling up (or down) their swimming costumes the better to get a tan. He called his invention the bikini after Bikini Atoll, where the first nuclear bomb had just been tested. But it wasn't until the Fifties that his design really took off: Brigitte Bardot posed in one during the Cannes Films Festival of 1953 and the world went mad for the idea. 'A swoonsuit that exposed everything about a girl except her mother's maiden name,' as Diana Vreeland, the fashion editor of *Harper's Bazaar*, put it. Vreeland thought the bikini was well named. It was, she said, 'the most important thing since the atom bomb'.

For a colourful account of some aspects of the British fashion industry and of daily life on a glossy magazine in the late Forties and early Fifties, I recommend *In the Mink* (1952) by Anne Scott-James, who was the editor of the British edition of *Harper's Bazaar*. The book caused a mild stir on its publication, the critic Harold Hobson describing its references to sexual behaviour in the fashion world as 'shocking and disgraceful'. It seems tame now but, on the other hand, some things never change. Her account of the Paris collections – 'just when you felt you *must* faint, the show would start' – will seem uncannily familiar to anyone who has ever read a twenty-first-century newspaper report on the same subject. It's all here: the clichés, the tantrums, even the difficulty of writing a properly interesting beauty feature when 'this year's Pink Blush is really just last year's Old-fashioned Rose rechristened'.

Some Good and Richly Subversive Novels by Women 1950–60

Iris Murdoch: 'Running over with purpose and intelligence'

1950   *Some Tame Gazelle*, Barbara Pym
        Pym's first novel, a comic tale of spinsters and the clergy-
        men on whom they dote, is not quite as cosy as it might
        first appear. Its women would rather be unmarried than
        submit to the limitations imposed by pompous husbands.

1951   *School for Love*, Olivia Manning
        Fantastic, little-known book set in Jerusalem in 1945, in
        which Felix, an orphan, comes to live with the miserly
        Miss Bohun. A radical novel for its unsentimental refusal
        to deal in female characters who are comfortable, let alone
        likeable.

1952   *The Sugar House*, Antonia White
        The third novel in the sequence that began with *Frost in
        May*. Not White's best, but a brave portrait of a doomed
        marriage and a woman who is slowly disintegrating. Shot
        through with fear, and claustrophobic as a padded cell.

1953   *The Echoing Grove*, Rosamond Lehmann
        Structurally ambitious, and exceedingly dark, this is a
        novel about sibling rivalry and sexual jealousy – a pair of
        sisters, Dinah and Madeleine, having been widowed by the
        same philandering bastard.

1954 *The Tortoise and the Hare*, Elizabeth Jenkins
Imogen, the once-beautiful wife of Evelyn Gresham, barrister, is powerless to defend her marriage against her
neighbour, the stout and tweedy Blanche. A fine study of
female self-esteem: where it comes from, and how it dis-
appears.

1955 *A World of Love*, Elizabeth Bowen
A deliberately short novel set in a heatwave about a young
woman who discovers a cache of love letters in the attic,
and of their startling effect both on her and her extended
family. Passion distilled.

1956 *The Towers of Trebizond*, Rose Macaulay
A group of eccentrics travel in Armenia 'hawking the C of E
to infidel dogs who thought we were mad and were probably
right'. Fantastical, funny, plangent – and featuring a number
of highly pleasing gags about the emancipation of women.

1957 *Angel*, Elizabeth Taylor
Angelica Deverell is a snobbish and deluded popular
novelist who believes fervently in her own epic spoutings
– a monstrous creation, then, but also, perhaps, an example of the willpower and wilful blindness involved in being
a writer, even a very bad one.

1958 *The Bell*, Iris Murdoch
A singular novel that combines a (for Murdoch) convincing plot with her fondness for symbolism (the bell at
its heart clangs for love, and for self-knowledge). Set in a
religious community led by a man whose sexuality has
prevented his becoming a priest, this is part caper and part
thoughtful treatise on personal morality.

1959 *The Vet's Daughter*, Barbara Comyns
Why isn't Comyns better known? Perhaps because her books follow no pattern, each one so different from the last. Bizarre and horrifying, this is the story of Alice, oppressed daughter of the title, whose ability to levitate first imprisons, then liberates her.

1960 *The L-Shaped Room*, Lynne Reid Banks
A young woman, pregnant and unmarried, struggles to survive in a run-down boarding house. The Fifties do not emerge from this novel well, but the courage of its heroine is just as vividly wrought as its infested mattresses and yellowing wallpaper.

It's worth noting, too, that the decade is bookended by the publication of Stevie Smith's two finest collections of poetry, *Harold's Leap* (1950) and *Not Waving but Drowning* (1957).

Select Bibliography

Adam, Ruth, *A Woman's Place: 1910–1975* (1975; Persephone Books, 2000)

Atkinson, Harriet, *The Festival of Britain: A Land and its People* (I. B. Tauris, 2012)

Bailey, Paul, *Three Queer Lives: An Alternative Biography of Fred Barnes, Naomi Jacob and Arthur Marshall* (Hamish Hamilton, 2001)

Bell, Melanie, *Femininity in the Frame: Women and 1950s British Popular Cinema* (I. B. Tauris, 2009)

Box, Betty, *Lifting the Lid: The Autobiography of Film Producer Betty Box, OBE* (Lewes Book Guild, 2000)

Box, Muriel, *Odd Woman Out* (Leslie Frewin, 1974)

Brome, Vincent, *J. B. Priestley* (Hamish Hamilton, 1988)

Bullock, Nicholas, *Building the Post-War World: Modern Architecture and Reconstruction in Britain* (Routledge, 2002)

Chivers, Susan and Suzanne Woloszynska, *The Cottage Garden: Margery Fish at East Lambrook Manor* (John Murray, 1990)

Collins, Diana, *Time and the Priestleys: The Story of a Friendship* (Alan Sutton, 1994)

Collis, Rose, *A Trouser-wearing Character: The Life and Times of Nancy Spain* (Cassell, 1997)

Cook, Judith, *Priestley* (Bloomsbury, 1997)

Cooper, Artemis, *Writing at the Kitchen Table: The Authorized Biography of Elizabeth David* (Michael Joseph, 1999)

Cooper, William, *Scenes from Provincial Life* (1950; Penguin, 2010)

David, Elizabeth, *A Book of Mediterranean Food* (Lehman, 1950)

————, *Summer Cooking* (Museum Press, 1955)

————, *French Provincial Cooking* (Michael Joseph, 1960)

Delaney, Shelagh, *A Taste of Honey: A Play* (Methuen, 1959)

Dundy, Elaine, *The Dud Avocado* (1958; Virago, 2011)

————, *Life Itself!* (Virago, 2001)

Festing, Sally, *Barbara Hepworth: A Life of Forms* (Viking, 1995)

Fish, Margery, *We Made a Garden* (1956; Faber, 1983)

Friedan, Betty, *The Feminine Mystique* (1963; Penguin, 2010)

Garfield, Simon, *Our Hidden Lives: The Remarkable Diaries of Post-War Britain* (Ebury, 2005)

Gibbons, Stella, *Westwood* (1946; Vintage, 2011)

Gibson, Trish, *Brenda Colvin: A Career in Landscape* (Frances Lincoln, 2011)

Gray, Patience, *Plats du Jour* (1957; Persephone Books, 2006)

————, *Honey From a Weed* (1986; Prospect Books, 2001)

————, *Ring Doves and Snakes* (Macmillan, 1989)

————, *Work Adventures Childhood Dreams* (Edizioni Leucasia, 1999)

Harper, Sue, *Women in British Cinema: Mad, Bad and Dangerous to Know* (Continuum, 2000)

Harrison, Martin, *Transition: The London Art Scene in the Fifties* (Merrell, 2002)

Harwood, Elain, *England: A Guide to Post-War Listed Buildings* (2000; Batsford, 2003)

Hawkes, Jacquetta, *A Land* (1951; Collins, 2012)

————, *A Quest of Love* (Chatto & Windus, 1980)

Heilbron, Hilary, *Rose Heilbron: The Story of England's First Woman Queen's Counsel and Judge* (Hart Publishing, 2012)

Heilpern, John, *John Osborne: A Patriot for Us* (Chatto & Windus, 2006)

Henry, Joan, *Who Lie in Gaol* (Gollancz, 1952)

————, *Yield to the Night* (Gollancz, 1954)

Hodgson, Vere, *Few Eggs and No Oranges: The Diaries of Vere Hodgson, 1940–45* (1976; Persephone Books, 1999)

Horwood, Catherine, *Gardening Women: Their Stories from 1600 to the Present* (Virago, 2010)

Kellaway, Deborah (ed.), *The Virago Book of Women Gardeners* (Virago, 1996)

Kynaston, David, *Family Britain 1951–57* (Bloomsbury, 2009)

Laski, Marghanita, *To Bed with Grand Music* (1946; Persephone Books, 2009)

Maddox, Brenda, *Rosalind Franklin: The Dark Lady of DNA* (HarperCollins, 2002)

Malcolmson, Patricia and Robert (ed.), *Nella Last in the 1950s: Further Diaries of Housewife, 49* (Profile, 2010)

Meades, Jonathan, 'Ian Nairn', in *Museum Without Walls* (Unbound, 2012)

Minns, Raynes, *Bombers and Mash: The Domestic Front, 1939–45* (Virago, 1980)

Mortimer, Penelope, *Daddy's Gone A-Hunting* (1958; Persephone Books, 2008)

——————————, *The Pumpkin Eater* (1962; NYRB, 2011)

——————————, *About Time Too: 1940–1978* (Weidenfeld & Nicolson, 1993)

Myrdal, Alva and Viola Klein, *Women's Two Roles: Home and Work* (Routledge, 1956)

Nicholson, Virginia, *Millions Like Us: Women's Lives in War and Peace 1939–1949* (Viking, 2011)

Panter-Downes, Mollie, *One Fine Day* (1947; Virago, 2011)

Powers, Alan (ed.), *Robin Hood Gardens: Re-Visions* (Casemate UK, 2010)

Reed, Paula, *Fifty Fashion Looks that Changed the 1950s* (Conran Octopus, 2012)

Rickards, Jocelyn, *The Painted Banquet: My Life and Loves* (Weidenfeld & Nicolson, 1987)

Rowntree, Diana, *Interior Design* (Penguin, 1964)

Sandbrook, Dominic, *Never Had It So Good: A History of Britain from Suez to the Beatles* (Little, Brown, 2005)

Scott-James, Anne, *In the Mink* (Michael Joseph, 1952)

Smithson, Alison, *A Portrait of the Female Mind as a Young Girl: A Novel* (Chatto & Windus, 1966)

Smithson, Alison and Peter, *The Charged Void: Architecture* (Monacelli Press, 2002)

——————————, *The Charged Void: Urbanism* (Monacelli Press, 2004)

Spain, Nancy, *Poison for Teacher* (Hutchinson, 1949)

——————————, *Why I'm Not a Millionaire: An Autobiography* (Hutchinson, 1956)

——————————, *The Nancy Spain Colour Cookery Book* (World Distributors, 1963)

Spanier, Ginette, *It Isn't All Mink* (Collins, 1959)

——————————, *And Now It's Sables* (Hale, 1970)

Spicer, Andrew, *Sydney Box* (Manchester University Press, 2011)

Summerskill, Edith, *Letters to my Daughter* (Heinemann, 1957)

Thomas, Dylan, 'The Festival Exhibition', repinted in Ralph Maud (ed.), *On the Air with Dylan Thomas: The Broadcasts* (New Directions, 1992)

Tomalin, Claire, *Several Strangers: Writing from Three Decades* (Viking, 1999)

Uglow, Jenny, *A Little History of British Gardening* (Chatto & Windus, 2004)

van Damm, Sheila, *No Excuses* (Putnam, 1957)

——————————, *We Never Closed: The Windmill Story* (Hale, 1967)

van den Heuvel, Dirk and Max Risselada, *Alison and Peter Smithson: From the House of the Future to a House of Today* (010 Publishers, 2004)

Wheeler, Mortimer, *Still Digging: Interleaves from an Antiquary's Notebook* (Michael Joseph, 1955)

Whitehorn, Katharine, *Selective Memory* (Virago, 2007)

Wilcox, Claire (ed.), *The Golden Age of Couture: Paris and London 1947–57* (V&A Publications, 2007)

Wise, Damon, *Come By Sunday: The Fabulous, Ruined Life of Diana Dors* (Sidgwick & Jackson, 1998)

Wyndham, Joan, *Anything Once* (Flamingo, 1992)

Acknowledgements

My primary sources for the essays in this book were my subjects themselves: their published memoirs and other works (see the Select Bibliography – almost all are long out of print) and, where such documents existed, their diaries and letters. But I also relied hugely on the recollections of their families, friends and former colleagues, many of whom were kind enough to talk to me at length, sometimes more than once. To this end, I offer heartfelt thanks to Frances Atkin, Sir Henry Boyd-Carpenter, Chris Brickell, Miranda Amour-Brown, Susan Angel, Tony Box, Morris Bright, Iris Chapple (ever a Windmill Girl!), Trevor Dannatt, Leonora Dossett, Carol Gardiner, David Gentleman, Neville Goldrein, Nicolas Gray, the late Richard Hamilton, John Hare, Nicolas Hawkes, Norman Hudis, George Kasabov, Jane Kerner, Dick Laurie, Sandra Lousada, Leslie Phillips, Tom Priestley, Simon Relph, Sir Christopher Rose, Ronald Simpson, Samantha Smithson, Soraya Smithson, Simon Smithson, Barbara Thomas, Jeremy Thomas, Tim Tinker, Nick Werner Laurie, Maureen Whitty, the late John Winter, Christopher Woodward and Elizabeth Young.

The introduction, meanwhile, would not have been possible without the help of the remarkable and inspiring women who talked to me with some honesty about their lives in the Fifties: Wendy Bray, the textile designer; Grace Robertson, the photographer; and Sylvia Syms, the actor. Thank you to them. As I write, all three are still doing the work they love.

Thank you to Gail and Mike Werkmeister for inviting me to East Lambrook Manor, and to Derek Sugden for giving me lunch and letting me snoop around his enviable home.

I am grateful to Gavin Green for explaining to me the ins and outs of rally-car driving, and to Giles Smith for putting me in touch with him.

Thank you to Hilary Heilbron for giving me such a fine photograph from her family collection. Thank you also to the estimable Brenda Hale, the new deputy president of the supreme court, for legal advice – and to Nicola Lacey for putting in a good word for me with her.

Ben Dossett kindly provided me with many excellent photographs of Muriel Box.

Thank you to Jonny Davis at the BFI Special Collections for helping me during the long days and weeks that I spent reading Muriel Box's vast diaries; to Lucy Waitt at the RHS Lindley Library; to the staff of the Fashion Museum, Bath, for enabling me to examine close up Alison Smithson's fabulous clothes; to (the marvellously enthusiastic) Alison Cullingford and John Brooker at the J. B. Priestley Library, University of Bradford; to all at the library at RIBA; to the staff of the sound collections at the British Library where I listened, rapt, to the voices of, among many others, Jacquetta Hawkes and Peter Smithson; and to the Women's Library, home of the papers of Helena Normanton, QC. I would also like to acknowledge the important work of the Twentieth Century Society, of which I am an enthusiastic member.

It was David Kynaston's marvellous *Austerity Britain* which first put me on the trail of some of the women in this book, a debt I am pleased to acknowledge. I was inspired in terms of my approach, if not my subject matter, by Phyllis Rose's peerlessly good *Parallel Lives*, Katie Roiphe's superb *Uncommon Arrangements* and Alexandra Harris's thoughtful *Romantic Moderns*. From them, I learned the value of the group, and was happily released from beginning at the beginning and ending at the end. During the writing of *Her Brilliant Career* I read several new books about certain aspects of the post-war years, and while I might not have made mention of them in my final text, they certainly influenced my thinking. In particular, I admired *Handsome Brute*, Sean O'Connor's powerful and sensitive account of the horrifying career of Neville Heath, and *A Fine Day for a Hanging* by Carol Ann Lee, a fine book about the life and sad death of Ruth Ellis. Discovering Rona Jaffe's 1958 novel *The Best of Everything* – a tale of young women looking for love and rewarding work in New York – convinced me that my search for her characters' real-life British equivalents would not be in vain. Like many readers, I am indebted to Nicola Beauman, the founder of Persephone Books, for bringing so many fine novels to my attention.

For keeping me in work and editing me brilliantly down the years, I would like to thank my dear friends Jeremy Langmead, Nicola Jeal and Harriet Green. It goes without saying that I am greatly in the debt of John Mulholland and many other colleagues at the *Observer*, but without Jane Ferguson, patient and loyal to a fault, this book simply could not have been written. Thank you to Jason Cowley and all at the *New Statesman*. For conversations down the years about work and life, and for encouragement all round, I would like to thank Carmen Callil, Rachel Kitt, Claerwen James, Anna Murphy, Juliet Soskice and, especially, my agent Peter Straus. India Knight read an early chapter, and her enthusiasm for it kept me going through some gloomy moments. I am, of course, hugely grateful to Lennie Goodings and to everyone at Virago for believing in this book right from the off. The indefatigable, beady-eyed and endlessly patient Zoe Gullen deserves particular thanks for going way beyond the course of duty in helping me with the editing of this book. Zoe Hood is more pal than publicist, and I have loved working with her. Thank you to my extraordinary family, and sorry to you all for having been so absent. The biggest debt of all, however, is owed to Anthony Quinn, who fired the starting gun on this book and on the best years of my life; thank you to him, from the bottom of my heart, for everything.

Credits

Pictures

6: Digging for Victory
© Derek Allen/National Portrait Gallery, London: 217
Getty Images: 220
Special Collections, University of Bradford: 225, 229, 232, 234, 244, 251
© National Portrait Gallery, London: 249
© Mark Gerson/National Portrait Gallery, London: 254

7: All Rise
© National Portrait Gallery, London: 259
Keystone: 263
Daily Herald: 267
© Mary Evans Picture Library/The Women's Library@LSE: 269
Reynold's News: 278
Manchester Evening Chronicle: 285
Daily Mail: 289
Evening Telegraph: 291
Courtesy of Hilary Heilbron: 293
© June Mendoza. By permission of the Honourable Society of Gray's
    Inn: 296

Fashion in the Fifties
© 2005 Credit: TopFoto/AP: 299
Roger Viollet/Getty Images: 304

Some Good and Richly Subversive Novels by Women 1950–60
Mary Evans Picture Library/IDA KAR: 307

Jacket
Front: © MARKA/Alamy; Mirrorpix; Retrofile/Getty Images
Back:
Betty Box: From Betty Box, *Lifting the Lid*
Muriel Box: © reserved; collection National Portrait Gallery, London
Margery Fish: Sir Henry and Lady Boyd-Carpenter
Patience Gray: Courtesy of Miranda Armour-Brown and Nicolas Gray
Jacquetta Hawkes: © Derek Allen/National Portrait Gallery, London
Rose Heilbron: © National Portrait Gallery, London
Alison Smithson: © National Portrait Gallery, London

Nancy Spain: Photography by Yousuf Karsh, Camera Press London
Sheila van Damm: From Sheila van Damm, *No Excuses*
Joan Werner Laurie: © Nick Werner Laurie

Text

Extracts from the letters of J. B. Priestley are reprinted by permission of
United Agents on behalf of The Estate of the Late J. B. Priestley.

Extracts from material by Jacquetta Hawkes are reprinted by permission
of Peters Fraser & Dunlop (www.petersfraserdunlop.com) on behalf
of Peters Fraser & Dunlop, Drury House, 34–43 Russell Street, London
WC2B 5HA Tel: 020 7344 1000 Fax: 020 7836 9539 www.petersfraser
dunlop.com permissions@pfd.co.uk. The Peters Fraser & Dunlop
Group Limited Employment Agents VAT 503209687 Registered in
England 218 5448

With thanks to Special Collections, University of Bradford.

Extracts from the papers of Vita Sackville-West are reproduced with
permission of Curtis Brown on behalf of The Estate of Vita Sackville-
West. Copyright © Vita Sackville-West, 1959.